SAC LIBRARY RY
D0196637
011

Advance Praise for

WITHDRAWN FROM COLLECTION

This book draws our attention to a critical, but often unrecognized, environmental challenge facing society in developed countries such as Australia and the United States: managing urban water supply. He makes a crucial connection that global policy makers should be aware of: Increasingly people understand that a comprehensive approach to the climate change challenge must look at water issues as equally important as curbing excessive energy use.

— Tony Arnel, Chair,
Green Building Council of Australia

Dry Run is a compelling analysis on the full spectrum of one of our most precious resources, water. Yudelson has the unique ability of synthesizing the historical, present day and available technologies/solutions for the impending struggle we are and will face in regards to water conservation. A must-read for the novice and experienced as we move towards a "new water" sector.

— Ronald W. Hand, AIA, CSI, E/FECT.
Sustainable Design Solutions

Dry Run provides a much needed and welcome examination of our impending water crisis and provides workable solutions to prevent it. It is a must-read for water resource planners and water conservation professionals.

— Bill Hoffman, PE,
H.W. (Bill) Hoffman & Associates

Jerry Yudelson's book, *Dry Run*, will become an excellent "nonstandard" reference manual for water efficiency. It provides a basic understanding of past, current, and potential water issues. Whether you live in an area of drought-potential or not, *Dry Run* provides knowledge and benchmarks for the consumer, the engineer, the operator, and the politician to help us become more water efficient.

— Greg Towsley,
GRUNDFOS Pumps Corporation.

This is the first book that provides the specific information that you need to "future-proof" your house and your business against water scarcity. If you act on the information in this book, you will save money today. More importantly, you will prevent dramatic losses in the future when droughts, severe storms and infrastructure decay reset our approaches to building.

— Laura Shenkar,
The Artemis Project

This book provides the most comprehensive overview about water-related knowledge and potential strategies I've ever seen. This is a must for every engineering and architecture practice with a serious focus on sustainability. It will boost the reader's consciousness and will give this topic the necessary attention in building design.

— Thomas Auer,
Transsolar Energietechnik,
Stuttgart, Germany

I can't emphasize enough how important it is that people read this book... not just some people — ALL PEOPLE. Water is *the* declining and under-valued resource of our time, and in 5 years we'll all be wondering why we took so long to realize that water's value to us as human beings will far out-strip our current worries and hand-wringing about oil. We are not 70% oil, we are 70% water. Jerry's book is the right message and the essential refer-ence guide for us to accelerate this idea and this awareness in this time of profound transformation and change — everyone needs to know what is in this book.

— Clark Brockman, AIA,
Director of Sustainability Resources,
SERA Architects

Once again, Jerry Yudelson has taken a critical complex issue and presented it in a readable manner. This is the next environmental crisis and Jerry is sounding the battle cry, while offering tangible solutions. I applaud the ef-fort and his graceful manner in presenting the material.

— Ron van der Veen, AIA,
Mithun, AASHE Board

Jerry Yudelson's *Dry Run* is an urgently needed manifesto. It makes a com-pelling case to shift from a pattern of careless water dependencies to stra-tegic alignment with water cycles and balance, and is an imperative for immediate action.

— Gail Vittori, Co-Director,
Center for Maximum Potential Building Systems

This book is the best summary of a comprehensive overall coverage of the entire urban water crisis context I have seen yet. Read it — whether you are planning for water, managing it or using it. You will understand why water will be the gold of the 21st century and what you can do to help avoid the crisis, mitigate or generate new business.

— Guenter Haber-Davidson,
Water Conservation Group,
Sydney, Australia

Clear — as water should be — is the message of this book. A serious topic is presented in a manner to make you curious, not anxious. It is possible to run through the book's pages in a hurry and anyway get the good impression that we can (still turn the problem to the good). It is also possible to take more time and stay with one aspect in one of the chapters and find information and unknown details like exploring deep water area in nature. Excellent figures make this book being an appetizer to join the group of active planning people, introduced by interviews. Nice to see by the presented examples, that people (let us call them colleagues) around the world already started in a common sense to prevent the next Urban Water Crisis, by using their skills, their brain and their heart at the same time.

— Klaus W. König,
Architectural Office of Klaus W. König,
Ueberlingen, Germany

Urban water utilities have long prided themselves on quietly providing reliable water at affordable prices. As a result, there's limited awareness about the challenges of providing water to ever-growing populations. Yudelson strips away complacency with a sobering look at the past, present and future challenges to our water supply. Yudelson shares his sustainable design and construction expertise to explain practical concepts for reducing our water footprint without compromising our standard of living. Whether you're a green-living novice or a seasoned professional, you'll find *Dry Run* enlightening.

— Doug Bennett,
Southern Nevada Water Authority

Jerry Yudelson continues to provide genuine thought leadership and support for the global green building agenda. *Dry Run: Preventing the Next Urban Water Crisis* delivers a comprehensive analysis of the issues surrounding urban water use and offers clear evidence of why we must change the way we view and value water.

— Romilly Madew,
Chief Executive,
Green Building Council of Australia

Setting the bar for new developments in our cities and towns is of utmost importance to ensuring a sustainable water supply for future generations. *Dry Run* truly hits the spot when it comes to water conservation in the Arid Southwest.

— Dr. Rodney Glassman,
Tucson City Council

Dry Run is a matter-of-fact book with evidence that screams Urban Water Crisis. It clearly outlines why we need to use existing attempts to respond to water shortages in other countries as well as parts of our own country that are already starting to feel the effects of low water supplies as a "dry run" for dealing with the looming Urban Water Crisis. A grounded effort to speed our vital response.

— Heather Kinkade, RLA, author,
Design for Water: Rainwater Harvesting,
Stormwater Catchment and
Alternate Water Reuse

An outstanding book covering today's very significant concerns over water availability and use in North America. Very importantly, though, Jerry also gives us an all-encompassing picture of "solutions" to these concerns in the form of 21st century products, technologies, and practices that can definitely lead to water sustainability. I highly recommend this book for both the new practitioner in the field of water use efficiency *and* the experienced water professional.

— John Koeller, P.E.

This book is the wakeup call we all needed to realize the grave challenge we face and the potential of the building industry to curb water consumption. From home designers and builders to city and national policy makers, this resource is the compass we all needed to navigate and guide our destiny over this century of transition from black to blue gold. I hope all sector stakeholders read it, soon!

— Donna McIntire, AIA

This book's incredible. It covers everything you need to know about water, and I mean everything, and will go a long way towards helping save this world. Jerry has already tackled sustainability in buildings but now he's taking on our world's biggest challenge of providing enough water for future generations.

— Steven Straus, PE, Glumac

DRY
RUN

DRY RUN

PREVENTING
THE NEXT
URBAN
WATER
CRISIS

JERRY YUDELSON

Foreword by Prof. Sharon B. Megdal

NEW SOCIETY PUBLISHERS

Copyright © 2010 by Jerry Yudelson. All rights reserved.

Cover design by Diane McIntosh.
Cover images: © iStock: Background — Mark Kostich;
Water — Michael Jay; Paper — Royce DeGrie

Printed in Canada. First printing April 2010.

Paperback ISBN: 978-0-86571-670-4

Inquiries regarding requests to reprint all or part of *Dry Run*
should be addressed to New Society Publishers at the address below.
To order directly from the publishers, please call toll-free
(North America) 1-800-567-6772, or order online at newsociety.com

Any other inquiries can be directed by mail to:
New Society Publishers
P.O. Box 189, Gabriola Island, BC V0R 1X0, Canada
(250) 247-9737

New Society Publishers' mission is to publish books that contribute in
fundamental ways to building an ecologically sustainable and just society, and
to do so with the least possible impact on the environment, in a manner that
models this vision. We are committed to doing this not just through education,
but through action. This book is one step toward ending global deforestation
and climate change. It is printed on Forest Stewardship Council-certified acid-
free paper that is **100% post-consumer recycled** (100% old growth forest-free),
processed chlorine free, and printed with vegetable-based, low-VOC inks, with
covers produced using FSC-certified stock. New Society also works to reduce
its carbon footprint, and purchases carbon offsets based on an annual audit to
ensure a carbon neutral footprint. For further information, or to browse our
full list of books and purchase securely, visit our website at: newsociety.com

Library and Archives Canada Cataloguing in Publication

Yudelson, Jerry

    Dry run : preventing the next urban water crisis / Jerry Yudelson ;
foreword by Sharon B. Megdal.

Includes bibliographical references and index.
ISBN 978-0-86571-670-4

    1. Water scarcity—Prevention. 2. Municipal water supply. 3. Water
conservation projects. 4. Water efficiency. I. Title.

TD388.Y93 2010   333.91'16   C2010-902483-4

NEW SOCIETY PUBLISHERS
www.newsociety.com

Mixed Sources
Cert no. SW-COC-001271
© 1996 FSC

FSC

Contents

Acknowledgments

First, I want to thank more than two dozen water experts, engineers, contractors, manufacturers, building owners, water agency staff and building professionals who allowed us to interview them for this book, supplied project information and have led the way in water efficiency and water conservation around the world. Those we interviewed are acknowledged individually in Appendix III: List of Interviews. I also want to thank the staff at New Society Publishers for supporting this book and seeing it through to timely publication.

Thanks as well to the many companies, engineers, building owners, developers, architects, architectural photographers and others who generously contributed project information and photos for the book. Thanks also to Heidi Ziegler-Voll for providing illustrations created specially for this book.

A special note of thanks goes to my long-time editor, Gretel Hakanson, for conducting the interviews, sourcing all the photos and permissions (a never-ending task), reviewing the manuscript drafts, drafting the Australia case study in Chapter 3 and, above all, making sure that the final production was as accurate as possible. This is our ninth book together; she has been an invaluable contributor to each work. A special thanks also goes to Yudelson Associates' research director, Jaimie Galayda, PhD, for organizing the research, preparing appendix material, gathering the information used in various chapters and reviewing the entire manuscript, and to Todd Leber for drafting the water agency case studies, sourcing some of the data and reviewing the final manuscript. Thanks also to manuscript reviewers Heather Kinkade, Jessica Yudelson and Joanna Nadeau.

I especially appreciate Professor Sharon B. Megdal of the University of Arizona, one of the best-known water resources experts in the Southwest, for taking time from her incredibly busy schedule to write the Foreword for this book.

A special thanks to the Mechanical Contracting Education and Research Foundation (MCERF) for supporting research into new water technologies for buildings that is sprinkled throughout this book, especially in

Part II, The Colors of Water. I especially acknowledge the support and encouragement for the research project from Dennis Langley at MCERF.

While I am appreciative of all the reviewers' work, as always, I must claim any errors of omission or commission as mine alone. Thanks also to my wife, Jessica, for indulging the time spent writing yet another book and for sharing my enthusiasm for sustainable living.

Foreword

by Professor Sharon B. Megdal

Water availability is of great interest to the public, especially in places where water shortages have been experienced or are anticipated. As a frequent speaker on water policy, I find that urban residents first and foremost want good-quality water to flow reliably from their taps. Many think about their use and are thirsty for information on how they can be more efficient water users. Many do not know where their water comes from and what treatment and engineered water distribution and treatment systems are in place to deliver the water and take the wastewater away. They often do not know whether the water they drink is being pumped from aquifers or diverted from rivers or both. They may not know how scarce freshwater supplies are or how vulnerable supplies may be.

The reality is that water supplies are being stressed by many factors simultaneously and in different ways than ever before. These factors include drought, climate change and growth in population and in water withdrawals. Water planners and policy makers are working diligently throughout the United States to make sure communities have safe and reliable water for the future. The goals are no different from the past, but achieving them is getting more challenging in the face of ever-increasing competition for water and more uncertain climate conditions. The changing of water practices will be required; for example, adoption of water conservation practices may not only reflect new regulations, but also represents an important cost reduction strategy for water users. Landscapes may change as people understand how communities can economize on water use without sacrificing their livability. This book will help the reader understand how water use practices are and should be changing, as well as how individuals and communities can contribute to a sustainable water future.

People frequently comment that water prices are low. Transplants to semi-arid Arizona, for example, often wonder why water does not cost more than it does. Water prices throughout the United States reflect the costs of delivering water to the customer. There is no cost to the water molecules themselves. If you own your own well, the primary cost is for water extraction, which is cheaper than water from a local utility. In fact, in Tucson, Arizona, some households from a wealthy established neighborhood left the public water system and drilled their own wells to save money. Their solution to high water cost was to find a cheaper alternative. (State law was later changed to stop this practice.)

Water prices can vary considerably within a given region if there is significant variability in the cost to water companies for water extraction, treatment and delivery. I often hear people state that the era of cheap water is over. Contaminant removal, seawater or brackish groundwater desalination, water rights acquisition and water storage and transportation systems will be more costly in the future. Water planners expect that customers will see water rates increase significantly. By how much is a significant unknown.

Rate structures, such as tiered rates that increase as water use increases, have been adopted to encourage water conservation. In response, some consumers have changed their water use practices. Interest in rainwater harvesting by individual households and businesses is growing. Installation of graywater systems can likewise match water quality with the type of water use and also reduce the costs of water and wastewater treatment. Tax policies and city ordinances are additional factors stimulating changing water use practices.

While individuals can contribute to avoiding future crises by reducing their own water use, there are community and regional level issues to be addressed. Water regulations are decentralized in the United States. The federal government sets standards for drinking water quality and for discharges of pollutants into streams and waterways. The Endangered Species Act impacts some water diversion and use practices. Most water supply and utilization management and treatment decisions and regulations are made at the state or local level. In some cases, there may be strict limits on groundwater withdrawals by community water providers. In others, groundwater withdrawals are unregulated, and wells can be drilled without consideration of the impacts to a neighbor.

Population growth is usually accompanied by growth in water use, but that does not always have to be the case. Agricultural water use remains significant in many regions of the country, as does industrial water use. Competition for water supplies is growing. Urban populations are spreading to agricultural lands. People demand more food, fiber and energy, all of which require water supplies for production. States such as Florida and California, for example, are explicitly considering environmental implications of water withdrawals. Long-term arrangements that transfer water from agricultural use to municipal use, like those agreed to in Southern California, are evidence of the scarcity of water compared with growing demands.

An important part of the water use picture is the environment. The degraded riparian environments in many areas of the Southwest are evidence that water withdrawals often occur without consideration of the environmental implications. *The environment is often the unrecognized water customer — the water customer not at the table.* Although there is heightened awareness of the importance of environmental preservation and state laws that require consideration of the environmental impacts of water use, there are still states and communities where water use can occur without such consideration. Once degraded, even partial restoration of a watershed or aquifer can be costly, and full restoration may never occur. Therefore, as we look to our water future, we must remember that the environment is part of our communities and care for it.

It can be overwhelming to think about what individuals and communities can do in the face of significant uncertainties and challenges, but *the key to making good decisions is good information.* This book provides key information for individuals and businesses as they look to becoming better water stewards. The book identifies "no regret" water use practices, that is, practices that are resilient to alternative future conditions. For example, rainwater harvesting at the individual user level can help a community avoid the high costs of treating water to potable standards only to have that water used for landscaping. If, at the same time, individuals are educated regarding landscaping practices suitable for their local environment, we have policies that make sense regardless of the climate or drought conditions that are experienced. We will be glad we adopted them whether we encounter severe and prolonged droughts or unexpected short ones.

Water managers and policy makers recognize the many challenges associated with providing safe and reliable water supplies. They are working hard to avoid water crises in the face of growing competition for water supplies and significant uncertainty about future rainfall, runoff patterns and water availability. This book can help individuals, businesses and communities adopt more sustainable water use practices. We can all participate in avoiding the next urban water crisis.

Professor Sharon B. Megdal
University of Arizona, Tucson

Preface

I've been writing books about green buildings, green homes and green developments since 2005; each has focused mostly on broad aspects, especially on energy use and making the business case for substantially increasing our investments in green building. Green building growth appears now to be self-perpetuating, expected to achieve more than a 20 percent market share of the new non-residential construction market in 2010. And, in the worst environment for homebuilding since the Great Depression, green homes are still selling well.

For this book, I've chosen to focus on my first love in the professional world, water, a subject to which I devoted a considerable part of my early professional career. With the arrival of renewed worldwide concern about water supply and quality, the time has certainly come to focus on water issues in the built (urban) environment, which after all is the world in which most of us live. Moreover, as people become more aware of the many connections between water and energy issues, sustainable building design will increasingly come to include both water and energy issues as primary concerns.

In fact, many vanished ancient civilizations disappeared because of their inability to manage water resources and the environment: Mesopotamian, Mayan and Indus River civilizations all disappeared. Protecting soil and water is essential to protecting civilization, since everyone must eat and we can't yet produce food in chemical factories in a way that would compete with natural ecosystem services. For most of us, the image that clearly conjures up water supply is the aqueduct (Figure P.1), bringing water to cities from afar, since the days of ancient Rome. For those living in Southern California and Arizona, the long-distance aqueduct continues to bring the lifeblood of water to our largest cities.

Similar conclusions about the importance of water use in undergirding economic and environmental health hold true not just for the United States, but for other developed and rapidly growing economies: Australia, Canada, western Europe, Japan, China, India and other countries. Water use in the built environment is going to be a larger issue in future public

policy discussions for all advanced economies. Increasingly, people understand that a comprehensive approach to the climate change challenge must
look at water issues as equally important as curbing excessive energy use.

Water is a vast subject: it is the elixir of life, one of the four basic elements of human existence. Anyone who writes about water has to make
choices about subject matter. Writing this book, I decided to focus strictly
on urban water use, neglecting major water uses in agriculture and industry in favor of a more focused approach on water use in the built environment — something I know we can substantially improve upon within the
current political, economic and environmental context.

In 2009, a major statewide drought emergency gripped California's 38
million people, reprising similar conditions in recent years in Texas and
Georgia, and forcing cities, water districts, counties and millions of people
to undertake unprecedented conservation restrictions, policies and programs. People in the US are getting a taste of what 20 million Australians
have battled in the first decade of what will become the "water century."
They are encountering the scarcity of available fresh water, sufficient to
supply not only the needs of cities but also the needs of agriculture, industry, energy production and (what should be in first place) a healthy environment. You'll read about many of these contemporary water crises in this
book.

I focus on lessons learned in actual projects, in urban and suburban
conservation programs and in developed countries that have already con-
fronted the inevitable consequence of global warming, population growth,

FIGURE P.1 For centuries, the aqueduct has symbolized water supply from
rivers to distant cities.

economic growth and environmental degradation: more erratic and most certainly reduced fresh water supplies. As a professional engineer with a master's degree in water resource development, I know we can do a much better job of conserving and protecting our water supplies. We've lived too long with the idea of unlimited water abundance, and now we need to change our ways. It's not too late for us to start looking at our water resources as finite, precious, recyclable and deserving of far better treatment.

Fortunately, change in our antiquated approach to developing and using water resources is well underway, at local, national and international levels. I hope that this book will give readers information that's accurate, timely, specific and motivating. In fact, I hope that you will take this information and put it to use in your own buildings, facilities, factories, hotels, hospitals, homes, schools and campuses, to reduce water use and to advocate for more enlightened policies and programs wherever you can.

As a country, and as a world, we need to get moving to dramatically change how we deal with water issues in the built environment. By profiling a large number of successful projects, programs and technologies, by demonstrating the business case for water efficiency, and by featuring the wide range of specific strategies reducing water use in cities, I hope to motivate you, the reader, to begin taking action now wherever you live, to prevent the next big urban water crisis.

Jerry Yudelson
Tucson, Arizona
Sonoran Desert Bioregion, January, 2010

A Short History
of Water

Whiskey's for drinking,
water is for fighting over.[1]

IN THIS CHAPTER you'll learn a little of the fascinating history of water and civilization and how politics, economics and water have been part of the history of the US, especially of the West, from the very beginning. The chapter also points out that water is not just for people, but natural water flows are a critical part of a healthy environment, something that water planners, politicians and engineers have mostly ignored, not just in North America, but throughout the world.

That's All There Is: There Ain't No More

We live on a watery planet, with seawater constituting some 97 percent of Earth's total water supply, undrinkable without considerable cost and energy expense, leaving 3 percent as fresh water. Most (two-thirds) of the world's freshwater supply is locked up permanently in ice caps, with less than 1 percent available as surface water, as shown in Figure 1.1. Of all surface water, only 2 percent is readily available in rivers; the balance is found in swamps and lakes. Of course, all surface waters require pumping and treating before we can use them.

The good news, of course, is that the Earth's fresh water is always available, a renewable resource evaporating from the oceans and falling as rain over land before returning to the oceans or atmosphere, a phenomenon known as the hydrologic cycle, shown in Figure 1.2. Solar energy drives this endless cycle with the sunshine falling on our planet, and thankfully, we've had four billion years without a sunshine shortage! Unlike solar energy, where the amount of sunshine falling on the planet is several thousands of times *more than* our current energy demands,[3] the amount of available fresh water is already *less than* our needs in many parts of the world.

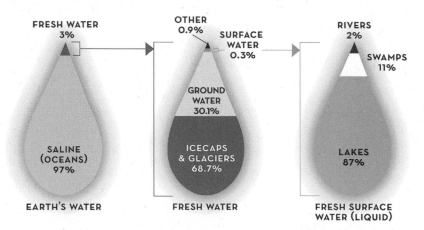

FIGURE 1.1 Very little of the Earth is fresh water and much of what remains is mostly inaccessible for people's needs.[2]

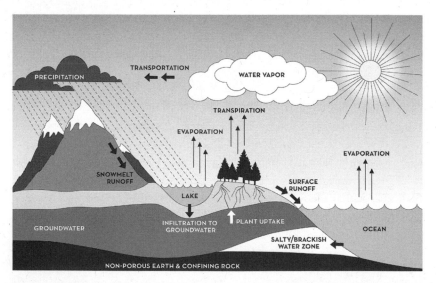

FIGURE 1.2 Driven by solar radiation, water cycles endlessly between ocean and land.

Even though endlessly renewable, water supplies are inherently finite in the short term. One way to understand this is to realize that no new fresh-water supply has been created since the beginning of recorded time. More-over, in many places, humans have essentially been "mining" groundwater for farms, buildings and factories, using up both current resources as well as water left over from eons ago that will take ages to be recharged.[4] We've taken a once renewable resource and a finite stock of fossil water[5] and have made it a non-renewable resource, much as we've done with hydrocarbons from the Jurassic era, 65 million years ago. This book will show you how we can bring our water use back into balance with our available supplies, and for most urban places, the first step is to stop using so much water. As many have noted, when you're standing at the edge of a cliff, the first act of wisdom is to take a step back, to move away from the precipice!

Water, Soil and Civilization

Water, soil and civilization have been intricately intertwined since the dawn of time.[6] The ancient great civilizations of Egypt, Mesopotamia and India relied on strict social controls over water to promote a productive irrigated agriculture. With the exception of Egypt, all early civilizations disappeared because of their misuse of water and soil; for millennia in Egypt, the annual Nile flood brought new topsoil to agriculture along the lower Nile Valley. In the United States, westward migration brought about a loss of topsoil, as farming took over the fertile prairie grasslands. The Dust Bowl era of the 1930s, a time of record droughts that led to massive dust storms, from which soil from the Midwest blew onto the steps of the US Capitol in 1935, brought about new laws and a new ethos of soil conservation that began to reclaim the productivity of the land.[7] To live sustainably in North America, we must relearn the lessons of every civilization: a country that destroys its soil and degrades its water resources is slowly committing environmental, economic and social suicide.

Water in the American West

Water has always been scarce in the American West, with an annual rain-fall dropping below 20 inches west of the 100th meridian, a line roughly 250 miles west of Omaha, Nebraska.[8] Because of this geographical fact, water law and politics in the West are quite different from those in the more humid East, where rain falls every month of the year. In the West, long droughts and months without rain are quite common. On the West Coast of the United States, for example, the rainy season typically runs from November through March, with little or no rain from April through October.[9] For this reason, most crops in the West must be irrigated in summer with water captured during the rainy season. This fact led to the construction of many water supply dams during the previous century, a few of which are now being removed to restore migrating habitats for fish.

In the West, conflicts over water rights have been the rule for more than 150 years. Water conflicts abound even today, for example, between Native American water rights and water uses for agriculture, mining, industrial users and cities.[10] We fight over dams, fish, wells and just about anything that involves diverting water from streams or underground. These conflicts will intensify in the future, as a growing population fights for control of a dwindling resource. In the Colorado River basin, seven states were allocated water rights in 1922, based on what we now know as record years of high flows. Long-term average stream flow in the Colorado may be as much as 20 percent below current allocations. Americans continue to fight with Mexico over the quality of the remaining 1,500,000 acre-feet[11] of water that flows past Yuma, Arizona, into Mexico on its way to the Sea of Cortes, a quantity that a 1944 treaty requires the US to deliver.[12]

But many societies have even less water and more contention than the American West. Considering how rivers demarcate many boundaries between different countries, with some controlling all upstream flows, the potential for conflict is clear. For example, the Tigris and Euphrates rivers have their headwaters in Turkey, then flow though Syria and Iraq into the Persian Gulf. At this time, Turkey's plans to build water supply and hydroelectricity-generating dams on the upper reaches of the Tigris, to enhance agriculture in southeastern Turkey, are causing significant concern in Iraq, which already has trouble getting enough water for its people.[13] Today, the flow in the Euphrates River is significantly smaller than just a few years ago.[14]

In the fictional world of *Dune*, Frank Herbert's 1965 science-fiction masterpiece, the desert planet of Arrakis is so dry that the local inhabitants, the cave-dwelling Fremen, have complex rituals and systems focusing on the value and conservation of water. They conserve the water rendered (distilled) from the dead and consider tears as the greatest gift one can offer to the dead. Herbert's world is one of a vast, dry, sand-dune ecology that in some ways resembles the world of Mars, as it was known before unmanned exploration of the Martian surface began.[15] In many ways, it presages what will likely happen in the 21st century: as water becomes more precious and scarcer, driven by continued population growth and accelerated global warming, water wars may well erupt between neighboring countries, or along entire river basins.

In his classic poem, "The Rime of the Ancient Mariner," Samuel Taylor Coleridge gave us the indelible memory of a seafaring man driven mad by his rash act of killing an albatross that was bringing good luck. The classic line, "Water water everywhere, Nor any drop to drink," describing his fate of being becalmed without freshwater in an ocean full of salt water, and being unable to satisfy his thirst, is indelibly etched in the memory of everyone who ever had to read this poem in an American high school.[16] We live in a world similar to the Ancient Mariner's, surrounded by oceans, but unable to drink much of it without great expense.

In the deserts of the American Southwest, prior to the European invasion of the 16th and 17th centuries, many Native American tribes made a living with irrigated and even dryland agriculture. Some civilizations flourished for many centuries but were eventually forced out by periods of both drought and extensive flooding. The hydrology of desert areas is characterized by long droughts, some up to a quarter-century long, and by sudden massive downpours, leading to flash floods that, in the case of the Hohokam civilization of the Salt River Valley of Arizona (the present Phoenix metropolitan area), wiped out their extensive system of irrigation canals. Some experts speculate that excessive salinization of the soils caused by the leaching of salts from high groundwater tables destroyed the fertility of the soil.[17] A similar situation occurred in Pakistan in the 19th and 20th centuries, in the Indus River Valley, compounded by a saline groundwater and flat topography. Such salinity can only be cured by massive drainage of the soil, to carry away salts from the upper layer of soil.[18]

At the Mesa Verde National Park cave dwelling in the Four Corners area of the Southwest, one can see evidence of a successful Native American civilization that succumbed to a long drought near the end of the 13th century. Tree ring studies, which originated nearly 100 years ago as the science of dendrochronology,[19] has allowed researchers to compile records of rainfall in the desert Southwest going back well over 1,000 years. These records show extensive periods of drought, enough to drive away a civilization dependent on irrigated agriculture. In modern times, much of the Southwest depends heavily on flows in the Colorado River, which show considerable historical variation. In fact, the currently allocated flows in the Colorado, especially among the "lower basin" states of Arizona, Nevada and California, significantly exceed historically measured flows, a situation that has led to long-standing feuds between these states.

But, as you will read in the case study of water issues in the Atlanta area (Chapter 3), even wet regions can have water feuds. The states of Georgia,

Alabama and Florida are currently fighting over rights to water from the Chattahoochee River, which forms the border between the southern parts of Alabama and Georgia, and which, as the Apalachicola River, flows into the Gulf of Mexico through the Florida Panhandle.[20] In 2009, a federal judge ruled that Atlanta had no water claim on Lake Lanier, a reservoir on the upper Chattahoochee that supplies the city with much of its drinking water. Florida claims that Atlanta's voracious use of water reduces freshwater inflows to the Gulf of Mexico so much that it harms the livelihood of oyster harvesters there.[21]

Water Variability

Rainfall and stream runoff are highly variable, making water a renewable resource dissimilar from solar power that is relatively constant in both space and time. Early in my career, I studied water resources engineering at Harvard University and learned about water's extreme variability in both space and time through the work of the late Professor Myron Fiering, whose book *Streamflow Synthesis*[22] was an original analysis of the extreme range of stream flows. Rainfall and runoff are characterized by statistics of extreme events (something we have seen in the 2008–2009 global financial crisis[23]). By contrast, in the "normal distribution" (the classic bell-shaped curve most of us remember from statistics class) of outcomes, like rolling dice or assessing people's heights, most events occur near the middle (average) with fewer than five percent occurring outside two standard deviations. Water flows don't follow those rules; as a result, planning for future water supplies must deal with more dramatic and unexpected events.

The Los Angeles metropolitan area, the country's second largest, is almost completely dependent on water imported from hundreds of miles

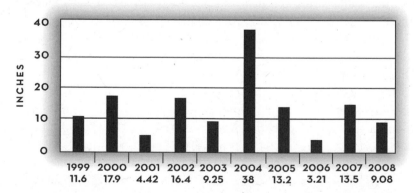

FIGURE 1.3 Annual rainfall in Los Angeles has varied by a factor of nearly 12 over a recent decade.[25]

away to smooth out its natural variation in annual rainfall, shown in Figure 1.3. Observe, for example, that between 2004 and 2006, rainfall varied by a *factor of 12*, with totals ranging from 3.2 inches to 38 inches! Without imported water from the Colorado River to the east, from the Owens Valley east of the Sierra Nevada and from the California Aqueduct to the north, which brings water from the western side of the same Sierra Nevada range, Los Angeles would still be the small semi-arid town it was 100 years ago, when the population barely topped 300,000, less than ten percent of today's nearly four million.[24]

California Water Wars

The growth of Los Angeles, greatly facilitated by imported water for the past 100 years,[26] is the stuff of legend; witness the movie *Chinatown* (1974), inspired by the water war between the Los Angeles metro area and the rural Owens Valley, left high and dry by the city's theft of its water in 1913.[27] Without imported water, other important western cities such as Phoenix, Las Vegas and San Diego would still be small towns, limited by the annual rainfall and surface runoff in their desert and semi-arid coastal regions.

California's water battles continue even today, intrastate as much as interstate. After nearly 50 years of political standoff between Northern California, which has most of the water but only about 30 percent of the state's population, and Southern California, which needs more water, the California Legislature in 2009 passed several new water laws, one that provides for an $11.1 billion bond for water supply and related environmental conservation measures.[28] The severe statewide drought of 2009 forced the issue; as Dr. Samuel Johnson observed: "When a man knows he is to be hanged in a fortnight, it concentrates his mind wonderfully."[29] For the first time, state law now requires urban water conservation of 20 percent by 2020, based on water consumption. (Each city can choose its own baseline year, from 2004 to 2008, so similar cities may adopt different policy measures depending on where they place the starting point.) Additionally, the package of five bills provides for new water reservoirs in the Sierra Nevada and may lead to a "peripheral canal" around the Sacramento-San Joaquin River Delta. California voters must still approve bonds for funding of the new water projects, in an election that will be in May 2010.[30]

Water and the Environment

The California water wars derive, at least in part, from a series of federal court decisions protecting the environment of the Sacramento-San Joaquin River Delta, a vast wetland of high biological productivity, from water withdrawals that would induce salt water to move inland from San Francisco Bay to the freshwater Delta. Wherever we look at water issues, we also find environmental issues. They are inseparable. By treating surface water as a "free good," we ignore the "ecosystem services" provided by free-flowing rivers. For example, in the Pacific Northwest, a century of dam-building in the Columbia River basin and its tributaries has decimated the native salmon runs, so that most of the free-ranging salmon still left in the region originate in small coastal rivers along the Pacific Ocean. Fresh water provides habitat for fish and wildlife, even in the Sonoran Desert, where the San Pedro River in southeastern Arizona passes through the San Pedro Riparian National Conservation Area.[31] In the future, water supplies will be constrained by the need to provide protection for ecosystem services, a subject too vast for this book.

Summary

With the world's population increasing almost fourfold, from about 2.5 billion in 1950, to an expected 9.3 billion in 2050,[32] water and soil resources have come under unprecedented stress in every country. Simply feeding all these people will require major increases in water withdrawals, even more dramatic than those from 1961 through 2001, shown in Figure 1.4. In the US, with a projected population increase of nearly 110 million between 2010 and 2050,[33] we will have to be more concerned with the quantity and quality of

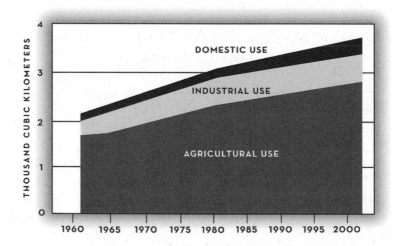

FIGURE 1.4 Spurred by population and economic growth over the past 50 years, the rate of water withdrawals worldwide continues to increase.[34]

urban water supplies and agricultural productivity than at any time during the past 50 years.

Water is both a renewable and a non-renewable resource. Thanks to the sun, the hydrologic cycle is constantly "making" water flow again as rain; however, there are times and places where water is being consumed faster than it is being renewed. Variations in precipitation, such as droughts, drain groundwater reserves and make fresh water availability even more precarious. Intellectually we know that life and the health of the environment depend on water, but that fact is easy to forget when most of us in North America have inexpensive drinking-quality water available at the flick of a wrist just about everywhere we go. Looking back at history helps to call attention to water's effect on past civilizations and helps us understand cultural and political animosity over ownership, so we aren't condemned to repeating past mistakes. In this book, you will find many reasons for hope, learn about promising new technologies and management approaches and discover many things that you can do to offer positive solutions to the urban water crises that lie before us.

PART I

THE COMING WATER CRISIS

Patterns of
Water Use

More than one-half of the world's major rivers
are being seriously depleted and polluted,
degrading and poisoning the surrounding
ecosystems, thus threatening the health and
livelihood of people who depend upon them. [1]

— Ismail Serageldin,
Chairman of the World Commission
on Water for the 21st Century

IN THIS CHAPTER, we look at where water comes from, how it is allocated among various uses and how much each individual uses. We'll look
briefly at water use in cities, homes and offices, compared with other uses
such as agriculture and food processing. We'll also look at a very interesting
new idea that extends water use, going beyond the direct consumption of
various end-users, to consider the total "water footprint" of various products.

Where does our water use go? In most of the world, water is used primarily for agriculture and food production; secondarily for mining, electric
power and industrial production and lastly for buildings (homes, offices,
schools, colleges, retail and the like). While this book focuses on the smallest category of water use, it is nonetheless important because it's the use in
some ways that is the easiest and most cost-effective to change.

Freshwater Withdrawals

Let's take a look at water use in 2005 in the US (the most current data available at this time).[2] According to the US Geological Survey, 2005 freshwater withdrawals were about 350 billion gallons per day (Bgpd), with 270 Bgpd from surface waters and 80 Bgpd from groundwater. Of these withdrawals, about 41 percent was used for thermoelectric (mostly coal-fired and nuclear) power plants, typically for "once-through" cooling (so most of the water was not "lost" or "consumed" except for some evaporative losses totaling about 10 percent of total withdrawals). You can see already that without water, little energy production is likely to occur. Water withdrawn for irrigation was 128 Bgpd, about the same as in 1970, indicating that agricultural water use has become much more efficient since that time. (Excluding power plants, agriculture accounted for 62 percent of all freshwater withdrawals in the US.) Water withdrawals for public water supplies were 44 Bgpd in 2005, about 13 percent of the total. Table 2.1 summarizes the available data on freshwater withdrawals in 2005.

Water use also varies dramatically by location, as shown in Figure 2.1. The average water use for household and commercial use in the US is 150 gallons per capita per day (gpcd). But the range is from about 100 gpcd in Vermont, where not much irrigation is needed, to more than 300 gpcd in Nevada, where irrigation is needed for almost everything, due to scant annual rainfall. As we'll see later in this book, the real variable in urban water use is the amount of water used for landscape irrigation, including small-scale food, fruit and flower growing.

Water Pricing and Water Demand

Water use is also determined to some degree by what people have to pay for water. Figure 2.2 shows national variations in water rates. The most expen-

TABLE 2.1 Freshwater withdrawals in the US, 2005, billion gallons per day (Bgpd).

End Use	Water Use (Bgpd)	Percentage of Total, with Power Plants	Percentage of Total, without Power Plants
Power plants	144	41	—
Agriculture	128	37	62
Public water supplies	44	13	21
Industry	18	5	9
Livestock/aquaculture	10	3	5
Private water supply	6	2	3
Total	350	100%	100%

sive water prices are in Western Europe, with Germany the highest at above $1.50 per cubic meter (265 gallons, or about $5.66 per 1,000 gallons), with the average US rate about one-third of that, about $0.50 per cubic meter ($1.89 per 1,000 gallons). In Western Europe, taxes account for much of both water and energy prices, a typical measure used by governments to reduce demand for these commodities (and to increase revenues).

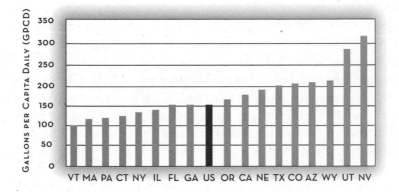

FIGURE 2.1 Average water use varies by state, from a low of 100 gallons per capita per day (gpcd) to a high of more than 300 gpcd.[3]

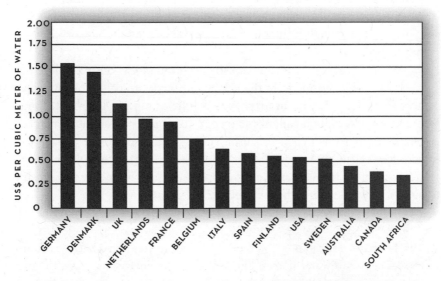

FIGURE 2.2 Average water prices tend to be quite a bit higher in Western Europe than in the US or Canada. Prices have a significant influence on water demand.[4]

We'll find out later in the book that *marginal* water prices (what you pay for the highest quantity, or tier, of water use) are even more important than *average* water prices in determining demand for water in cities. This result is in line with the thinking of most economists, which is that once we go beyond the 30 gallons per day or so that we need for drinking, cleaning and washing, water is an economic commodity whose use is determined primarily by its cost. We also recognize that cultural factors play a major role in determining water use: washing cars in the driveway, irrigating lawns in the desert and running the sprinklers of commercial buildings on a fixed daily schedule regardless of rainfall or soil moisture. For example, it's common in older sections of Phoenix to "flood irrigate" lawns in the intense heat of the desert summer, so they'll stay green all year round.

I live in Tucson, a metro area of a million people in the hot, arid Sonoran Desert of southern Arizona. A single-family homeowner in the city of Tucson will pay $1.86 per 1,000 gallons for the first 11,000 gallons of monthly use, but then will pay $6.86, nearly four times as much, for all subsequent water use.[5] This is an example of a fairly extreme *increasing block rate* pricing mechanism that water agencies use to dampen consumer demand in water-short cities. From my viewpoint, rationing *by price* is far more effective and much fairer than rationing *by regulation* to reduce demand. Price signals lead to permanent behavioral changes, investments in more efficient irrigation systems, changes in landscaping to reduce water use and purchases of water-efficient appliances and fixtures, whereas rationing by government edict is usually viewed as a short-term unpleasant measure and typically doesn't really result in permanent changes in water use psychology or practices.

Water prices also vary dramatically according to who is providing the water and who is using it. In the US, government projects subsidize agricultural water use, with users paying as little as $10 per acre-foot, about one-third of a million gallons ($0.03 per 1,000 gallons), about 1.5 percent of my first-tier water cost, with urban users paying an average of $450 per acre-foot ($1.50 per 1,000 gallons). In California, agricultural water prices in 2000 ranged from $10 per acre-foot to more than $100 per acre-foot, still substantially less than urban water costs.[6]

Water Use in Buildings

This book has a substantial focus on urban water uses and what you can do to reduce urban water demand and prevent the next water crisis in your town, city or state. Water use patterns are complex. Understanding them is the first step toward designing effective strategies to reduce water demand.

Consider Figure 2.3, which shows the various end uses of water in five different types of commercial and institutional buildings.

Hospitals and office buildings have the largest percentage of water use for heating, ventilating and air conditioning (HVAC), which you might have guessed, whereas restaurant water use is heavily concentrated in the kitchen. For schools, the largest water users are restrooms and showers, which you might expect, but almost as large a water user is landscaping, which you might not have expected. In hotels, water use is more balanced between laundry, kitchen, landscape and showers, and HVAC is a lesser contributor, perhaps because many of the rooms are unoccupied during the day. It's easy to see that some of the significant water uses may stem from older, inefficient fixtures, such as restrooms in restaurants, whereas others are built into the very fabric of the enterprise, such as laundry in hotels, HVAC in office buildings and restrooms and showers in hospitals.

Effective policies for reducing water use in these varied end-use categories should combine price signals, fixture and appliance retrofits, behavioral changes and incentives for purchasing newer equipment. In this book, you will discover that each water conservation measure is effective in particular circumstances and with particular end-users, meaning a comprehensive water use reduction program must encompass a wide variety of measures.

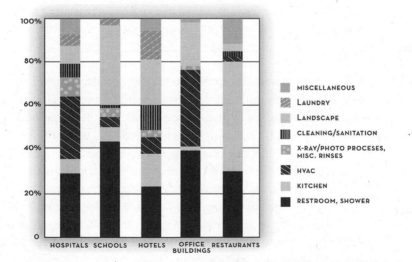

FIGURE 2.3 End-use demands vary greatly in commercial buildings, and in some surprising ways. Courtesy of *Environmental Building News*; data from American Water Works Association.

Your Water Footprint

Good water conservation management is essential to prevent drought from crippling a major city. However, water use patterns are integrated with lifestyle choices, economic values and even the foods we eat and the beverages we drink. An emerging idea, the "water footprint" looks at water consumption through a broader lens. In the broadest sense, a national water footprint shows not only water use inside the country, but also the induced or indirect water use in the products imported. According to the Water Footprint Network:

> The water footprint of a nation is defined as the total amount of water that is used to produce the goods and services consumed by the inhabitants of the nation. Since not all goods consumed in one particular country are produced in that country, the water footprint consists of two components:
> - Internal water footprint, i.e., the water use inside the country for consumption.
> - External water footprint, i.e., the water use in other countries for production.
>
> Traditional water use statistics show the water supply per sector (domestic, agriculture, industry). The approach has always been supply and producer-oriented. The water footprint concept [was] introduced to have a demand and consumer-oriented indicator as well, including not only the water used within the country but also the virtual water import.[7]

Similarly, a company's water footprint refers to the total volume of fresh water that is used directly and indirectly to run and support the business, consisting of direct water use in its own operations plus the water used by the company's suppliers. If a company takes in agricultural products, for example, to make its product, it can have a supply-chain water footprint much greater than the operational footprint.[8] Consider a very common product, beer. A liter of beer can have a very large water footprint, as shown in Figure 2.4, one that will vary depending on whether the crops that make the beer come from irrigated or non-irrigated sources. In this case, beer makers in South Africa must rely on the products of irrigated agriculture, which is a much greater water user, while beer makers in the Czech Republic can rely on mostly non-irrigated crops to make their beer. Proponents of water footprint accounting hope that you will eventually use this criterion to de-

1 LITER OF BEER   45 LITERS OF WATER   150 LITERS OF WATER
PILSNER URQUELL   CARLING BLACK LABEL
(CZECH REPUBLIC)   (SOUTH AFRICA)

FIGURE 2.4 If you're going to drink beer, be aware that it carries a large "water footprint."[9]

cide which beer to buy. South African beer makers, of course, hope that you will *chug-a-lug* without regard to the water footprint of the malt and hops.

Figure 2.5 shows the water footprint of common foods, such as meat, grains, fruits and other vegetables. In all cases, the water footprint of meat is two to five times that of vegetables, fruits and grains, lending an additional benefit to the choice of a vegetarian diet, or one in which animal products are condiments, not main dishes. Of course, there are other beneficial food choices, such as that of "locavores" who want to eat only food grown close to where they live, within a radius of 100 to 250 miles.[10] In the same way, an "aquavore" is someone who wants only to use water that actually falls on or near his or her property (but more on that later in the book).

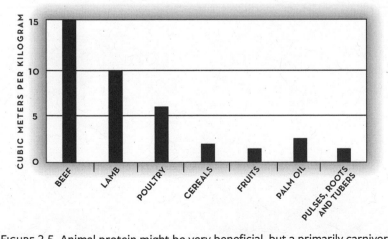

FIGURE 2.5 Animal protein might be very beneficial, but a primarily carnivorous diet has a much larger water footprint than a mostly vegetarian diet.[11]

Summary

To avert urban water crises, as a society we need to reduce our total water footprint by modifying our patterns of water use. An awareness and understanding of water withdrawals as well as national and personal demand patterns will go a long way in assisting with that effort. City, state and regional water agencies are leading this charge by implementing programs and incentives to encourage individuals and businesses to reduce their water usage. The next chapter looks at what happens when an entire country, in this case Australia, undergoes a major drought brought on by the effects of climate change. We also look at recent drought responses by two major US cities, Atlanta and San Diego.

Urban
Water Crises

Water is the only drink for a wise man.[1]
— Henry David Thoreau

URBAN WATER CRISES are not just a thing of the future, they are happening all around us as long-term reductions in rainfall and runoff tie in with short-term multiyear droughts. In this chapter, you'll read case studies of three crises, in three very different regions: Australia, which has endured its most severe drought in history; Atlanta, whose water supplies are under stress from both drought and water fights with neighboring states; and San Diego, at the end of a long pipeline bringing water to Southern California, which dealt with a statewide drought in 2009. From these crises we can learn lessons for handling future droughts in urban areas of the US and Canada.

Australia: Drought of a Lifetime and an Early Warning to the US

Australia's current multiyear drought is the most devastating in the country's 117 years of recorded history. Australia was already the most arid inhabited continent in the world,[2] and most are pointing to climate change as the main culprit of the current drought.[3] Increasing temperatures (1.35°F over the past 15 years) caused greater evaporation from vegetation and reservoirs, depleting further already penurious water supplies.[4] Some authorities are warning of permanent drought in certain areas. Figure 3.1 shows a map of the major cities of Australia and of the Murray-Darling River system, a key water source.

The country's water supply was precarious before the drought. Agricultural irrigation overuse and other restrictions have altered flows in the 1,600-mile Murray River, a major water resource. Flows have been as low as 25 percent of capacity while salinity levels have surged beyond the World Health Organization's (WHO) recommendations for safe drinking. The acceptable level of salinity for safe drinking water, according to WHO, is 800 EC (electrical conductivity) units, but the salinity in parts of the Murray is now around 1,200 EC units. If salinity levels rise to 1,400 EC units, the water authority will be forced to import water.[5]

In Western Australia, inflows to Perth's largest reservoir have fallen 75 percent from an 85-year average of 320 gigaliters (GL) (84.5 billion gallons) per year to about 80 GL per year since 2003 and as low as 60 GL in 2007. Even with extensive conservation measures and a planned increase in treated wastewater reuse from 13 to 30 percent, the region requires new supply sources such as seawater desalination. Perth is often described as the most isolated large city in the world, some 2,000 miles away from the next

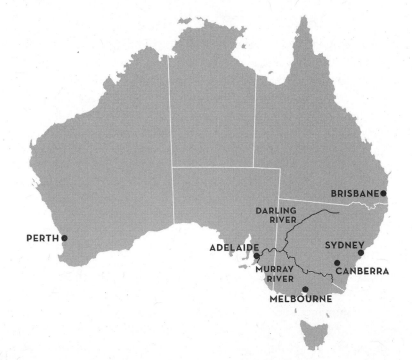

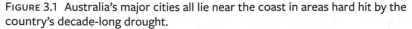

FIGURE 3.1 Australia's major cities all lie near the coast in areas hard hit by the country's decade-long drought.

largest city, Adelaide. There is nowhere else to look for water, except to the sea. One explanation for the region's drought is a shift in weather patterns caused by higher ocean water temperatures that has moved storm tracks south toward Antarctica and away from southwest Australia.[6]

Drought Side Effects

Not only has the cost of water increased and available supply decreased, the ongoing drought is also blamed for a reduction in food reserves and an increase in potential health risks. Australia's food reserves are at their lowest level in 30 years, while population continues to rise. This situation is not unique to Australia. World food demand is predicted to double by 2050, while the amount of available water for irrigation is predicted to shrink by almost 50 percent. Many observers blame increased water draws from cities, combined with climate change.[7] Of course, one disturbing implication of this forecast is that food prices will inevitably rise, making it more difficult for the world's population to get enough to eat without massive government subsidies.

Increased collection of rainwater and changes in temperature and rainfall could lead to more outbreaks of dengue fever, the most common insect-born viral infection in tropical areas. Dengue-fever-carrying mosquitoes reproduce in stagnant water, and experts predict a growth in the number of breeding cycles with rising temperatures.[8]

FIGURE 3.2 Water flows in the Murray-Darling River system, critical to agriculture as well as ecology in southeastern Australia, have diminished greatly during the country's drought.

National Response

National Water Initiative (NWI), the country's "blueprint for water reform," was established in 2005 by the Council of Australian Governments.[9] Administered by the National Water Commission, NWI is a shared commitment by national and state governments to develop a cohesive approach to the managing, pricing, planning and trading of water. Each state and territory government is required to prepare an NWI implementation plan that outlines their water management strategy.[10]

In 2008, the Australian government introduced Water for the Future, a national plan that integrated rural and urban water issues to secure the country's long-term water supply. The $12.9 billion plan has four priorities: taking action on climate change, using water wisely, securing new water supplies and supporting healthy rivers. Besides policies and programs, a key focus of the plan is the Murray-Darling River Basin; the plan will establish a sustainable and legally enforceable limit on surface and groundwater extractions within the Basin.[11]

Over the past three years, most major urban areas instituted water restrictions, both permanent and temporary, based on rainfall, reservoir storage levels and other conditions. According to the *National Performance Report 2007–2008*, the average volume of water supplied to urban residential customers fell by 37 percent over the prior six-year period.[12] Brisbane Water recorded the largest reduction, 50 percent.[13]

Effect on the Economy

The water and wastewater treatment sector has annual revenues of about AUD$4 billion (US$3.7 billion). Ninety percent of the country's 20.8 million people are connected to a public water supply, and 85 percent are connected to one of the 700 sewage treatment plants. The drought has severely affected the farming industry; economists estimate that it has reduced the country's GDP by 1 percent.[14] Australian utilities reported a net profit decrease of AUD$1.73 billion in 2006–2007 and AUD$1.26 billion in 2007–2008. Water rates are expected to increase owing to reduced consumption combined with increased costs.[15] (This is a phenomenon that water utilities in North America are also encountering and one that is fraught with political consequences, since higher water rates affect everyone's budget.)

Product Labeling and Innovation

Requiring the use of more water-conserving plumbing is one component of the solution to what appears to be a permanent problem for Australia. A first start has been to label devices to indicate their water use. The Water Efficiency Labeling and Standards (WELS) Scheme is a mandatory regulatory rating system based on the 2005 Water Efficiency Labeling and Standards Act. Showers, sinks, toilets and urinals manufactured or imported after July 2006 are required to carry a WELS label. Products are awarded zero to six stars based on the product's water efficiency.[16]

The "Smart Approved WaterMark" is a labeling scheme for products and services that reduce water use in and around the home.[17] To receive a WaterMark label, products are reviewed by independent certifying authorities and must meet the requirements of the Plumbing Code of Australia and the specifications listed in relevant Australian Standards. The requirements are focused on the quality of the product, including health and safety characteristics, and confirm that it is fit for its intended use. Some state and territory plumbing regulations require the WaterMark certification before such products can be installed. More than 160 products and 17 services carry the WaterMark label.[18]

Drought and water restrictions have been the inspiration for some creative water-saving products. One of the recently WaterMark labeled products is the Every Drop Shower Saver, a paddle-like device that can be inserted into the base of an existing shower arm. It can pause the flow of water from the shower without turning the tap off and on again, or having to readjust the water temperature and pressure. The Squeaky Green Total Waterless Car Wash, also WaterMark labeled, includes biodegradable gloves and cloths for washing, waxing and polishing without the use of water. Smart Approved WaterMark services include irrigation consultants, waterless car cleaning services and plumbing certification programs.[19]

Industry Response to Drought

In 2007, the Plumbing Industry Commission of the state of Victoria developed the PlumbSmarter project that aims to "to identify strategies for tackling environmental sustainability through changing the framework and operation of the Victorian plumbing industry — and to begin pursuit of the strategies."[20] The PlumbSmarter report, *Path to a Greener Plumbing Industry*, contains contributions from more than 300 plumbers. The water- and energy-saving opportunities discussed in this report range from specific changes in plumbing practices and products to broad proposals that influence the nature of the industry. The report is organized into the following areas for action:

- Sustainability skills for plumbers in Victoria
- Innovation gateway
- Knowledge bank

- Hot water systems
- Fire sprinklers
- Swimming pools
- Sustainable plumbing systems design

PlumbSmarter estimates that plumbers in Victoria will deliver 200,000 sustainability retrofits, sustainability audits and information kits to homes and small businesses. As a result, the state will save an estimated four billion liters (1 billion gallons) of water per year directly as a result of the retrofits made over a five-year period based on the strategies identified in the report.[21]

Wastewater Treatment and Third-pipe Systems

Western Australia's Department of Water's State Water Strategy set a short-term target to recycle 20 percent of all wastewater by 2012; as of 2009, total wastewater recycling exceeded 13 percent. The long-term goal for wastewater recycling in Western Australia is to exceed 30 percent.[22]

In Sydney, many new homes are being outfitted with "third-pipe" circulation systems. These systems carry recycled water to homes from water recycling plants for typical graywater uses such as toilet flushing. Australia's largest residential recycling plant, Rouse Hill, supplies recycled water to more than 16,500 homes in Sydney. The plant, which began operation in 2001 and produces more than 1.9 GL (500 million gallons) of recycled water per year for reuse, is undergoing an AUD$52 million expansion. Capacity will be increased by an additional 4.7 GL (1,240 million gallons) per year of recycled wastewater for use in new housing developments in Sydney's suburbs.[23]

Targeting High Water Users

In South East Queensland, home to 14 percent of Australia's population, residential water use dropped from 70 to 34 gallons per person per day in 2007–2008, owing to voluntary conservation and water-use restrictions. By comparison, the average per capita per day use in California is 135 gallons.[24] These savings were not a result of conservation programs alone. The Residential Excessive Water Users Compliance Program, initiated by the local water agency, targeted the highest-water-using households. Beyond providing water conservation information, the program also required those households to account for their consumption and provide reasons for excessive use. In 2005–2006, 37 percent of households used more than

210 gallons per day; in 2007–2008, as a result of the program, the number of excessive users fell to 6.8 percent.[25]

Water Use in Commercial Buildings

The commercial and institutional sector accounts for nearly half of the country's non-agricultural water use, while offices and other commercial buildings are responsible for 11 percent of municipal water use. Wastewater produced by the commercial sector as a result of doing business (not from toilets and sinks) is called "trade waste water," and it makes up 10 to 15 percent of the country's sewage flows. Commercial water supply and discharge are a primary focus of governmental water management strategies. For example, the state government of New South Wales created a four-year AUD$120 million fund to help businesses implement water-efficiency and recycling projects. Also in New South Wales, as one example, the Metropolitan Water Plan includes initiatives to encourage participation in Sydney's water and wastewater industry by simplifying the process of *sewer mining* (treating and recycling wastewater).[26] (See Chapter 10 for an extended discussion of sewer mining.)

In 2003, the Green Building Council of Australia released the Green Star system that rates the environmental attributes of buildings based on nine categories including water management. One office building rated at the highest level of the Green Star system (6 Star) reduced potable water use 90 percent, compared to a typical building, through blackwater recycling, sewer mining and a cooling system that uses harbor water instead of cooling towers. A 6-Star-rated shopping center reduced potable water use by 62 percent by using a rainwater harvesting system designed to supply 100 percent of the project's water needs for irrigation, toilet and urinal flushing and cooling tower makeup water.[27]

Securing Future Water Supplies

Since most of Australia's population lives near the ocean, nearly every state is implementing or seriously considering desalination. The first large-scale desalination plant opened in April 2007 in Perth and supplies 45 GL (12 billion gallons) of water per year. Western Australia is planning a second plant, projected to have a 50 GL per year capacity. In Sydney, the local water utility, Sydney Water, expects that 15 percent of its water supply will come from desalination by 2015.[28] A new AUD$1.9 billion plant to supply 250 million liters (66 million gallons) of drinking water per day (90 GL per year) to Sydney Water customers is expected to be operational by summer

2010. A 67-turbine wind farm will supply the plant's energy needs.[29] In East Queensland, the Gold Coast Desalination Plant supplies more than 135 million liters (36 million gallons) of drinking water per day.[30] A number of other plants are under construction (or under serious consideration) around the country.[31]

The Australian Guidelines for Water Recycling first appeared in November 2006. Phase 1 focuses primarily on the industrial and agricultural sectors but anticipates that recycled sewage water will be used for drinking purposes in the near future. For example, the Western Corridor Recycled Water Project in Queensland, one of the country's largest completed projects, plans to supply drinking water when dam levels fall below 40 percent. Other utilities such as Sydney Water set targets to increase recycled water use, with Sydney Water's planning to supply 70 GL per year (18.7 billion gallons) of recycled water by 2015.[32]

Sewer mining, the process of extracting wastewater from urban sewers and treating it onsite for reuse as recycled water, is still in the initial stages of consideration and adoption. The development of additional non-potable water supplies through sewer mining would reduce the demand for potable water.[33] Melbourne's 6-Star Green Star building, Council House 2, already has implemented this approach for a 9-story public office building, using an in-house treatment system to provide recycled wastewater for toilet flushing, a roof garden and other uses. (See Chapter 10.)

Atlanta: Facing the Prospect of Continuing Water Shortages

The Metropolitan North Georgia Water Planning District (Metro Water) serves 16 counties and more than 90 cities in and around the Atlanta metropolitan area, delivers approximately 652 million gallons of water per day. Metro Water District relies on surface water (streams, rivers and lakes) for 98 percent of its water needs, with the Chattahoochee River Basin providing about 70 percent of the district's total water supply.[34] The Atlanta region averages 50 inches of rainfall each year; however, the district periodically experiences extreme drought, such as in 2003 and 2007–2008. The impacts of drought periods for north Georgia are severe because the region does not import any water and relies mostly on surface water supplies.[35]

In September 2007, Georgia's Environmental Protection Division (EPD) imposed Level 4 drought restrictions, banning most types of outdoor water use in northern Georgia. The greatly depleted Lake Lanier (Figure 3.3) came to symbolize the seriousness of one of the worst droughts in the region's history.

Figure 3.3 Lake Lanier, the primary water supply reservoir for metro Atlanta, was heavily affected by a recent drought.

The EPD officially lifted drought watering restrictions on June 10, 2009, after the second-wettest spring on record significantly replenished the region's lakes and reservoirs.[36] Upon announcing the end of the drought, Carol A. Couch, EPD Director, stated, *"The decision to ease outdoor watering restrictions should not be seen as a license to waste water, but as a vote of confidence in Georgians' ability to conserve and use water efficiently."*[37]

As the state transitions from mandatory drought management to more voluntary water conservation, district, local and state water officials in Georgia intend to achieve sustained water conservation savings by continuing to foster positive water use choices. This includes developing a "culture of conservation" in the region.[38] In fact, the Metro Water District's *Water Supply and Water Conservation Management Plan* shows that, without aggressive ongoing water conservation, *water usage will reach the limits of projected available supply by 2030.*

The Metro Water District's Water Conservation Actions expect to reduce average annual water demand by an estimated 20 percent, to satisfy the needs of a growing regional population and to guarantee reserve water supplies through 2030.[39]

The District's planned Water Conservation Actions include:

- Establish conservation pricing by all District water utilities.
- Replace older, inefficient plumbing fixtures.
- Require pre-rinse spray-valve retrofit education programs (for commercial users).
- Enact legislation to require rain sensor shutoff switches on new irrigation systems.
- Require unit sub-meters in new multifamily buildings.
- Assess and reduce water system leakage.
- Conduct residential water audits.
- Distribute low-flow retrofit kits to residential users.
- Conduct commercial water audits.
- Implement education and public awareness plans.[40]

The water conservation framework and objectives established by the Metro Water District guide the formation of specific water policies enacted by local water agencies, such as the City of Atlanta's Department of Watershed Management.

Water Management in the City of Atlanta

Mayor Shirley Franklin created the City of Atlanta's Department of Watershed Management (DWM) in September 2003 to consolidate the city's drinking water, sewer and stormwater management services. This marked the de-privatization of Atlanta's water system from United Water, a private water corporation that secured a water management contract with the City of Atlanta in 1999.[41] The DWM serves 142,000 accounts with over 2,400 miles of pipe in the distribution system, some of which was first built in the 1870s. Atlanta's DWM is in the midst of a $4 billion Clean Water Atlanta initiative to overhaul its antiquated water and sewer infrastructure.[42]

City of Atlanta Drought Response 2007–2008

In response to the 2007–2008 drought, the DWM aggressively pursued water conservation measures, which generated average monthly water savings of about 15 percent and earned DWM Commissioner Robert Hunter the US Environmental Protection Agency's Water Efficiency Leader award. These measures:

- doubled the price for irrigation water use;
- limited landscape watering exceptions and eliminated exceptions for newly installed sod;

- invited Atlanta's 50 largest water customers to learn about water-saving options, after which all 50 cut their water consumption, some by up to 45 percent (invitees included Delta Airlines and Atlanta City Hall);
- irrigated street trees by reusing water originally used to flush fire hydrants, in partnership with Trees Atlanta; and
- initiated a high-efficiency toilet (HET) rebate program.[43]

Institutionalizing Ongoing Water Conservation Practices in Atlanta

Although the statewide Drought Alert has been officially lifted, Atlanta's DWM continues to use a range of mandatory and voluntary water conservation policies and programs.

- **Conservation water pricing:** The DWM uses conservation pricing where customers using 1 to 3 CCF (1 CCF equals 100 cubic feet or 748 gallons) monthly pay $9.77 per CCF for water and sewer; those using 4 to 6 CCF monthly pay $15.07 per CCF; and those using 7 or more CCF pay $17.34 per CCF, about double the base rate.[44] The City of Atlanta has found that conservation water pricing is an easily understood and powerful means of signaling the value and scarcity of water to its customers.[45]
- **Rainwater harvesting barrels:** The DWM launched an online rain barrel tutorial providing step-by-step instructions for residential customers to construct a safe and effective rain barrel for outdoor watering uses.[46]
- **Free water conservation kit:** The kit includes a low-flow shower head, kitchen and bathroom aerators, flow measurement bag, toilet dye tablets and instructions.
- **Residential toilet rebate program:** In January 2009, Mayor Shirley Franklin allocated $1 million toward a toilet rebate program for Atlanta residents to replace old toilets with new, low-flow models.[47]
- **GreenPlumbers training:** The DWM's GreenPlumbers Caring for Our Water Metro City Challenge Certification Workshops emphasize water conservation and efficiency training for Atlanta's professional plumbers.[48]
- **WaterSmart** is a statewide education program and water conservation branding effort designed to help Georgia residents understand how to maintain their landscapes while using less water.[49]
- **Meter replacement:** The City has replaced 66,855 of its 153,000 water meters with ones capable of remote reading. As part of an ongoing $34 million replacement program, the new meters will ensure more accurate billing and reduce illegal water use.

Table 3.1 Progress in improving Atlanta's water supply under renewed public ownership

2002	2008
750 leak repairs per year (avg.)	9,600 leak repairs per year (avg.)
20,000 malfunctioning water meters	4,000 malfunctioning water meters
9 boil water advisories	0 boil water advisories
No financial plan	Detailed financial plan

- **Measured progress:** Table 3.1 compares statistics from 2002 to 2008 and highlights the DWM's accomplishments since assuming responsibility for Atlanta's water distribution system from United Water in 2003.[50]

Regional and State Leaders Focus on Georgia's Long-term Water Challenges

Disputed water rights at the regional level — between Alabama, Georgia and Florida — also complicate Atlanta's future water security. In July 2009, a US District Court judge ruled that nearly all of Georgia's water withdrawals from Lake Lanier are illegal because the lake was originally built for hydroelectricity not for consumptive water storage. As a result of this ruling, the Governors of Alabama, Georgia and Florida are expected to return to the negotiation table, after decades of stalemate, where Atlanta's long-term water consumption and conservation will be major points of contention.[51]

In 2007, Governor Sonny Perdue's executive order created Georgia's Water Conservation Implementation Plan (WCIP). The document's opening statement says: "The ultimate goal of water conservation is not to discourage water use, but to maximize the benefit from each gallon used. Georgia's Water Conservation Implementation Plan (WCIP) is designed to create a culture of conservation and guide Georgians toward more efficient use of our state's finite water resources."[52]

Chapter Five of the WCIP, Conserving Water Used in Industrial and Commercial Facilities, outlines goals, benchmarks and 13 Best Practices (BPs) ranging from water management plans to recycling and reusing water. Best Practice 5, recycle and reuse water, suggests:

Industrial and commercial (IC) facilities can minimize their need for new water withdrawals by: 1) using reclaimed water for 50 percent or more of total outdoor water needs where practical and reasonably available; 2) implementing stormwater capture to collect clean rainwater as a substitute for freshwater in and around the facility. Stormwater ponds must be constructed according to local and state environmental regulations; and 3) counterflow cooling/rinsing methods (for manufacturing industries).[53]

At the local, district and state level in Georgia, water conservation remains a social, political and economic priority. However, as the region emerges from its most recent drought and the pressure for immediate water savings lessens, Georgia is still experiencing the challenges of maintaining its policies for aggressive water conservation that accompany undisputed water scarcity and drought-induced crisis. In 2010, Governor Perdue proposed and secured major new legislation, the Georgia Water Stewardship Act, intended to institutionalize water conservation practices.[54]

San Diego County Water Authority

The San Diego County Water Authority (CWA) is a wholesale water supplier serving the San Diego region. CWA supplies water to 24 member water agencies including six cities; irrigation, municipal and public utility water districts; and the Camp Pendleton Marine Corps base. In 2008, CWA supplied 710,000 acre-feet of water to the area's 3 million residents.[55] In 2008, more than 300 miles of pipeline from northern California and the Colorado River delivered about 88 percent of San Diego's water supply.[56] Owing to the region's dependence on imported water and projected population growth of one million people by 2030, CWA's central priorities include water supply diversification, storage and infrastructural improvements, and water conservation.[57]

Since 1990, CWA and its member agencies have saved about 560,000 acre-feet of water and have kept urban *per capita water use below 1990 averages,* with an investment of more than $1.8 million annually in conservation programs. Some notable water conservation achievements over this period include:

- 518,000 ultra-low-flush toilets installed.
- 600,000 water-saving shower heads installed.
- 53,000 high-efficiency clothes washers installed.
- 7,200 acre-feet of water saved through commercial-industrial-institutional hardware replacements.[58]

California's Interconnected Water Supply
Spurs Statewide Conservation in 2009

San Diego County receives more than 70 percent of its water from the Metropolitan Water District (MWD) of Southern California. On April 14,

2009, the MWD announced that it would cut water deliveries to San Diego County by 13 percent (down from a worst-case scenario that would have cut water deliveries by 20 percent).[59] New restrictions on surface water pumping in the Sacramento-San Joaquin River Delta (a major water source for Southern California) prompted the reductions. The restrictions aim to help protect endangered fish species. On April 23, 2009, CWA issued a similar announcement to cut water deliveries to its member agencies by 8 percent effective July 1 and declared a Level 2 Drought Alert.

Drought Management 2009: Public Outreach and Level 2 Drought Alert Restrictions

In response to the reduced water allocation from MWD, CWA launched a series of water conservation public awareness campaigns to complement the traditional Level 2 Drought Alert public announcements. The 20-Gallon Challenge is a region-wide, voluntary water conservation campaign challenging San Diego County businesses and residents to reduce their water use by 20 gallons per person, per day.[60]

San Diego County's local water agencies are required to meet or exceed the CWA's model drought response ordinance defined under a Level 2 Drought Alert.[61] The City of San Diego adopted the following drought ordinance:

- **Landscape irrigation limits and day assignments:** Sprinklers (limited to ten minutes per watering station) and tree and shrub watering are allowed no more than three assigned days per week from June 1 to October 31, and before 10 AM or after 6 PM, according to a specified schedule.
- **Leak Repair:** All leaks must be stopped or repaired upon discovery or within 72 hours of notification by the City of San Diego.
- **Construction Use of Water:** When available, use of recycled or nonpotable water is required for construction purposes.
- **Car Washing:** Vehicles may only be washed at a commercial car wash or by using a hose with an automatic shutoff nozzle or with a hand-held water container.
- **Single Pass-through Cooling:** The City will not provide new water service connections for commercial customers using single pass-through cooling systems (all systems must use water more than once).
- **Water Recirculation Systems:** All new conveyer car wash and commercial laundry systems connections will be required to employ a recirculation water system.
- **Hotel Laundering:** Guests in all hotels, motels, and other commercial

lodging establishments must be provided the option of not laundering towels and linens daily.

- **Restaurant Water Refills:** Restaurants and other food establishments shall only serve and refill water for patrons upon request. [62]

City of San Diego Water Conservation Initiatives

Within San Diego County, all 24 local water agencies develop, implement and enforce the water ordinance for their communities. The following examples from the City of San Diego Water Department illustrate how a local water agency translates the countywide objectives of the CWA into specific water ordinances and programs.

Plumbing Retrofit Upon Sale Ordinance. San Diego Municipal Code section 147.04 requires that all buildings, before a change in ownership, be certified as having water-conserving plumbing fixtures. This ordinance affects all residential, commercial and industrial water customers who receive water service from the City of San Diego Water Department.[63] Plumbing fixture retrofit requirements include:

- **Toilets** that use more than 3.5 gallons per flush (gpf) must be replaced with ultra-low flush toilets (ULFTs) that use 1.6 gpf or less. Modifications intended to reduce the flow of an existing toilet, such as the use of toilet bags, dams, bricks, or other alternative flushing devices, are not permissible and do not comply with Code provisions.
- **Shower heads** that emit more than 2.5 gallons of water per minute (gpm) must be replaced with low-flow shower heads that use no more than 2.5 gpm. Shower head flow restrictors are not acceptable substitutes.
- **Sink faucets** (bathroom, bar, and kitchen sink faucets) that use more than 2.2 gpm must be retrofitted with either a new fixture or faucet aerators to reduce the water flow.
- **Reverse osmosis systems (for home water purification)** need automatic shut-off valves.
- **Urinals** that use more than 1.0 gpf must be replaced with low-flush models. The entire fixture must be replaced, not just the flush valve.

Commercial Landscape Survey. The Commercial Landscape Survey Program provides a free onsite irrigation system audit and water-use recommendations for commercial, industrial and institutional customers who have more than one acre of landscaped property. Qualifying participants also receive a written evaluation of the system's performance, aerial photos of the property, a water-use estimate for the upcoming year, and an irrigation controller schedule for each month. The program has generated landscape water savings between 20 and 40 percent on participating properties.[64]

Future Planning

Future planning is an important part of the work of every water agency. In San Diego County, in the coming years, the CWA will shift its focus from indoor to outdoor uses, particularly landscape water conservation. In 2009, about 50 percent of San Diego County's urban water use was for landscaping.[65] In April 2008, the CWA published a strategic plan that defined the following countywide water supply and conservations goals:

> By January 1, 2015, the average regional residential per capita water consumption will be reduced by 10 percent from the current 10-year regional average.
>
> By January 1, 2020, the Water Authority will have facilitated and/or developed local seawater and brackish groundwater desalination facilities that meet 10 percent of the region's total water supply requirements.
>
> By January 1, 2025, the member agencies, with the assistance of the Water Authority, will supply at least 6 percent of the region's total water supply through water recycling.[66]

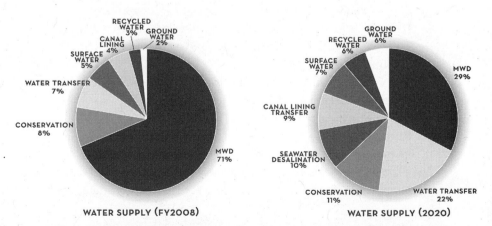

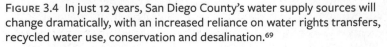

FIGURE 3.4 In just 12 years, San Diego County's water supply sources will change dramatically, with an increased reliance on water rights transfers, recycled water use, conservation and desalination.[69]

Table 3.2 shows expected sources of water conservation and new water supplies, based on the 2005 San Diego County Urban Water Management Plan, while Figure 3.4 shows expected water supply sources in 2020, compared with those in 2008.[67] You can see that San Diego County is relying heavily on new and "exotic" water sources such as inter-basin water transfers from irrigation districts, a proposed desalination plant in Carlsbad (North County), recycled water and conservation to meet its current and expected requirements. Water deliveries from MWD, the regional wholesale water supplier, are expected to fall from 71 percent of demand in 2008 to less than 30 percent of demand in 2030.[68] This is a bold experiment for a growing metro area with more than three million people today (and a population of four million expected in 20 years), but as the "end of the pipeline" county in a water-short and water-stressed area, San Diego County has few viable alternatives.

TABLE 3.2 Potential Water Conservation Savings through 2030 Within the San Diego County Water Authority Service Area (Acre-feet)

Best Management Practices (BMPs)	2005	2010	2015	2020	2025	2030
Existing BMPs						
Residential Surveys	1,620	1,620	1,620	1,620	1,620	1,620
Residential Retrofits	8,100	8,100	8,100	8,100	8,100	8,100
Landscape	3,524	18,484	21,793	24,783	27,744	30,718
Clothes Washer Incentives	495	1,281	1,672	1,672	1,672	1,672
Commercial/Industrial/Institutional	2,260	3,328	5,056	6,801	8,533	10,272
Toilet Incentives	17,553	23,616	23,616	23,616	23,616	23,616
Subtotal	33,551	56,792	61,857	66,593	71,826	75,998
Potential BMPs and Efficiency Standards						
Efficiency Standards	19,837	23,137	25,409	27,526	30,598	32,323
Graywater	0	25	30	40	50	50
On-demand Water Heaters	0	5	10	15	20	25
Subtotal	19,837	23,167	25,449	27,581	30,668	32,398
Total	53,389	79,960	87,306	94,174	101,954	108,396

Summary

Urban water crises are caused by various factors including drought, supply reductions and ownership conflicts. Along with restrictions and changes to water policy, to reduce water usage a "culture of conservation" needs to be cultivated in the public's mind. Many water agencies are also finding it necessary to locate new supply sources to meet demand.[70] Four million people in the Atlanta metro region face continuing uncertainty over water supplies, having barely survived the 2007–2008 drought when reserves were reduced to a mere 90-day supply of water. Recognizing its existence at the "end of the pipeline" and not wanting to endure permanent drought restrictions, San Diego County needs to embrace just about every available new and exotic source of water to supply the needs of a population expected to grow from three to four million over the next 20 years. Each of these case studies provides ample warning and good lessons for urban areas throughout the American southeast, south, southwestern and western states, home to considerable population growth in the past 20 years and likely to see a continued influx of new residents for the next 20.

Urban Water Management

*What makes the desert beautiful
is that somewhere it hides a well.*

— Antoine de Saint-Exupery[1]

WHAT ARE THE OPPORTUNITIES for urban water management in the coming decade, the second of this century? Where should cities be looking for means and methods to meet their water supply requirements? What is the relationship between water supply and energy supply? What should water cost in the new era of scarcity and uncertainty? What will be the effects of global warming on water supplies? In this chapter, we'll explore these themes and see what lessons, best practices and good examples we can elicit for urban water management. Let's start with the big picture, global warming induced by climate change.

Global Warming and Water Supply in North America

Most experts believe that much of the US will get warmer and drier in the decades ahead, as global warming phenomena begin to manifest. Figure 4.1 shows current "best guess" average temperature predictions, although subject to a great deal of uncertainty, for the year 2100. Even averages can disguise a lot of variation — consider the value of the Dow Jones Industrial Average (DJIA) in April 1998 (9000) to July 2009 (9000), and you will see the same numbers, meaning that there was no growth of a basket of the

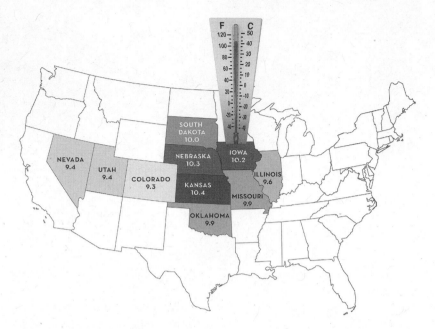

FIGURE 4.1 US temperatures in the central regions might increase as much as 10°F over the next 90 years.[3]

DJIA stocks over that 11-year period.[2] However, who won't remember the collapse of the US stock market not once but twice within that decade?

Because of the higher temperatures, most people expect more annual precipitation to fall as rain rather than as snow, leading to greater spring floods and reduced summer streamflows; areas dependent on summer flows will likely experience droughts in summer and be forced to rely more on groundwater wells or new sources of water. In many areas of the West and Southwest, current models also predict lower overall precipitation, with a greater probability of multiyear droughts.[4] The highest predicted temperature increases, shown in Figure 4.1, are west of the Mississippi in the middle latitudes of the country, which may adversely affect crop and livestock production.[5] The warming will differ by season, with winters warming more than summers in most areas.[6]

So, a simple equation might be: higher temperatures + less rain + lower soil moisture + lots more people = greater water demands on a finite resource. Even without global climate change, most regions of the southern tier of the United States will find themselves in San Diego's predicament, having to rely more on new and exotic sources of water supply to meet growing demands.

Nega-gallons and Water Demand

More than 20 years ago, the scientist and energy expert Amory Lovins introduced the term "negawatts" to indicate that conservation of energy would be a reliable alternative way to supply "megawatts" of projected electricity demand.[7] Lovins pioneered a "least-cost, end-use" approach that distinguished between the supply of energy and the services for which people wanted the energy (the end-use demand). For example, you really don't want to buy "electricity" from the utility company; you want "illumination" from electric lights. It is a lot cheaper to install more efficient fluorescent lighting (with a higher output in lumens per watt) than to buy more kilowatt-hours of electricity to run an inefficient incandescent light.

In the same way, water users don't really "need" water for more than basic physiological needs (a few gallons per day for bathing, drinking and cooking); what they really want are green plants (using irrigation), clean clothes and dishes, sanitation and clean bodies, clean cars, clean driveways, etc. If water is priced expensively, people will try to conserve it, by purchasing more water-efficient appliances and fixtures, fixing leaks, using drip irrigation instead of sprinklers, recovering and reusing rainwater and graywater and finding alternatives such as xeriscaping (landscaping with low-water-using plants). There is also a strong movement toward more natural landscapes that do not require more water than what nature provides.

In the San Diego County case study in the previous chapter, the county water agency expects the contribution of water conservation and recycled water (*nega-gallons*) to increase from 11 percent of total supply in 2008 to 17 percent in 2020, while supporting a larger total population. If the projected 10 percent of supply from seawater desalination does not develop by 2020, the important role of conservation will likely grow. In many respects, to continue the analogy, depending on expensive desalination for new water supply in coastal areas is similar to trying to reduce carbon dioxide emissions from coal plants with expensive nuclear power. In both cases, the expensive new supply source may be necessary, but planners should not regard it as a primary option or even a total solution.

In California, a study of water use efficiency calculated the capital cost as $0.13 per annual kilowatt-hour (kWh) saved, which would amortize at $0.013 per kWh on a ten-year basis, about one-fifth the cost of new electric power supplies. Water use efficiency also trumped the state's energy-efficiency programs, which cost an estimated $0.22 per annual kWh saved in 2006 to 2008, or about $0.022 per kWh (annualized), also far cheaper than new power sources. It certainly appears that *nega-gallons* trump even negawatts as an energy source![8]

The outcome: in today's world, *it's far cheaper to conserve water than to provide for new supply; nega-gallons are always going to be cheaper than new infrastructure solutions.* Consider a public agency, which is losing 5 to 15 percent of its supply to "unbilled" water, i.e., leaks. Wouldn't it be cheaper to find and fix the leaks today, thereby providing immediate additions to supply, than to build an expensive desalination plant that would require energy and maintenance into the far future? Wouldn't it be far cheaper to pay to fix leaks in public and private buildings, than to import water from hundreds of miles away, even if it were available?

Virtual Reservoirs: Why Water Efficiency Is the Best Solution for Water Shortages

As I have shown already, many parts of the United States face unprecedented challenges to water supply, caused by growing populations, reduced summer streamflows from the effects of global warming and lack of future infrastructure planning and financing.

Traditionally, building more dams and reservoirs was the first and only answer to water supply problems, but today it would be just about impossible to get a new large dam and reservoir permitted anywhere in the US. But in a typical American fashion, we still want to fight the future water supply problems with measures that worked in the past (but won't work anymore). These 19th- and 20th-century approaches don't work any more because they don't address many root problems. Though rainfall is a fundamentally renewable resource, surface waters are already over-allocated, groundwater is often finite and overdrawn, capturing and storing rainwater in large reservoirs costs quite a bit of money for the resulting benefit, and we are not using wisely the water we do have.

Relying solely on building large new dams or desalting brackish water or seawater is not cost-effective and won't solve today's water needs, which are really driven by poor water-use efficiencies in agriculture. Here's why: Per gallon of water supplied, dams cost up to 8,500 times more than water efficiency ("nega-gallon") investments. Dams are fixed in one place, take years to fill up and hold only a limited amount of water; they eventually fill up with sediment and become useless. When dry seasons abound, reservoirs can't even be used for recreation. Even when sufficient rains fill reservoirs, these giant pools can (and do) lose tremendous amounts of water through evaporation and seepage into surrounding rocks, particularly in the arid West.

For these reasons, building new dams or desalination plants should be a last alternative for solving most of our urban water supply needs. Water efficiency is our best source of affordable water and needs to become the core tenet of water supply planning. By implementing regionally appropriate water-efficiency policies, urban areas across the country can maintain cost-effective supplies that will meet the economic demand for water.

The Economics of Water Demand

Water is still very cheap, except when we buy it in bottled form, in which case it's about four times the cost of gasoline per gallon and 4,000 times as expensive as tap water! (Figure 4.2) To the degree that water in North America is an economic commodity, the more expensive it is, the less will be consumed. That's why one easy way to reduce water demand is just to charge more for it, beyond a minimum quantity for basic water needs.

In Tucson, Arizona, the increasing block rate structure kicks in above a monthly consumption of 1,500 cubic feet (11,200 gallons, or 374 gallons per day) per household.[10] For two people, that's 187 gallons per capita per day (gpcd), or about 20 percent more than the household average in the US.

In the early 1990s, the Irvine Ranch Water District (IRWD) in Orange County, California, used price as a primary method to ration scarce water supplies. The experiment was so successful that it put to rest the notion that "rationing by price" wouldn't work. The key factor was clear price signals sent in advance, generating a rapid feedback loop between water use and water cost. The "increasing block rate" structure was created in 1991, and by 1995, the district's per capita water use dropped from around 115 gallons to 90 gallons a day. It remains at that level today despite the area's rapid suburban growth.[11] IRWD gives each residential lot a water budget based

PUBLIC WATER SUPPLY
$2 - $5/1,000 GALLONS

GASOLINE
$3,000/1,000 GALLONS

GLACIER/VOLCANO WATER
$12,000/1,000 GALLONS

FIGURE 4.2 Tap water is still cheap, but bottled water is four times as expensive as gasoline![9]

on the size of the lot and the time of year. Customers who stay under that allowance pay around $1.15 for each 100 cubic feet (CCF) of water they use. IRWD users who use more water than they are allocated can see their water rate double three times before they hit the top of the rate structure at 201 percent of their allocation. Water at the "wasteful" tier costs $9.30 per 100 cubic feet, about eight times as much as their base rate. Figure 4.3 shows the IRWD rate structure. The District especially targeted landscape water use, resulting in a 46 percent reduction in that use from 1992 to 2004 on an "acre-foot per acre" basis.[12]

With "smart meters" coming into vogue as a means for recording and communicating electricity consumption via the Internet, it won't be long before "smart water meters" start appearing.[14] However, the key is not just the information, but how and when it's communicated to the end-user. If you "see," using a household meter or linked Internet site, 75 to 150 gallons of water use every time the lawn sprinklers operate, you may decide to reduce the amount of watering. Once the monthly bill arrives, it's too late to make changes retroactively, and it's also too late to connect a particular water use behavior with a specific amount of water consumption.

Higher prices are most effectively communicated by an increasing block rate pricing system, in which water rates ratchet up fairly dramatically at each new threshold of water use, as Figure 4.3 shows. This type of rate structure also answers the social equity, or fairness, concern that access to clean

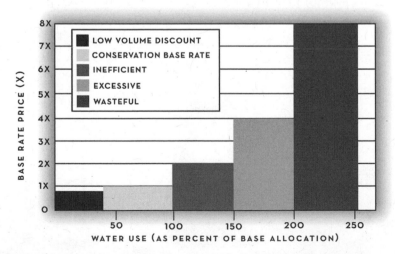

Figure 4.3 The Irvine Ranch Water District in Southern California was a pioneer in using increasing block rate pricing structures to induce water conservation.[13]

water should be a fundamental right of humanity. Having a subsidized low-volume discount makes it cheap for lower-income consumers to have an affordable water supply, especially in apartments and smaller homes without much landscaping. As usage increases and each threshold is exceeded, consumers pay increasingly more per gallon for what are essentially lifestyle choices about water use. Of course, lower-income consumers may live with very water-inefficient bathroom fixtures and kitchen/laundry appliances, so water utility conservation programs often focus on replacing these older fixtures with newer models, cutting water bills for the consumer and reducing overall water demand for the utility.

In place of using pricing to ration water use, water utilities are forced to rely in the short term on water rationing and policing of water use. I experienced this in Portland, Oregon, in the early 1990s, when a drought forced summer water rationing in the Portland metro area. The irony, of course, is that the City of Portland is located along the Columbia River, one of the largest rivers in North America, so there should never be a water emergency. However, the local water utility had for years relied on pure glacier meltwater from the Mount Hood/Bull Run Watershed, a gift to the city dating back to the second presidency of Grover Cleveland in 1893. Even though they had some wells located along the Columbia River, local planners had not adequately prepared for a major drought and were forced to impose rationing on the public. Price signals would not work, since water use was only billed quarterly. I found the specter of neighbors reporting the excessive water use of other neighbors so disagreeable that I prepared an alternative "water abundance" plan, which became a prize-winning essay.[15] It was then that I became a convert to the idea that a "water pricing" solution is a far better alternative to "water rationing" for handling drought occurrences and for encouraging lasting conservation.

Water Issues in Wet Regions and Dry Regions

Professor Sajjad Ahmad studies water policy and water supply issues in both wet and dry regions and currently teaches civil engineering at the University of Nevada in Las Vegas. Previously, he taught at the University of Miami in Florida, a very wet region, with a fair amount of rainfall each month of the year.[16] In Florida, water use for environmental purposes is far more important than in Las Vegas. Ahmad says,[17]

> There are many differences between Florida and Nevada but some commonalities too. Florida is a flat area with a long coastline and high rainfall. (The average annual rainfall in South Florida is about 55 inches. It

is about .5 inches in Las Vegas.) Agriculture is a major activity in South
Florida, with citrus and sugarcane farms. Another major difference is
that they have very large environmental flow requirements because of
the [need to replenish the] Everglades. So they have three major competing users: agriculture, municipal, and environmental flows. In Las
Vegas, we are of course a semi-arid area that is inland with low rainfall.
We don't have much agriculture competing with municipal use, at least
in the Las Vegas Valley.

Ironically, Las Vegas has about 50 percent higher per capita water use than
Florida, even though the water situation is much more constrained. Ahmad
says,[18]

> Florida and Nevada are also different in terms of per capita water use.
> Las Vegas numbers are high because we are in a warmer climate where
> humidity is considerably less. To compare, Las Vegas' average water use
> is about 250 gallons per capita per day (gpcd). In Florida it was about
> 170 gpcd. Another difference would be that Las Vegas has a much
> higher outdoor use. We have probably around 55 percent of total water
> use for outdoor purposes for lawn irrigation and things like that, with
> the remaining water used indoors. In Florida, it was quite the oppo-
> site because there's a lot more rainfall and it's humid. There, only about
> 30 percent of total water use is outdoors.

Florida has different water issues than Las Vegas. Southern Nevada depends almost entirely on one source of water — the Colorado River, whereas
Florida's water sources are diversified into various groundwater basins.

> For Florida, saltwater intrusion and rising sea levels are significant is-
> sues, and both states face flooding and drought issues, but for Nevada,
> it's mostly drought. The common thread in both states is the tremen-
> dous growth. Both portray themselves and compete with each other as a
> destination for retirement and tourism. [Las Vegas is] dependent on the
> Colorado River, so it's a single source system that supplies 90 percent
> of our water. South Florida is diversified in the sense that about 96 per-
> cent of the municipal use is from groundwater and about 38 percent of
> the agricultural use is from surface water sources. [But], even though
> Florida's groundwater and surface water are pretty tightly connected be-
> cause the water table is high, if you don't have much surface runoff, the
> groundwater also declines.

Florida is more focused on water reuse, whereas Las Vegas isn't. In a unique way, Las Vegas's treated wastewater is "credited" against its Colorado River allocation when it flows back into the Lake Mead reservoir. However, Professor Ahmad doesn't believe that water conservation alone can solve water supply problems in Las Vegas in the long run.

> If we continue growing at the current pace, conservation alone will not do it. An aggressive reduction in outdoor use — 20 percent or more (bringing water consumption below 200 gpcd) — will buy us probably 20 more years. Either we have to revisit our growth model with conservation or, if we don't want to do that, we'll have to look at some other sources to increase our supply. There are several options on the table. The most advanced one right now is transferring water from northern Nevada. They are going ahead with building a pipeline from the northern counties. It is, I believe, more than 300 miles long with several pumping stations. They originally requested around 170,000 acre-feet of water to be transferred and got permission for about 75,000 acre-feet. They are going ahead with that. Other options include putting a desalination plant in California or Mexico and doing a paper [water rights] trade with them.[19]

With these comparisons in mind, let's take a closer look at what Las Vegas has done and consider its future prospects.

Case Study: Las Vegas

Las Vegas has among the highest water use per capita in North America, as a result of importing a suburban American lifestyle based on 30 to 50 inches of rain per year into a desert where the annual rainfall averages only 4.5 inches.[20] Add swimming pools and golf courses to green lawns and you have water use that far exceeds what nature supplies; only the mammoth nearby Lake Mead allows Las Vegas a reasonably reliable water supply. Lake Mead is the 16th-largest artificial lake in the world and the largest such lake in the Western Hemisphere. Built in the 1930s along the Colorado River, Hoover Dam created Lake Mead, which occupies about 1.5 million acres — twice the area of Rhode Island — and creates about 820 miles of shoreline.[21]

Southern Nevada Water Authority
Established in 1991, the Southern Nevada Water Authority (SNWA) is the wholesale water provider collectively governed by representatives from southern Nevada's seven water agencies. SNWA provides water and

wastewater service to nearly two million residents in the cities of Boulder City, Henderson, Las Vegas and in areas of unincorporated Clark County.[22] Southern Nevada receives nearly 90 percent of its water from the Colorado River and the remainder from groundwater that is pumped from wells located throughout Clark County.[23]

Colorado River Basin Drought

Between 1999 and 2008, the average annual inflow to the Colorado River Basin was 44 percent below long-term averages. As a result, the combined storage of Lake Mead and Lake Powell — the two primary reservoirs in the Colorado River system serving southern Nevada — stood at 52 percent of their total combined capacity in early 2009.[24] Major consequences of lower water levels include less Colorado River water to supply southern Nevada and greater operating challenges associated with Nevada's water intake facilities at Lake Mead.

Water Conservation Goals
and Demand Management Tools

In response to ongoing drought conditions and long-term water supply concern, in 2009 the SNWA Board of Directors adopted a new conservation goal: reduce consumption to an average of 199 gallons per capita per day (gpcd)[25] by 2035. Achieving this goal will reduce overall use, compared with 2008 levels, by more than 50 gpcd and save the community approximately 276,000 acre-feet of water per year.[26] This goal builds upon SNWA's past conservation efforts, which have reduced water use from approximately 350 gallons per capita per day (gpcd) in 1990 to approximately 250 gpcd in 2008.[27] Since 2002, the Las Vegas Valley has reduced its overall annual water consumption by about 20.5 billion gallons, despite the arrival of 400,000 new residents and nearly 40 million annual visitors.[28] SNWA organizes its water conservation programs and policies according to the water demand management framework shown in Figure 4.4.[29]

The SNWA's range of incentive programs offers customers the opportunity to choose and implement relevant and attractive water conservation measures.

Water Smart Homes: Developed in partnership with the Southern Nevada Home Builders Association, the Water Smart Home Program certifies new homes that can save as much as 75,000 gallons of water per year (100 CCF), compared with a conventional home built at the same time. Launched in 2005, this is the nation's largest program for water efficiency in new homes, with almost 7,000 Water Smart Homes certified so far.[31]

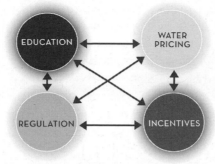

FIGURE 4.4 Four basic demand management tools are
regulation, education, water pricing and incentives.[30]

Water Efficient Technologies (WET): Rebates of up to $150,000 per
property are available to business customers who choose from a menu of
proven water conservation technologies or select a custom technology that
conserves at least 500,000 gallons of water per year. The program can be
used to retrofit existing equipment or to purchase certain approved technologies for new installations. Southern Nevada businesses have already
conserved about 1.75 billion gallons (5,370 acre-feet) since the program's
inception in 2001.[32]

SNWA's menu of pre-approved water-saving technologies include:
- High-efficiency toilet, urinal and shower head retrofits
- Conversions of sports fields from grass to an artificial surface
- Retrofit to standard cooling towers with qualifying, high-efficiency
  drift-elimination technologies
- Performance-based incentives (PBIs) for commercial customers installing eligible custom water efficiency technologies
- Consumptive-use[33] technologies (those that cause water to evaporate
  or become wastewater) earn up to 50 percent of the product purchase
  price (excluding labor and installation) or $25 for every 1,000 gallons
  conserved annually
- Non-consumptive-use[34] technologies earn up to 50 percent of the product purchase price (excluding labor and installation) or $8 for every
  1,000 gallons conserved annually.

Water Pricing

SNWA's member agencies set water rates independently, but all agencies
use similar rate-setting principles to manage demand. The Las Vegas Valley
Water District (LVVWD), which delivers nearly 70 percent of the public

water supply in Southern Nevada, has a long history of encouraging conservation through progressively tiered water rates, shown in Figure 4.5. These include expanding from two tiers to four, increasing the rate for upper-tier water use and compressing upper-tier thresholds to put water users more quickly into higher-rate tiers. Since 1990, LVVWD has increased the upper-tier rate by roughly 500 percent.[35] Although water pricing effectively signals the value of water use and conservation, public water agencies must carefully balance price-driven water conservation with its predictable, adverse effect on water agency revenues.[36]

Education

The SNWA sponsors a range of targeted education and outreach programs to elicit community buy-in for the region's water regulations, pricing mandates and incentive programs.

Water Conservation Coalition: Established in 1995, the Water Conservation Coalition is a public-private partnership tasked with identifying water conservation opportunities that are most beneficial to southern Nevada's business community. For instance, the Coalition has partnered with local resorts on the Linen Exchange Program where linens are changed only on the third day of a guest's stay, unless otherwise requested.[38]

Demonstration Gardens: Located three miles from downtown Las Vegas, the Las Vegas Springs Preserve is a 180-acre natural wetland and cultural institution designed to commemorate Las Vegas' history and to provide a model for sustainable desert living. Owned and operated by the Las Vegas Valley Water District, the Springs Preserve is one of the state's

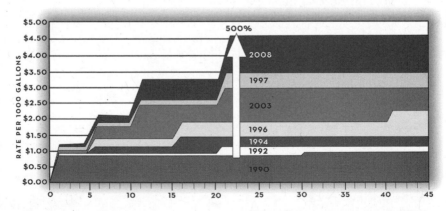

FIGURE 4.5 In Las Vegas, the current increasing block rate structure has evolved over time, always in the direction of higher rates at even lower thresholds.[37]

showcase demonstration gardens for water conservation. The Springs Preserve is also a LEED Platinum-certified green building.

Regulations
In 2005, a citizen advisory committee recommended that the SNWA permanently adopt the stringent, temporary landscape watering restrictions put in place during the region's 2003 drought. Regulations that have been permanently adopted by many SNWA water agencies prohibit lawn installation in new residential front yards, limit lawns to a maximum of 50 percent of the landscaped area in new residential backyards and prohibit turf in new commercial developments.[39] Many southern Nevada water agencies attribute their ability to transition from temporary to permanent water conservation policies to a shift in public opinion where residents, for instance, are choosing desert instead of "oasis" landscaping and removing rather than planting new grass. "For many of the drought measures, they tend to look like common sense for living in the Mojave Desert," said Rick Holmes, director of environmental resources for the Southern Nevada Water Authority.[40]

Water Conservation: One Component
in Southern Nevada's Future Water Security
The SNWA has one of the most comprehensive water conservation programs in the nation. However, the SNWA acknowledges the diminishing returns from water conservation, where the more responsive a community is to requests for conservation, the more difficult it becomes to realize additional conservation gains.[41] In a growing arid region with ever-changing drought and water resource circumstances, southern Nevada regards water conservation as a valuable and near-term priority, but no substitute for the development and diversification of alternative long-term water supplies.

Doug Bennett is water conservation manager with the SNWA. He thinks that conservation measures such as incentives must be linked with public education to be effective.

In my opinion, incentive programs are not usually going to radically change the water use of a community. You're more likely to make those changes through codes and policies such as development policies, plumbing codes and landscape codes for new construction. Then you use the incentive programs to help pick up the stuff that doesn't meet that most current code and get it converted. In many respects, incentive programs are, more than anything, an expression of goodwill and partnership between an agency and the community which is being asked to embrace water efficiency. Very few people would tell you that their incentive programs alone took them from point A to point B in water efficiency. It's a tool, but it's not the most productive tool. By providing incentives and good information, people are more likely to embrace the ethic of conserving a resource because they feel like you are helping them, holding their hand and giving them a little push.[42]

During recent drought periods, SNWA's community goodwill has become an important conservation asset, according to Bennett, since people will even go beyond your goals if they feel motivated.

You can get anywhere you need to go [with conservation]. The key question is, "How aggressive do you need to be and how do you do that without having the community turn against you?" *When the community is working with you, they'll do far more than any of your calculations say they will.* During the early stages of the drought, our landscape program really took off, water rates got moved and we looked at the individual components and estimated how much water each of them was going to save. For example, we estimated how many billion gallons would be saved by changing the rate structure; with a certain number of people participating in a landscape program and other program components. Well, *we wound up saving three times more water* than we could account for in any one of our individual initiatives, meaning that people just made choices on an everyday basis — "I used to hose off the sidewalk, but I'll get out the broom" or "I'm going to dump this water on a plant [instead of down the drain]" — things that are not [our] programs or initiatives, just choices people started making.

Since 2007, SNWA has worked to develop an Intentionally Created Surplus (ICS) within the Colorado River system. To this end, SNWA has been the principal financier for the construction of the new Drop 2 Storage Reservoir just north of the US/Mexico border. When brought online in 2010, the Drop 2 Storage Reservoir will add temporary storage capacity in the lower Colorado River basin for agricultural water, thus reducing the required water withdraws from Lake Mead and offering greater water management flexibility throughout the Colorado River system. In return, SNWA will receive 400,000 acre-feet of water, at a maximum rate of 40,000 acre-feet a year, until 2036.[43]

Southern Nevada currently reclaims all of its wastewater, primarily through return-flow credits. Direct water reuse for golf courses and parks in Southern Nevada is still fairly minimal. In 2007, total reuse for the City of Las Vegas was 5,538 acre-feet and about 27,000 acre-feet for the entire SNWA area.[44] To earn return-flow credits, wastewater treatment facilities throughout southern Nevada treat sewage, then redirect the treated water back to Lake Mead. Nevada's Colorado River allocation is based on consumptive use, which allows for return-flow credits, enabling SNWA to divert up to 70 percent more water supply than its primary allocation.

Water and Energy: Siamese Twins

Water and energy are inextricably linked, now and forever. It takes electric power to move water from one place to another, to pump it from rivers and groundwater, to treat it before use and to treat it after use. It takes water to provide cooling for thermoelectric power plants, both fossil and nuclear, and (surprisingly to some) for concentrating solar power plants, the most cost-effective solar power technology.[45] Without a reliable energy supply, there can be no water supply; without a reliable water supply, there can be no energy production. This relationship is called *the water/energy nexus*.

A center of excellence for the water/energy nexus is Sandia National Laboratories in New Mexico. Mike Hightower is an engineer who is leading many of Sandia's studies of water and energy.

> To say that the water/energy nexus is "critical" [is not] really the case now, but probably in the next five to ten years, we will see significant changes in energy systems and their need and use of water. The planning for power plants that are going to go online five or six years from now is beginning, and people are starting to look at their older plants, when they're going to have to refurbish them in five, six or eight years. The reason behind [this renewed interest in water use and consumption in electric power generation] is a combination of older infrastructure needing to be replaced and new power infrastructure needing to be built that could significantly impact water use and consumption in the next decade and beyond.[46]

The key point for Hightower and other broad-scale thinkers on this issue is that there's no magic bullet that is going to provide energy supply for growing water demands and water supply for growing energy demands. What's required is a planning effort that considers future water and energy needs together, one that develops different solutions for different regions and relies heavily on conservation investments and integrated planning of the water and energy infrastructures.

> The big concern is that there is no single technology that's going to solve the water problem for power plants. Many people suggest, for instance, that we could just go to dry cooling, saying, "Dry cooling will solve all the problems of thermal electric power plants." The problem with that is dry cooling doesn't work in all parts of the country equally well. The Southwest and the Southeast have real problems with current dry cooling approaches. Many people say, "Let's go to renewable energy like wind and solar that doesn't require much water." But, in some cases, solar does require considerable water, and these distributed energy technologies are intermittent, so they have to be balanced with gas and coal and nuclear plants, which require water, or storage capacity to get a reliable base-load electric supply.

Like many water supply planners, Hightower is also concerned about the effects of climate change on our ability to deliver adequate water supplies to meet the demands of a growing population, not just the direct demands for urban water supplies, but for agricultural, energy, and biofuel production.

> Climate change will likely decrease our surface water supply capacity, and because of the overpumping and drawdown of aquifers, the availability of groundwater supply is going to decrease. Therefore, while we're seeing an increasing demand for water for agriculture, people and energy, we're also seeing freshwater supplies likely decreasing. So you've got water supply going in one direction with available supplies going down, and you've got water demands going up. That's not a good situation. We're going to have to look at matching our water demands with water supplies much better than we've done in the past. These additional competing demands are quite large, and our available and additional freshwater supplies that we can develop are limited. This will likely lead us to move to coastal desalination, brackish groundwater desalination or some of these other [newer] things, [such as reclaimed water use], which will be more energy-intensive.

One approach is a clever combination of wastewater treatment and power production at CPS Energy's power plant in San Antonio, Texas. The San Antonio Water System's (SAWS) Dos Rios sewage treatment plant sends all of its treated sewage to a lake that provides cooling for the nearby electric power plant. In this way, wastewater treatment costs can be combined with power plant cooling costs, to the benefit of the public, while at the same time reducing water demand for power production. Beyond this use, SAWS delivers 35,000 acre-feet per year of highly treated sewage plant effluent to commercial and industrial users throughout the city, with a planned 64-mile pipeline going around the entire city delivering recycled water to customers for non-potable purposes.[47] CPS Energy is the nation's largest municipally owned energy company, providing both natural gas and electric services.[48] In this respect, San Antonio illustrates how urban energy and water suppliers can cooperate, to the betterment of both operations.

Power Requirements for New Water Supplies

According to Mike Hightower, current water supplies require much less than 1,000 kWh per acre-foot (326,000 gallons) of supply, roughly 1 to 2 kWh per 1,000 gallons. Treating brackish groundwater or sewage treatment plant effluent to drinking-water quality currently requires 2 to 4 kWh per 1,000 gallons (two to three times as much energy), while seawater desalination currently requires more than 10 kWh per 1,000 gallons (five to ten times as much energy). So there is no easy solution for developing new freshwater supplies, even though many have proposed combining desalination with solar and wind power plants. Considering that solar and wind are intermittent supplies and that solar power is expensive at present, relying on these sources could actually drive up the price of new water supplies.[49]

Going Carbon-neutral as a Water Supplier

Western Water, an Australian water supplier serving parts of suburban and rural Victoria northwest of Melbourne, developed a plan to become carbon neutral by 2017, by increasing the energy-efficiency of their many pumps, using solar-powered mechanical aerators at sewage treatment plants and buying green power (from solar, wind and biomass resources) from outside suppliers. The net annual reduction in carbon emissions is estimated at 23,000 metric tons. This is a program that any North American water supplier and sewage treatment operator could easily emulate. Based on ratepayer surveys, Western Water found that consumers were willing to pay up to AUD$30 per year, about $2.50 per household per month, to achieve these reductions.[50]

The Water/Energy Nexus in California

Studies by the California Energy Commission in 2005 calculated the energy intensity of the water use cycle in the state, shown in Table 4.1. Energy use for the water cycle in Southern California is dominated by conveyance (transportation), because of both the distances involved and lifting water more than 3,000 feet to get over the Tehachapi Mountains. In Northern California, most of the water supply flows by gravity from the Sierra Nevada to the urban centers. California's main water/energy issue is that two-thirds of precipitation falls in the northern part of the state, whereas two-thirds of the water demand is in the southern part.[51]

In California, water supply and wastewater treatment accounted for *19 percent of statewide electricity use* and 32 percent of all natural gas use, generating 106 million annual metric tons of carbon dioxide-equivalent emissions. While California might be an extreme case of the energy cost of water supply and treatment, this example illustrates how future energy planning has to be jointly considered.

Summary

Expected global warming in this century will cause significant problems for urban water managers unless more water agencies begin to incorporate conservation and water use efficiency as integral parts of their future supply planning. We know that water supply, distribution and treatment use significant amounts of energy; in California it's nearly 20 percent of all energy use. We also have learned that "nega-gallons" (supply gains from conservation and efficiency programs) are far cheaper than most water supply and efficiency programs now in place nationwide. We also learned that pricing is a key tool for reducing water demand, one that is just beginning to be employed in many parts of the country. In Las Vegas, there are programs in place to reduce water use by 50 percent from 1990s levels, to account for a dwindling supply of water from the Colorado River's Lake Mead, its main water supply source, using four specific methods: pricing, education, incentives and regulation. The water/energy nexus will continue to challenge both water and energy planners in the decades ahead. By recognizing their interaction, we'll be able to make better water resource decisions for the future.

TABLE 4.1 California Water Supply Energy Requirements, kWh/million gallons, 2005[52]

Supply Component	Northern California kWh/million gallons	Southern California kWh/million gallons
Conveyance	150	8,900
Water Treatment	100	100
Distribution	1,200	1,200
Wastewater Treatment	2,500	2,500
Regional Total	3,950	12,700

Water Use in Commercial and Institutional Buildings

Water flows uphill toward money.

— Anonymous[1]

BEFORE TURNING to different ways to reduce urban water demand, in this chapter we'll get better acquainted with patterns of water use in the commercial, industrial and institutional (CII) sectors. These sectors together account for the majority of urban water uses and respond to quite different incentives than do people in homes and apartments. I visited Melbourne and Sydney during the winter of 2009 (their summer) to find out how Australians were contending with difficulties in preparing for present and future water supply crises and learned a great deal about their water use situation. Sydney is a large metropolitan area with about four million inhabitants, about 20 percent of Australia's total population. Known worldwide for its water sports and for the elegantly designed Sydney Opera House (Figure 5.1), Sydney is also home to one of Australia's major responses to its continuing drought — new desalination plants to provide water to major cities.

Figure 5.2 addresses water use in office buildings in Sydney, Australia's largest city. Almost 30 percent of water delivered to office buildings there is lost through leaks inside the building. Restrooms consume 35 percent of the total, so upgrading them to more-efficient fixtures would considerably

FIGURE 5.1 The Sydney Opera House has symbolized Australia's largest city for 40 years.

reduce the total amount consumed. Because Sydney temperatures can reach 100°F in summer, and many office buildings run cooling towers most of the year, almost 20 percent of water use derives from cooling towers, a level of consumption susceptible to reduction through improved technology and more efficient operations.

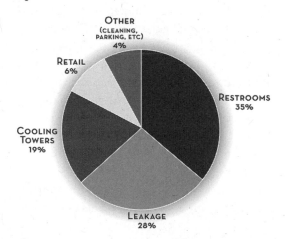

FIGURE 5.2 Internal leaks are an important aspect of water use in Sydney office buildings. This situation suggests a major priority for water conservation efforts in all major cities.[2]

With so much water lost to leaks, rather than building an AUD$2 billion desalination plant, wouldn't it have been far cheaper for Sydney Water, the city utility, to go into each commercial property, replace the fixtures and fix the leaks, to get the same amount of "new" water supply (from "nega-gallons")? To help pay for the desalination plant, water rates are projected to increase 30 percent by 2012.[3] The plant is expected to produce 90 billion liters per year by 2012, equivalent to 65 million gallons per day. Interestingly, Sydney Water intends to run this expensive desalination plant only when local reservoir levels fall below 70 to 80 percent of capacity, so it is intended only as an emergency (and very expensive) supply of water.

How Much Water Should a Building Use?

To find out how much water a commercial office building should use, I examined data from three countries: Australia, Germany and the US, shown in Table 5.1. Australian data come from a study conducted in 2006 by the Australian government; US data are representative from public and private offices; German data are from unpublished studies supplied by a German building engineering firm and research group. The data represent both average use and "best practices." As we will see in this chapter, increased water use can result from hot climates that require significant cooling tower operations for large office buildings. Interestingly, German water use data are quite a bit lower than either Australian or US data, reflecting perhaps a milder climate as well as more water-efficient building operations. From these data, building managers in the US can get a good idea about establishing best practice goals, ranging from 5 to 10 gallons per year per square foot for buildings without irrigation or cooling towers, and up to 20 to 25 gallons per square foot for buildings in hot areas with site irrigation and cooling towers. In my view, it's better to focus on absolute water use (gallons per square foot) rather than just on relative improvement (e.g., saving 20 percent compared with a reference or "code" building).

Water Use and Green Buildings

The relative importance of water conservation has increased lately as a topic among green building professionals. As energy-efficiency measures have become more widely adopted, the green building industry has shifted more of its focus to water conservation issues. A recent survey found that 85 percent of real estate professionals believed that water efficiency would be a very important aspect of green building in 2013, compared to 69 percent who said that it was in 2008.[13]

Table 5.1 Annual Water Use in Office Buildings

Use	Australia[4]	US	Germany[5]
Average private office: no leaks, with cooling towers	1.01–1.125 kL/sq.m. (24.8–27.6 gal./ sq.ft., gsf)		
Average public building	3.34 kL/sq.m. (82.0 gal./sq.ft.)		
"Best practices": private office, with cooling towers	0.50–0.77 kL/sq.m. (12.3–18.9 gsf)		
"Best practices": private office, no cooling towers[6]	0.40 kL/sq.m. (9.8 gsf)		
"Best practices": public building	2.0 kL/sq.m. (49.2 gsf)		
NABERS[7] 5-star (highest level)	0.35 kL/sq.m. (8.6 gsf)		
1,500 buildings, both private offices and public[8]			0.15–0.20 kL/sq.m. (3.7–4.9 gsf)
Large insurance company (6 offices)[9]: office only			0.15–0.20 kL/sq.m. (3.7–4.9 gsf)
Large insurance company: office with cooling tower and irrigation			106 L/person/day 0.8–1.2 kL/sq.m. (19.5–29.5 gsf)
Large office building, Nashville, TN[10]		24.7 gsf (2006) 17.7 gsf (2009)	
Large office buildings, Portland, OR[11]		14.0 gsf (2007) 26.5 gsf (2009)	
Federal buildings in NE, TN, CA and CO[12]		3.6–16.2 gsf (2007)	

Early adopters of new water-conservation technologies are building owners/occupiers, with 42 percent of owners reporting in the same survey that more than three-quarters of their projects have water-efficient practices incorporated in the design. This compares with only 28 percent of architecture and design firms and 20 percent of contractors who reported that they used water-efficient technologies in their projects. One possible explanation is that owner/occupiers have likely inflated their own adoption figures owing to the utility cost saving they have already decided to pursue. We'll discuss in later sections of this chapter specific requirements for water

conservation now incorporated in the US Green Building Council's LEED®
green building rating system.

Water Use Patterns in CII Buildings in the US

Figure 5.3 shows water use patterns in CII buildings in California. One-third
of the use goes to landscaping (a pattern similar to residential use that we'll
see in Chapter 6), about one-sixth each to process water (non-fixture, non-
cooling) uses, restrooms and cooling towers, with the balance for kitchen,
laundry and miscellaneous uses. Recall the variety of water uses in different
commercial buildings such as hotels, schools, restaurants, hospitals and offices (shown in Figure 2.3), as well as industrial applications such as food,
and you'll understand why there is such a large use for process water.

Restaurants, ranging from coffee shops to large full-service facilities, use
from 500 gallons to 10,000 gallons per day. A full-service restaurant can
consume 5,000 gallons daily, with a 50–50 split between hot and cold water
(with no hard and fast rule on either total use or the breakdown between
hot and cold). Typically there is less cold water used in the winter and more
used in the summer. The Food Service Technology Center estimates that
water use can be reduced by 20 percent or more by making cost-effective
changes to water-using equipment, landscaping strategies and cleanup
practices.[14]

What is the total water use in the CII sector? For example, in California
in 2000, the commercial and institutional sectors used about 2.2 million

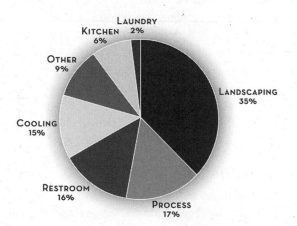

FIGURE 5.3 Water use in commercial, institutional and industrial buildings in
California shows important demand sources: landscaping, process water, restrooms and cooling towers.[15]

cubic meters of water, while the industrial sector consumed about 0.8 million cubic meters for a total of about 3.0 million cubic meters (2.5 million acre-feet), about 30 percent of all urban water use.[16] The largest commercial and institutional users were, in order from highest total use, offices, schools, golf courses, restaurants and retail. In the industrial sector, the largest uses occurred in petroleum refineries, high-tech industries and food processing. Looked at in terms of the purpose of the water use, some 38 percent of the total CII water use went to landscaping in 2000 (representing about 10 percent of total urban water use, not even counting household water use for landscaping)! Clearly, the CII sector can reduce water use substantially over time just by focusing on landscaping, cooling towers and bathroom fixtures.

The definitive study of the CII sector in California estimated that widespread adoption of best practices could result in annual savings of about 39 percent or 1,200 million cubic meters (975,000 acre-feet) of water used in the year 2000. Half the savings would come from landscaping water use, while restroom and laundry use would also be cut by 50 percent.[17]

Water Efficiency Technologies

What are some new water efficiency technologies that might be of interest in the CII sector? There were many responses to the water supply crises engulfing parts of the US in 2009, particularly in California. Some involved creating new water supplies from desalting saline or brackish water; others derived from buying saved water or from investing in irrigation water efficiencies, and still others relied on reusing municipal wastewater. Presenting the details of all of these approaches is beyond the scope of this book. Here our concerns are specifically with the methods that show immediate promise, in both new and commercial buildings, as shown in Table 5.2 and Figure 5.4. Some are well-known, and their use is beginning to accelerate, while others are just coming into general distribution. Graywater reuse and rainwater harvesting are addressed in Chapters 8 and 9; this chapter discusses some of the benefits of low-flow fixtures and sub-metering, along with a few technologies specific to the commercial building sector.

Driving Forces to Use Water-efficient Products and Methods

What are the driving forces that make water efficiency an increasing concern for the built environment? Table 5.3 shows some of them, roughly in descending order of importance.

According to the survey report cited earlier, for some users concern over future climate changes and the possibility of further governmental regulations will drive adoption of new water technologies. Many building

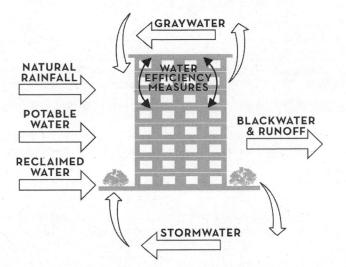

FIGURE 5.4 Commercial buildings have many opportunities to reduce water use, as well as to recycle and reuse currently wasted water.[18]

TABLE 5.2 New Water Technologies and Systems for Non-residential Buildings

Technology or System	Uses	Benefits or Drawbacks
1. Rainwater harvesting	Toilet/urinal flushing; cooling tower makeup and site irrigation	Interior use needs same treatment as drinking water due to code requirements; seasonal supply; needs on-site storage; hard to re-plumb existing buildings
2. Graywater reuse	Toilet/urinal flushing; site irrigation	Higher level of treatment required for interior use; constant supply source; hard to re-plumb existing buildings
3. Water-free or ultra-low-flow urinals	Replaces conventional urinals	Possible drainlines carry problems in older buildings; saves 87.5% to 100% of urinal water use; easy to retrofit
4. High-efficiency toilets (HET), typically 1.28 gpf or 1.12 gpf	Replaces conventional toilets	Saves 10% to 20% of water use for toilet flushing; easy to retrofit
5. Low-flow faucets and shower heads	Replaces conventional faucets	Cost-effective; easy to retrofit
6. Water sub-metering	Establish actual use patterns; change water use behavior	May be costly to retrofit in older buildings

Table 5.3 Driving Forces for Water Efficiency[19]

Driving Force	Importance
1. Water shortages and droughts in many states	Very important for short-run conservation efforts
2. Water pricing structures	Assists in the longer run in reducing per capita water use
3. Policies and regulations; incentive programs for efficient fixtures	Requires creation of minimum standards for all new projects; treats everyone equally
3. Green certification programs such as LEED	Important for projects pursuing LEED certification
4. Rising average costs of water supplies and sewage treatment	Economics is still the best motivator; higher water costs lead to fixture retrofits and changes in landscaping practices
5. Public concern over water issues; community mindset for water conservation	A weak motivator in most situations, except where regulations require the adoption of new technology

owners and facility managers are becoming aware that the built environment, both residential and non-residential, is a significant contributor to climate change, with buildings contributing 38 percent of US carbon dioxide emissions each year.[20] Rising water scarcity in some regions is leading engineers and architects to design new buildings with significantly reduced water demands.

A larger concern among building owners is risk management and risk mitigation, especially prevalent with concern over energy use in buildings. In the survey cited earlier in this chapter, 87 percent said that energy-use reduction was a motivator for water conservation (even though the financial correlation between the two is not that direct, except for service hot water and cooling towers), 84 percent cited operating cost reduction, while 79 percent cited directly the motivation to reduce water use. Higher costs for water and energy were the primary trigger for water conservation, especially in response to conservation pricing structures (increasing block rates) by municipal water providers.

Water Efficiency vs. Water Conservation

Many water experts distinguish between water-efficient devices and systems, which lower the water use per activity, and water conservation, which includes issues such as behavior and economics and can also result in a drop in water consumption, from whatever source. In other words, a low-flow or high-efficiency toilet could use *more* water if people feel they have to flush twice to get the bowl clean. Hence, the result is "efficiency but *not* "conservation!" John Koeller, an engineer and water expert, expands on this point:

> Efficiency versus conservation is an important distinction because people incorrectly use the terms interchangeably. In LEED, for example, the term that's used is "water efficiency" not "water conservation" because it's about designing green buildings, and among other things, efficiency is what you design into those buildings. You cannot design conservation into the building; perhaps you design that into the building managers through education and other means.[21]

Koeller also questions the value of some efficiency devices in achieving actual conservation, even if they are "working" correctly.

> In my presentations, I highlight a few things that people think are true that are actually false. My favorite one is sensor valves in restrooms on sinks, toilets and urinals in commercial buildings. People cannot believe that. They think that if you put an infrared motion sensor on a fixture, that it is automatically, by definition or design, a water-saver. Quite the opposite is true: the water waste when a sensor-activated valve is substituted for a manual valve is very significant. For example, in flush valves for toilets and urinals, we talk about "phantom flushes," the unnecessary flushes due to untimely activation of the sensor. We have all experienced phantom flushes, and our experiences tell us that these things don't save water.

I can relate totally to phantom flushes. How many times have you sat in a stall at an airport or some other location with motion sensors? Every time you lean forward, for whatever reason, there's a flush. Beyond the inconvenience, the water waste can be disconcerting.

Public Programs for Water Conservation in the US
Politics may wind up as the major driver, rather than the marketplace, particularly in drought-stricken areas and in jurisdictions with strong environmental constituencies. In the McGraw-Hill survey cited above, building industry respondents ranked government regulations on wastewater runoff (69%) and mandates and incentives for water efficiency (67%) as key drivers over the next five years for their efforts aimed at saving water in buildings. (Table 14.3 in Chapter 14 shows a representative range of such public agency programs for seven cities in the US.)

Ike Casey of the Plumbing Heating Cooling Contractors (US) national association agrees that politics is likely to be the driver and that the industry needs to be aware of potential problems, lest the plumbing contractor be left holding the bag for future problems.

> I think low-flow toilets are going to be the big driver. The water efficien-
> cies in toilets and urinals are going to be a big issue in our industry com-
> ing down the road because some states are already requiring it. At this
> time, California and Texas have passed legislation to phase out the sales
> of anything but HETs.[22] Washington made it a requirement [in April
> 2009]. Texas has a bill that's pending to require high-efficiency toilets.
> This is a political issue for us because [HETs] don't work all the time.
> When your toilet doesn't work, you don't look on the label and call the
> manufacturer. You call the plumber. The plumber is the one that's left in
> the middle.[23]

Increasing Importance of Controlling Water Losses

In discussing Sydney office buildings, I mentioned the large amount of water lost inside the building and how important it is for public water agencies to look at this as a "free" water resource that can extend the capacity of their systems. In addition, there is "unbilled water" that is lost in transit from the water treatment plant to end users. Water agencies need to redouble their efforts, especially in older systems, to reduce the amount of water lost into the ground from broken or leaking pipes. This loss is analogous to the prob-lem faced in sewage treatment by infiltration of ground and surface waters into sewer pipes, thereby adding to the burden of treatment plants. Fixing water losses is not glamorous stuff, for sure, but controlling water losses is essential to extending our water supplies to meet future demands.

Further attesting to the strong controls over public water supply, in Ger-many low water losses within the public drinking-water network are an im-portant indicator of the quality of pipelines and security of supply. During the past few years, water losses in this network have been decreasing. With less than seven percent, German water suppliers have by far the least water loss in Europe.[24] However, in Asian countries, this "non-revenue water" av-erages about 30 percent of all water produced.[25]

Water Considerations in Certified Green Buildings

The US Green Building Council's (USGBC) Leadership in Energy and Environmental Design (LEED) rating system is the national standard for certifying and classifying green buildings. Beginning in 2009, LEED required a 20 percent reduction in water use as a prerequisite for project certification. The fastest-growing LEED rating system is now LEED for Existing Buildings Operations & Maintenance (LEED-EBOM), with growth of more than 111 percent in the number of projects registering for LEED-EBOM certification (2,085 new projects, representing more than 400 million square feet of commercial and institutional space), in 2009.[26] The LEED-EBOM system requires CII projects in existing buildings to examine investments in water-efficiency and conservation measures to meet minimum savings goals.

Water Efficiency in LEED-EBOM

LEED-EBOM awards up to 14 points for efficient water performance, and a project can also attain bonus points for exemplary performance and for meeting regionally significant water-use reduction targets. Water is emerging as the next big environmental concern in the green building world for the two reasons discussed in earlier chapters: one is the relative scarcity of freshwater resources around the world, especially in the context of global warming and increasing world population. The second reason is that the process of capturing, storing, transporting, distributing and treating water is a large net consumer of significant amounts of electric power.[27] While the majority of water use is still in agriculture and industry, urban water resources are constrained by aging infrastructure, population growth and fast-rising costs. For example, wholesale water prices in southern California are projected to double between 2008 and 2013.[28]

LEED-EBOM Water Efficiency Prerequisite. LEED-EBOM contains one Water Efficiency category prerequisite: a project must reduce water use 20 percent below the LEED baseline. What does that mean? The baseline is a calculated number that assumes all building fixtures meet the 2006 editions of the Uniform or International Plumbing Codes.[29] The baseline is adjusted upward 20 percent from current code limits for buildings completed in 1993 or later and 60 percent for older buildings. For example, assume that a project is a 1990 building with 100 water closets flushing at 3.5 gallons per flush (gpf). The current code is 1.6 gallons per flush, and the baseline would be the equivalent of 2.56 gpf (1.6 gpf times 1.6 baseline adjustment). So the owner would have to reduce water use by about 27 percent to meet the prerequisite. That means changing out 50 of the toilets to fixtures that met the new codes (94 gallons required savings divided by 1.9 gallons per fixture savings). At today's water rates in most cities, this type of investment would typically pay off, because within a few years, future water savings would more than pay for the costs of the upgrade.

Table 5.4 LEED-EBOM Water Efficiency Credits and Points

Credit	Points
1. Water Performance Measurement: Whole Building or Sub-Metering	1 to 2
2. Indoor Plumbing Fixture and Fitting Efficiency	1 (at least 10% below baseline) to 5 (30% below baseline)
3. Water-efficient Landscaping	1 (50% below calculated baseline) to 5 (100% below baseline)
4. Cooling Tower Water Management	1 (chemical management via conductivity) and 1 (>50% non-potable makeup water)
Total Available Points	Up to 14 (plus additional credits for exemplary performance in category 2)

LEED-EBOM Credit Requirements

Table 5.4 shows how LEED-EBOM allocates points among various water issues. There are 4 credits and 14 total available points for water efficiency. Most projects should be able to get 5 to 7 of these points with minimal cost increases.

Metering and Sub-metering

What gets metered, gets managed. So if a building isn't metered for water use, it's just that much harder to justify water use reductions and to understand where to focus investments in water efficiency. Of course, for most commercial and institutional buildings (except perhaps in campus settings), there is at least a whole building meter. If sub-meters are provided for at least 80 percent of the total water use of one major water-using subsystem such as irrigation, indoor fixtures, domestic hot water or process loads (dishwashers, clothes washers, pools, etc.), then the project can earn two points in this section.[30] If cooling towers, a major water user, are submetered to earn this point, then LEED requires all towers to be metered.

What are the costs and benefits of sub-metering? Costs include installing meters that cost between $400 and $1,100, according to the Los Angeles Bureau of Sanitation.[31] There will also be personnel costs for data logging, tracking and meter maintenance. Whether you gain a net cost savings depends a great deal on how your water utility charges for sewage treatment. For instance, in its billing practices, the Los Angeles Bureau of Sanitation assumes that 90 percent of delivered water to a commercial customer is discharged to the sewer.[32] Benefits of sub-metering might include savings on water utility costs, leak detection (to help you see what you're using, compared with what you're paying for) and reducing overall use through direct billing of tenants. Even with metering and direct billing, changing tenant or occupant behavior is still challenging. In California, the new state building code, CALGREEN, beginning in 2011 will require both indoor and outdoor meters in all new non-residential construction.[33]

From Australia comes an interesting approach to sub-metering that might work for larger users, such as industrial plants. Andrew Forster-Knight of Melbourne's South East Water public utility reports:

> Utility Services (a division of South East Water in Melbourne) developed the Hydroshare Web-based monitoring system for large industrial users. We have currently got this system installed at over 500 sites across Australia monitoring water meters and sending the trends directly to the Web to help customers visualize their water usage at a level never before seen and to allow them to better manage their consumption. The system has no geographical barriers as the technology it uses can tap into the Internet from any country and send the data back to our hosting servers. We have the units running in Europe (Austria) as well as New Zealand. The units we install on a user's water meter are designed and manufactured in Melbourne and have a five- to ten-year battery life. They require no external power and can plug into any existing water meter (as long as it has a pulse output, which 95% of old ones do). We think this would be a great solution to help conserve water for companies in the US, just as it has helped saved millions of liters of water here in Australia.[34]

Water Use for Site Irrigation

The tie-in between sustainable site management and reducing potable water use for irrigation should be clear. By planting native and/or adapted vegetation, a project should be able to reduce potable water use for landscape maintenance and reduce pesticide/herbicide use, while increasing natural habitat. By calculating a baseline use for irrigation using regional averages, a project can demonstrate its relative reduction in water use.

Notice that LEED requirements address only potable water use, so if a building is capturing and treating graywater or rainwater, the owner can work with a landscape contractor to make it available for reuse in irrigation, so the project can reduce 100 percent of its landscape water use by relying solely on those sources.[35]

Water Use for CII Plumbing Fixtures

In commercial and institutional applications, many high-efficiency toilets (HETs) reduce water use 20 to 30 percent from a conventional 1.6 gallons-per-flush (gpf) toilet, down to 1.28 gpf (a 20 percent reduction) or even 1.12 gpf (a 30 percent reduction). Since most commercial toilets are valve-type (i.e., they have no tank), Sloan Valve has come up with the Uppercut® retrofit valve, a "dual-flush manual flushometer" that flushes with 1.6 gallons on the downward stroke, but uses only 1.1 gallons on the upward stroke (Figure 5.5).[36] The handle is green, to indicate an environmentally friendly product, and has an antimicrobial coating. However, there is one problem: most people don't want to touch

FIGURE 5.5 Pushing down on the Sloan Uppercut Valve triggers a normal 1.6 gallon flush, while pulling up uses only 1.1 gallons of water. Courtesy of Sloan Valve

the valve handle in a public toilet. Men typically operate a flushometer by pushing down on the handle with one foot. It's hard (and almost comical) to imagine myself standing there and attempting to lift up with one foot while standing on the other. As for what women might do, I'll have to plead ignorance.

Water-free Urinals

There are many brands on the market of both water-free and low-water urinals (i.e., those using 1 to 4 pints per flush) to reduce water use 50 to 100 percent below that of the standard 1 gpf urinal. Some companies have been making these for nearly 20 years. Water-free urinals capture plenty of attention, since they represent an obvious solution to a common water conservation opportunity. Since urine is basically all water, why use more water to flush it down? Water-free urinals are also a better alternative to the "If it's yellow, let it mellow" approach of my youth. Figures 5.6 and 5.7 show water-free urinals and the basic principles behind their operation. Water-free urinals work well in settings where there is frequent and anonymous use, such as airports, train stations, sports stadiums and schools, but perhaps not as well as in office buildings, where the use is a lot less frequent and the users are not anonymous. In addition, they work best when they are plumbed

FIGURE 5.6 The water-free urinal is becoming ubiquitous in places with large numbers of daily users, such as airports, train stations, stadiums, parks, hotels and schools. Courtesy of Falcon Waterfree Technologies.

"downstream" of the sinks, so that there is constant flow in the drainline, avoiding buildup of uric acid crystals, which can cause odors.

Instead of water-free urinals, most of the building managers that I interviewed seem to prefer the low-water-using urinals, shown in Figure 5.8, reasoning that they have fewer code-compliance problems, less maintenance cost and possibly fewer odor concerns. They still deliver most of the water savings of a water-free urinal: a 1-pint-per-flush urinal will save

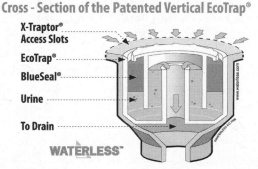

FIGURE 5.7 The key operating principle in a waterless urinal is letting urine pass by a sealant liquid or gel, preventing odors from rising back up. Courtesy of Waterless Co.

about 87 percent of water use compared with a standard urinal. (There's plenty of fluidity in the sanitary fixture business today, so these judgments may be subject to change.)

Water Audits, Plumbing Retrofits and Performance Contracting

There are also companies, similar to Energy Service Companies (ESCOs), that will pay for the entire water conservation installation and take their return from the savings on your water bill, a method called "performance contracting." Here's how one such company describes its approach. Mark Morello, president of Infinity Water Management based in Florida, says:

We do what's called performance contracting. Everything we do has to pay for itself in savings. If we go in and do a project, the utility savings — from water and energy — pays for the project. With some basic information such as water rate and population data, we can determine if there will be payback early on during the preliminary audit. If there's no payback, we don't have a project.

FIGURE 5.8 The 1-pint-per-flush urinal seems to be emerging as the consensus way to save almost 90 percent of the water used by conventional urinals, while still looking and working like a standard fixture. Courtesy of Zurn Industries.

We're taking toilets that have anywhere from 3.5 to 5 to 7 gallons per flush, and we're putting in anywhere from 1.6 gpf to a 1.28 gpf or a 1.12 gpf fixture, depending on the cost of the water in the area in which we're working. That gives us a little bit of flexibility in what we can put in. If we're working with a high water rate, we can use more expensive fixtures and equipment. We may be able to install newer HET toilets that use the lowest amount of water; also we may be able to install hands-free fixtures that although they do not save water are desired by many of our clients, and we need the savings to pay for the upgrades. If the water rate is not that high, we tend to use standard handle-flush valve, 1.6 gallon toilets, for example.[37]

For Morello, the key is to perform a detailed water-use audit, using at least three years of data (if it's available), and having specific information on end-uses for at least 95 percent of water use, to figure out exactly where water is being used. This is a good approach for all building and facility managers to emulate.

> We look at the bills for the past three years, and we'll determine with our proprietary software and historical data where all the water is go-ing — toilets, faucets, showers, urinals, pools, irrigation, etc. Once we determine where the water is going, we'll go in with our water-saving measures and determine how much water would be saved by changing them out with more efficient options, and that provides the payback. Our payback is usually within three to five years.

Morello says the quickest payback is to put 0.5 gpm (gallon per minute) spray aerators to replace conventional 2.5 gpm faucet aerators. The next quickest payback in older buildings is to replace the toilets. If there is a com-mercial kitchen, he likes to replace water-cooled icemakers and refrigera-tion/freezer units with air-cooled units to save water and improve overall energy efficiency.

Of course not everything in the water-fixture retrofit business is so easy. Sometimes, plumbing problems can vex even the most experienced build-ing managers. Wade Lange is vice president of property management for Ashforth Pacific in Portland, Oregon, which owns Liberty Centre, a 17-story Class A office tower situated in the heart of Portland's Lloyd District, with about 277,000 square feet of office space. Lange and his staff worked hard for more than two years to get a LEED-EB Silver rating. As for the plumbing fixtures, Lange says:

> We replaced all [toilet] flush-valves so they were low-flow. There was an investment there in materials, and we did it in-house. We had to have the low-flush valves because we couldn't qualify [for the LEED prereq-uisite] without them. The building was built [in 1997] with low-flush valves, but they didn't work and were taken out early on. So we had to go back and put in what was originally there. The staff came up with a fix to the low-flow issue (caused by a low water pressure problem); now it works, and we're saving considerable water as a result.[38]

The lesson here is obvious; some of this retrofit stuff can be quite technical, and owners really need to know their building. In this case, there was the virtue of having an in-house engineering staff committed to tackling and solving problems such as those described above. For other building owners, it may be useful to have a mechanical or plumbing service contractor conduct an entire building water-utilization audit, to determine the most cost-effective retrofits.

Water Use in Cooling Towers

Most chillers for large buildings have an associated cooling tower that uses water evaporation as part of the cooling process. The average water circulation is 3 gpm per ton of cooling.[39] A large commercial building with 1,000 tons of refrigeration will have 3,000 gallons *per minute* of water flowing through the tower and compressor heat exchanger. (Only a small amount of this evaporates.) Makeup water to the cooling tower must replace the evaporation plus the water that is discharged to keep mineral buildup under control and to replace drift losses. This amounts to approximately 2.25 to 3.0 gallons of water per ton-hour of cooling. While this does not sound like much, it adds up quickly. A cooling tower for a 1,000-ton chiller operating on a hot summer day can use more than 40,000 gallons of water per day. Consider that the average household might use only 300 gallons per day,[40] and you can see why focusing on reducing water use from cooling commercial buildings is so important.

Texas-based water expert and professional engineer Bill Hoffman believes that not enough people realize how much of the total water use of a large commercial building comes from the wet cooling process in cooling towers.

> The area that has considerable potential is the area dealing with thermodynamic processes — cooling towers and boilers. First, it will be about getting people to realize that the water costs for cooling towers are going up faster than electricity costs. If you look at the last eight years of the Consumer Price Index from the US Department of Commerce, you'll see that the cost for water and wastewater has gone up 1.45 times faster than electricity costs.
>
> This is very important because in the South and Southwest, for those buildings that typically have cooling towers, the cooling tower can be one-third to one-half the water use for the whole building. That includes plumbing, landscape irrigation and everything else all thrown together. I recently worked on a hospital in Florida where 43 percent of the water use for the hospital went to cooling towers; in a building in Austin, Texas, the water use for cooling towers was 49 percent, in an

office building that has modern fixtures such as 1.6 gallon flush toilets. In California, a study done on grocery stores with cooling towers found that approximately 40 to 45 percent of the water use went to the cooling towers. Those are huge numbers when you're looking in the commercial sector. Applying good technology to make sure that you're achieving the best cooling tower operation is going to be very important in the future.

The other thing that's going to be very important is to take a hard look at the overall cost-benefit analysis — life-cycle costing of dry versus wet cooling. Wet cooling in cooling towers is typically more energy-efficient in many cases. However, new technologies are coming on now such as geothermal systems and variable-refrigerant-volume types. These are dry systems that are more efficient than the old direct expansion (DX) systems found in many facilities. In some cases, especially for smaller systems, these dry systems are more cost effective.[41]

Building owners and facility managers need to be educated about the importance of changing their approach to cooling tower design and operations; they need to focus much more on the water use in the HVAC system to realize significant potential water savings.

LEED-EBOM awards one point for supplying at least 50 percent of the cooling tower makeup water from non-potable sources such as harvested rainwater, harvested graywater, swimming pool filter flush water and municipal reclaimed water. LEED also rewards careful water management that reduces the required amount of cooling tower makeup water.[42]

While small in the overall picture, recovering water from air-conditioning condensate would also be a good practice for most commercial buildings. Air-conditioning condensate is a prime source because it is generally as clean or cleaner than rainwater, graywater and process water; and it is cold, providing additional efficiency gains for the cooling tower function.[43] In large commercial buildings, condensate can supply a significant portion of makeup water for cooling towers. The Rivercenter Mall in downtown San Antonio uses a condensate recovery system. The system captures condensate water from four large air handlers that produce 250 gallons (950 liters) of condensate per day. This innovative system earned the 2003 WaterSaver Leadership Award from the San Antonio Water System.[44] The condensate recovery system paid for itself in less than six months.[45]

According to one source, "If condensate is being used only for cooling-tower makeup, the condensate can often be fed directly into the cooling tower without storage — because condensate produced in a building will never exceed the evaporative losses from the cooling tower. This can reduce costs significantly." Condensate production is about 0.1 to 0.3 gallons per hour per ton of A/C and is highest in regions of the US with high humidity during the cooling season. For a 100,000 square foot building in San Antonio, this would translate into production of about 50 gallons per hour while the cooling system is in operation.[46]

Some Unintended Consequences of Water Conservation Programs

Water rates are increasing in many metropolitan areas because of inflation, drought and growing demands to maintain infrastructure. Some water agencies are also raising rates to compensate for reduced water demand during the current Great Recession. For this reason, Tucson, Arizona, increased rates by 10 percent in June of 2009.[47] Every system has fixed costs that must be covered by water customer payments, so when demand falls, rates inevitably go up. The same concern exists when conservation programs reduce overall water consumption. The individual consumer gets a reduction in utility bills, but the overall system suffers reduced revenues.[48] In addition, conventional systems that were created during a period of increasing water use can sometimes create unintended adverse consequences when overall water use declines.

The "Drainline Transport" Problem

Considering the pressure for new onsite water sources, there is growing concern about public health implications of rainwater and graywater reuse, even in toilet flushing, as well as problems that might crop up with reduced water flows in commercial fixtures. In the plumbing trade, the latter is referred to as the "drainline transport" problem.[49] In announcing a research effort to study the impact of lower flows on solids removal, the industry stated:

> Recently, the need to find additional efficiencies in water consuming plumbing fixtures has resulted in the creation of voluntary specifications that eliminate another 20 percent from the flush discharge volume of water closets, bringing consumption down to a maximum average of 1.28 gpf. These toilets are known as high-efficiency toilets (HETs). Some water closet manufacturers are now voluntarily offering models that flush at 1.0 gpf. Many plumbing experts are concerned that we are at or approaching a "tipping point" where a significant number of sanitary waste systems will be affected by drainline transport problems, espe-

cially in larger commercial systems that have long horizontal runs to the sewer. Looking forward, newer technologies, such as non-water-consuming and high-efficiency urinals (HEUs), lower-flow-rate faucets and increasingly efficient water-consuming appliances, will further reduce the amount of water discharged into sanitary waste systems.[50]

Here we see at work the well-known Law of Unintended Consequences, reflecting one of my favorite adages: "You can't change a system without putting another system in its place." In this case, a single-minded focus on reducing water use in buildings and homes could have significant repercussions on public health, sanitation and sewage flows.

Russ Chaney, executive director of the International Association of Plumbing and Mechanical Officials (IAPMO), has similar but more pronounced concerns:

> The other primary concern, and it's a very vital concern that really hasn't been studied to a great extent to date, is the unintended complications from what we call low-flow plumbing fixtures or high-efficiency plumbing fixtures. The drainage lines on what we call the sanitary side of the systems have been designed to transport solids with a certain rate of flow. In other words, when you introduce low-flow urinals or low-flow toilets, they flush with a much lower flow-rate than has traditionally been used. As a consequence, we've not yet experienced a higher rate of stoppages or other circumstances that result from the reduction in water flow-rates. So we're coming to terms that we have to deal with the fact that we're introducing lower flow volumes into the sanitary side of our systems, and we're just now undertaking some studies to understand the long-term effect this phenomenon has on the sanitary side of our drainage systems. We call this effect "dry drains." It doesn't always mean dry drains, but it means that we're putting less water into the system, and as a consequence, if the pipe isn't sloped properly, you'll end up having conditions where the solids from the use of toilets will clog the drainlines because you're not getting an adequate flow of water to wash them away.[51]

Problems with Sewage Transport

It's also clear that those focusing on reducing water use haven't yet thought through some of the other implications. For example, most sewer pipes are sloped below ground just enough to be "self-scouring" on their way to the sewage treatment plant and require a certain minimum flow for solids transport. If there's not enough flow, the solids will build up, generating hydrogen sulfide, with emissions that are smelly and dangerous.

Even in Germany, a water-rich country but one with a strong conservation ethos, public agencies are resisting further water-conservation and water-reuse programs because of revenue shortfalls and concerns over the effect on sewerage systems.[52] Between 1990 and 2006, for example, total public water supply to customers declined by 22 percent.[53] Already, daily German water consumption averages only 123 liters (32 gallons) per person, about 20 to 25 percent of that in the US (some of which is explained by the higher percentage of apartments and the smaller lots that most homes occupy), leaving little room for further improvements. Even so, current levels of consumption are causing problems: "In 2009, the German Federal Association for Energy and Water (BDEW) warned that water conservation in the country is so effective that the insufficient water flow causes stagnation and corrosion in the water pipes that serve some of Germany's biggest cities," including Cologne (Köln).[54]

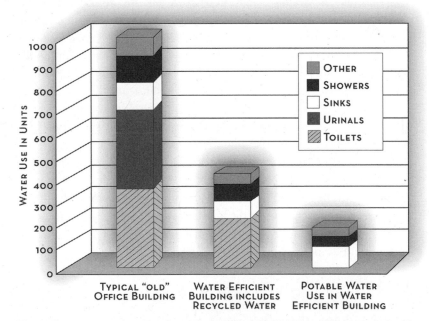

FIGURE 5.9 Potable water use in water-efficient buildings can be reduced nearly 80 percent with efficient fixtures and widespread use of recycled or reclaimed water.[55]

Summary

Water use in the CII sector can be cut substantially, to the economic benefit of everyone. Figure 5.9 shows what might be accomplished in older office buildings with the widespread use, not only of conservation measures but of recycled and reclaimed water: a total savings approaching 80 percent. There are many combinations of measures that will accomplish this goal, but in my view, *raising the price of water for CII users* is a first step, along with financial and technical assistance from water utilities and private service companies to help them make the most obvious changes. (Of course, finding and fixing leaks is still the prime method for reducing water use.) The US Green Building Council's LEED-EBOM rating system will likely spark a significant reduction in water use from office buildings, schools, colleges, hotels and retail enterprises, since the green certification has clear marketing and branding benefits for existing buildings. In new buildings and major renovations, the LEED system for new construction will likely push building teams to the same result.

Water Use in the Home

Water sustains all.

— Thales of Miletus, 600 BC[1]

L ET'S TAKE A LOOK now at residential water use, something that most of us are quite familiar with. Figure 6.1 shows the sources of water use inside the home. Almost 60 percent goes for shower, toilet and bath, our daily need for water for cleanliness. In Figure 6.1, you can see that leaks might account for as much as 12 percent of total household water consumption. Where do the leaks or non-specific uses come from? A leaky toilet, a dripping faucet, leaving the sink running while doing dishes or brushing your teeth, perhaps a drip irrigation system where some rodent has chewed a hole in the line, all contribute to household water use.

WaterSense Appliances

At this time, the US Environmental Protection Agency's (EPA) WaterSense® program's water-efficiency label only covers faucets and high-efficiency toilets for the home and flushing urinals and high-efficiency (tank-type) toilets for commercial purposes. You can expect shower heads, clothes washers and dishwashers to be added to the household list soon, along with pre-rinse spray valves and landscape irrigation controllers for commercial uses.[3] EPA has a calculator that allows you to estimate your savings in water and energy by using WaterSense appliances.[4] Figure 6.2 shows the reduction in water use from WaterSense toilets, urinals, shower heads and faucets.

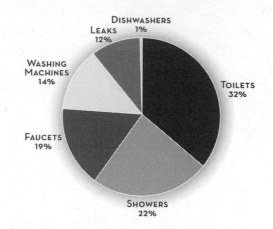

FIGURE 6.1 Toilets, showers and faucets account for three-fourths of water use inside a typical California home.[2]

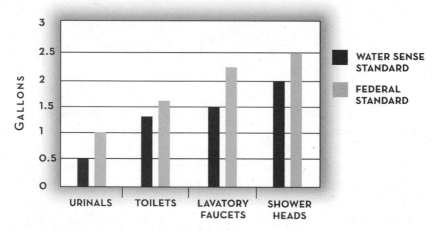

FIGURE 6.2 WaterSense appliances are designed to cut water use by 20 percent in flush toilets, 50 percent in urinals, 35 percent in faucets and 20 percent in shower heads.[5]

High-efficiency Toilets

Let's begin our home water conservation discussion with one appliance that we have to use every day: the toilet.

Background

The Energy Policy Act (EPAct) of 1992 mandated a maximum of 1.6 gallons per flush (gpf) for new toilets beginning in 1994. Nevertheless, quite a few homes and apartments still have older toilets that might use 3.5 or more gpf. During previous periods of water shortages, many people would put bricks or dams in these older toilets to cut water use per flush, without any noticeable decline in performance.

In January 2007, EPA released its first product specifications for high-efficiency toilets (HETs). The WaterSense specifications require that HETs use at least 20 percent less water than standard 1.6 gpf models (less than or equal to 1.28 gpf). The water-efficiency and flushing performance of Water-Sense HETs have to be tested and verified by an independent testing laboratory and manufactured by a company that has voluntarily partnered with the EPA and the WaterSense program.

Types of High-efficiency Toilets

HETs are available in various forms:

- Pressure-assist toilets compress air at the top of the refill tank to increase flush velocity.
- Flushometer (valve-type) toilets use direct water pressure to flush without a tank. These are common in commercial buildings.
- Dual-flush toilets use about 1.6 gpf for solids and 0.8 to 1.1 gpf for liquids.[6] I have two of the 1.6/0.8 gpf dual-flush toilets in my home, made by Kohler, and they work just fine.

Figure 6.3 shows estimated savings from dual-flush toilets, based on how much water your current toilet now uses.

5g/19l per flush
Uses 36,162 gallons (137,418 liters) per year*

3.5g/13l per flush
Uses 25,314 gallons (94,022 liters) per year*

2.5g/9.5l per flush
Uses 18,081 gallons (68,709 liters) per year*

1.6g/6l per flush
Uses 11,572 gallons (43,395 liters) per year*

Single-Flush Toilets

Caroma Dual-Flush toilets save millions of gallons of water every year.*

1.6/0.8g (6/3l) per flush
Uses 6943 gallons (26,037 liters) per year*

1.28/0.8g (4.8/3l) per flush
Uses 6480 gallons (24,301 liters) per year*

Dual-Flush Toilets

* Based on 1:4 solid/liquid usage. Figures calculated for an average family of four.

FIGURE 6.3 Dual-flush toilets potentially can save 25 percent or more of the water used in current flush-toilets and much more compared with older (pre-1992) models. Courtesy of Caroma.

Improved Performance and Testing

Due to advancements in hydraulic engineering and more-effective performance testing, the HETs currently on the market are far more reliable than
first generation HETs introduced in 1990s. Nearly every toilet component,
including the tank, flush valve, bowl rim and trapway, has recently been
re-engineered as a result of new tools such as Computational Fluid Dynam-
ics (CFD) computer modeling.[7] Although all toilets sold in the US meet
the minimum flush volume and performance standards of the American
National Standards Institute/American Society of Mechanical Engineers
(ANSI/ASME), these products receive only a pass or fail grade, making relative performance comparisons impossible.

In 2003, the Maximum Performance (MaP) test was established to
"identify how well popular toilet models perform using a realistic test media. A new testing protocol, cooperatively developed by water-efficiency and
plumbing fixture specialists in the US and Canada, incorporated the use of
soybean paste (miso) as a test media, closely replicating the 'real world demand' upon fixtures."[8] Actually, to conserve on soybean paste, the test me-
dium became miso wrapped in a condom, which replicates real-life turds
surprisingly well. The 14th edition of these MaP test results, released in May
2009, detailed the performance of more than 1,000 toilet models including
those that are WaterSense-certified HETs.[9] A MaP test exclusively for commercial products and applications is currently under development.[10]

Lessons Learned with HETs

The drainline carry of waste using HETs is not nearly as well-studied or
understood as HETs' initial flushing performance (the removal of all waste
from the bowl in a single flush). This is usually not a worry in homes, which
have steeper drainline slopes than in commercial buildings.

Where to Learn More

Both the Alliance for Water Efficiency[11] and the EPA websites provide extensive information on the WaterSense program, industry partners and
certified toilet tank and bowl combinations (which is a subtle yet important distinction since only specific tank and bowl combinations can achieve
WaterSense toilet certification).[12] The EPA's WaterSense Current,[13] a quarterly news update on WaterSense, is a valuable resource to keep current on
this maturing certification system. Your local water utility may have additional information on its website, along with possible incentive programs
that will pay all or most of the cost of replacing older toilets with Water-
Sense-labeled toilets.

Estimated Water Savings

In the 1970s, during times of water shortages, a popular motto was, "If it's yellow, let it mellow; if it's brown, flush it down." Now, with dual-flush toilets, we can accomplish the same goal. Assuming three liquid flushes per day and one solid flush per person in a four-person household, the average daily water savings of dual-flush toilets, per person, would be 2.4 gallons, a savings of 37.5 percent over a standard toilet's 6.4 gallons. For four people, the savings would be 9.6 gallons; for a full year (350 days at home), that would be 3,360 gallons. By reducing toilet use by 37.5 percent, overall household water consumption could be reduced by about 10 percent.

Low-flow Fixtures

There are myriad low-flow faucets and shower heads on the market; you only have to go to the EPA website and find a manufacturer who makes WaterSense-labeled fixtures. Figure 6.4 shows that a water-conserving fixture can still be very attractive while delivering a good flow rate.

Let's look at the total water flows through a home, as shown in Figure 6.5. In most homes, the basic inputs are water from the water mains (utility water) and rainwater that can be captured and used for outdoor watering. Inside the home are water-efficiency fixtures and appliances and, in some cases, graywater that can be recovered and used for outdoor irrigation. Wastewater flows from the home, a mixture of graywater and blackwater, into the sewer and then to a local sewage treatment plant.

FIGURE 6.4 Water-saving shower heads can be attractive additions to the bathroom. Copyright © Kohler Co. used with permission.

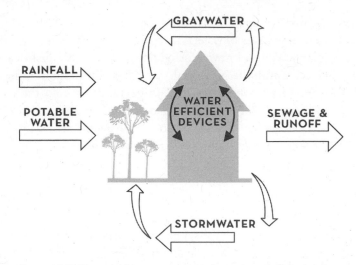

FIGURE 6.5 Household water use can be reduced with simple strategies that focus on efficient fixtures, rainwater harvesting and graywater reuse.[14]

FIGURE 6.6 This integrated sink/toilet fixture attempts to recycle graywater from hand washing and other sink use directly into the toilet tank. Courtesy of Caroma.

Figure 6.6 shows an integrated sink/toilet combination that effectively takes water from washing, shaving and other sink uses and puts it directly into the toilet tank as graywater for future flushing. I'm still having a hard time thinking that people will straddle a toilet to wash their hands, but as we enter a new era of water conservation thinking, anything's possible! Other units put the graywater storage under the sink and pump it into the toilet tank after each flush. This approach seems more user-friendly.

Still another example of striking design comes from Roca Sanitario in Barcelona, Spain. A combination of form and function that would work in a larger bathroom, the W+W — short for washbasin and water closet — from Roca[15] is currently only available outside the US. It reuses graywater from an attached sink for toilet flushing, helping to cut water use up to 25 percent, compared to a standard dual-flush toilet. Before the water is reused, it is filtered to take out bacteria and odors, along with any particles. Before being stored for flushing, the water is also chemically treated. Roca's W+W may cost more than $4,000. While that is far from cheap, according to blogger Jetson Green, "the product represents a striking combination of design, performance, and sustainability."[16]

Shower Heads

The EPAct of 1992 established a maximum of 2.5 gallons per minute (gpm) for shower heads at 80 psi (pounds per square inch water pressure). Efficient shower heads use 1.5 gpm or less. EPA's WaterSense program is working on a standard for shower heads that will likely use a 2.0 gpm flow rate. Efficient shower heads can pay for themselves in just a few months because they also reduce energy use. One concern is that flow restrictors are sometimes used to meet the EPAct maximum flow limit, but they can be easily removed and defeat the conservation goal.

Multiple shower heads and body-wash nozzles are trendy in newer bathrooms. They present a loophole for shower head-efficiency standards. Some manufacturers are marketing high-end "shower tower" systems that use as much as 20 gpm. This trend is contributing to a rise in water consumption in new homes and remodeled bathrooms.

Faucets

The EPAct of 1992 limited the flow rate of residential kitchen and bathroom faucets to 2.5 gpm at 80 psi or 2.2 gpm at 60 psi. In the case of bathroom faucets, WaterSense fixtures must meet a more stringent maximum flow rate of 1.5 gpm at 60 psi, a one-third reduction. Similar to shower heads, a concern is some faucets achieve mandated low flow rates with aerators or flow restrictors that could later be removed. The lower the flow rate, the longer it takes for hot water to reach the user, requiring greater amounts of energy. Aerators may also lose their effectiveness over time because of clogging and have to be serviced or replaced.

WaterSense Homes

In June 2009, EPA released a standard for the WaterSense New Home Certification,[17] usable by homebuilders to designate homes that reduce water consumption by 20 percent. This program should roll out in 2010 and 2011 to the home-building industry. I expect it to be especially popular in regions that have experienced significant water shortages in the past few years. The certification requirements deal with three key areas of household water conservation:

- Indoor water use, including plumbing, plumbing fixtures and fittings, appliances and other water-using equipment
- Outdoor water use, including landscape design and irrigation systems, if installed
- Homeowner education[18]

For indoor water use, a WaterSense Home will adopt the latest guidelines for various appliances and fixtures, including water pressure, hot water waste, bath and kitchen faucets, toilets, shower heads, clothes washers and dishwashers. If the builder provides evaporative coolers, drinking water (reverse osmosis) treatment or water softeners, they must also meet specific water-saving criteria.

For outdoor water use, landscape must be designed with no more than 40 percent turf or to meet a specific water budget. Irrigation systems, if sold with the home, must meet specific criteria, including guidelines for irrigation system controllers.

Homeowner education must include an operating manual for all water-using equipment or controls installed in the house and yard, including all relevant WaterSense materials on indoor and outdoor water use. Further, if an irrigation system is installed, the builder must provide the homebuyer with a schematic drawing of the system and copies of the recommended or programmed irrigation schedules.

Water Quality in the Home

This book is concerned mostly about the quantity of water available for urban uses, not its quality. Most of us take for granted that our drinking water is safe. Some of us want to get rid of chlorine and minerals, so we filter our drinking water using reverse osmosis and activated carbon filters. For the most part, we don't worry about what's in the water supply, since municipally supplied water has generally been quite safe in the US and Canada. However, as we start to reuse water, such as rainwater and graywater, in our homes, we should take all necessary precautions to make sure that contaminants don't enter the drinking water supply. Of course, if your water supply comes from wells, you can test the water regularly. In the US, the federal EPA requires all cities over 100,000 population to annually survey drinking water quality (called "consumer confidence reports").[19]

Table 6.1 lists some of the common contaminants that may be found in public and private drinking-water supplies. Some come from the chemicals

TABLE 6.1 Possible Water Supply Contaminants (partial list)[21]

Arsenic	Chromium	Nitrates
Bacteria	Copper	Radium
Carbufuran	Cryptosporidium	Radon
Chloramine	Hydrogen sulfide	Sulfates
Chlorine	Lead	Trihalomethanes
Chlorine by-products	Mercury	Volatile Organic Compounds

used to treat our drinking water supplies, such as chlorine. The EPA issues a maximum contaminant level goal (MCLG) for 90 contaminants, which shows the levels below which there is no known or expected risk to health. Water suppliers are not allowed to distribute water that exceeds any of these MCLGs.

A source of water contamination could be rainwater harvested and used for consumption or watering food crops. Researchers in Australia have found significant bacterial contamination of cisterns, which are very popular in Australia.[20] It's important that if you use rainwater in a way that could result in ingesting it, you decontaminate the water supply regularly. Chlorine bleach is a good way to do this.

Going Further with Water Conservation

Table 6.2 shows a full range of things you can do to save water, energy and money in and around the home. Each measure will provide both real and "psychic" benefits, reducing your water bills and showing your family and friends that you take water conservation seriously. Most of them are low-cost/no-cost measures; some require replacing appliances, such as dishwashers and clothes washers, which is best done during a normal replacement cycle as these wear out. Others require installing new systems, which will require some cash outlay. Still others require some lifestyle changes, such as taking shorter showers or putting up with less flow from faucets and shower heads. Some water treatment systems (such as reverse osmosis filters and water softeners) actually increase water consumption because of the required backflushing; these systems typically increase household water use by an average of 15.8 gallons per day.[22]

Recirculating Hot Water Systems

As one example, consider the amount of water wasted while waiting for hot water, especially first thing in the morning, something that upsets many people. There are many devices on the market now, that have an

TABLE 6.2 Range of Home Water Conservation Measures[23]

Measure	Potential Savings
1. Dual-flush or high-efficiency toilets	4,000 gallons per year[23a]
2. Low-flow shower heads	7.5 to 12 gallons per five-minute shower, about 7,800 gallons per year[23b]
3. ENERGY STAR dishwashers	3 to 8 gallons per load, about 1,250 gallons per year[23c]
4. ENERGY STAR clothes washers	18 gallons per load,[23d] about 11,000 gallons per year[23e]
5. Faucet aerators (bath and kitchen)	1,700 gallons per year[23f]
6. Hot water recirculation systems	7,300 gallons per year[23g]
7. Graywater reuse	30,000 to 40,000 gallons per year (of irrigation water)[23h]
8. Rainwater catchment	50% of domestic water consumption (if used for 100% of site irrigation)[23i]
9. Low-water-using native/adapted landscape or xeriscape; remove lawn; use artificial grass for green space.	Up to 40% of total household water use (assuming no irrigation water required)
10. Rain gardens or bioswales	Included in landscape measures
11. Lifestyle changes	Don't run water when shaving, brushing teeth (about 3 gallons each time[23j]), etc. Take shorter showers (a 1–2 minutes shorter shower can save 5 gallons[23k]), Wash dishes in dishwasher when full. Wash car at car wash, not in driveway.
12. Maintenance	Check for leaks (fixing leaky faucets can save 20 gallons per day[23l]); use dye for toilet (fixing toilet leaks can save 30 to 500 gallons of water per day).[23m] Check drip irrigation system.

electronically controlled pump-and-valve assembly system, that circulate the water back to the water heater that would normally go down the drain.[24] According to one expert, "The best pump system is one that has a temperature controlled by-pass valve under the farthest fixture sink and a timer on a pump that can be conveniently located next to the water heater. The timer can be set to go on and off at 15-minute intervals depending upon when you need hot water at the fixtures."[25] I installed this type of system in my home in January 2010, and it works just fine. I set it to run from 5:00 AM to 8:00 AM, so there would be instant hot water during the time our family is getting ready for the day.

The only issue I have with this system is that since most homes feature long plumbing runs from the water heater to point of use, there is going to be some energy wasted in circulating cold water through uninsulated water pipes, but I'd rather save the water. At a typical installation cost of $500 to $600, it's going to take some time to recover the initial investment with annual water savings, but the satisfaction of instant hot water might well be worth it. Besides, some water utilities have begun to offer rebates for this retrofit.[26]

For saving water by generating instant hot water, there are also tankless water heaters on the market that usually fit on the outside of the house, along with instant, on-demand water heaters that fit under a sink.

Later chapters will address rainwater harvesting, graywater recovery, landscaping for minimum water use and rain gardens and bioswales. You'll see how easily they can be adapted for home water conservation.

Solar Hot Water Systems

Mindful of the water/energy nexus first discussed in Chapter 4, you should consider using a solar water heater to supply 50 percent or more of your annual energy needs for water heating. I have a 40-square-foot solar thermal panel on my home, plenty big enough for two people, with the solar storage tank doubling as the (electric) water heater. In this way, even if you have to run the water for a while to get it hot, you won't be wasting as much energy. A solar water heater is a simple household appliance that has been perfected over the past century. The unit shown in Figure 6.7 also puts an electric water-storage tank (essentially the backup water heater) on the roof, so it also frees up room in your garage. With federal solar tax credits of 30 percent of installed cost, solar water heaters can typically provide a return on the net initial cost in less than five years, with just the hot water savings. In some cities and states, there are local incentives as well for solar water heating.[27]

Costs and Incentives for Household Water Conservation

Many residential water conservation measures are low cost and/or may be included in your water utility's incentive program. For example, faucet aerators are available from hardware and building supply stores, easy to install and cost a few dollars. Aerators can reduce faucet water flow from 2.2 gallons per minute to as low as 1 gallon per minute,[28] saving a family of four approximately 1,700 gallons per year.[29] Some water providers and utilities even give away faucet aerators as part of conservation programs.

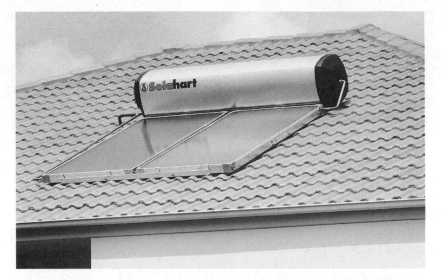

Figure 6.7 A solar water heater can help reduce annual energy consumption for providing hot water by 50 percent to 90 percent. Courtesy of Solahart.

Low-flow shower heads cost as little as $20 and can save 7.5 to 12 gallons per five-minute shower.[30] Replacing toilets will obviously cost more, with prices for HETs and dual-flush toilets starting at approximately $150 uninstalled. However, toilet replacement programs are a popular incentive offered by many water utilities. For example, Tucson Water in Arizona will rebate half the cost of installing new HET toilets up to $120 each with a $200 maximum per household.[31]

Water-efficient dishwashers and clothes washers are definitely investments, with prices starting at a few hundred dollars. The San Antonio Water System (SAWS) in Texas offers a rebate program for installing a high-efficiency washing machine. SAWS customers can choose from a list of approved models, mail in the application along with the original receipt, and SAWS will provide a $100 rebate on the customer's water bill.[32]

Rainwater harvesting systems vary in price depending on the type of system. You can acquire small-capacity (under 100 gallons) rain barrels for as little as $100 and attach them to a gutter downspout for garden watering. Larger, more-complex systems can range well above $1,000 installed. Currently, only a few incentive programs exist for rainwater harvesting systems, such as in the State of Arizona (a 25 percent tax credit up to $1,000), Santa Fe County (NM), Portland (OR), Cincinnati (OH), the state of Texas[33] and the City of Santa Monica, CA.[34]

Few jurisdictions offer incentives for residential graywater systems in the US. Arizona offers tax credits for "water conservation systems," which are defined as systems that harvest residential graywater and/or rainwater. Taxpayers can take a one-time tax credit of 25 percent of the cost of system, to a maximum $1,000 credit.[35]

Landscaping-related incentives and rebates are among the most common programs offered by utilities. The Santa Clara Valley Water District in northern California offers two types of rebates: landscape replacement and irrigation equipment upgrade. For example, a single-family property can be reimbursed up to $75 per 100 square feet of landscaping ($2,000 maximum) for replacing high-water-using plants (including turf) with approved low-water-using plants and/or permeable hardscape.[36] Alternatively, the agency offers rebates for high-efficiency irrigation hardware such as drip irrigation, rain sensors, weather-based controllers and landscape sub-meters.[37]

Most utilities provide information about their rebate programs online and are happy to discuss them with their customers because they are a win-win solution. The customer saves money, and the utility reduces demand on its water supply and treatment systems.

Saving Household Water in Australia

Queensland has been one of the hardest hit regions in the Australian drought and is home to the country's third-largest city, Brisbane, with a 2006 population of more than 1.6 million people.[38] Since southeast Queensland is heavily suburban, residential water demand consumes 70 percent of supplies. Beginning in 2007, state and local governments used extensive public promotions to persuade citizens to comply with a program called Target 140, a goal to reduce residential water use to 140 liters per day (37 gallons) per person. Beginning in the summer (January) of 2008, residential water use dropped below this level, to 34 gallons per day, a decline of 43 percent from pre-drought levels. With the easing of the drought last fall, average daily use has crept back up to 43 gallons per person per day, but is still well below earlier levels. Compared with American averages of 150 gallons per person per day, Brisbane and the rest of Australia show us how far we can go in reducing water use in the US. What worked in Brisbane? A shared sense of civic responsibility and strong promotional efforts by the authorities, along with personal decisions in favor of shorter showers, far less garden watering, less car washing and a host of small measures, reinforced by fines handed out by "water cops," along with a public display of water conservation measures in facilities such as parks and beaches.[39]

Summary

Do you know how your water use compares to the national average of 150 gallons per person per day (that's about 20 cubic feet per day, or 6 CCF per month)? Even though it's not currently a requirement, could you imagine reducing your water use to match Australian levels of 43 gallons (150 liters) per person per day? There are cost-effective, easy-to-install options for reducing water use inside the home, and many water utilities offer rebate programs for them. Today's HETs and dual-flush toilets work as well as traditional toilets and can reduce overall household water use by 10 to 20 percent. Consider replacing your faucets with those that are WaterSense-labeled and install shower heads that have a flow at or below 2 gpm. While more costly to buy and more complicated to install, hot water recirculation, graywater recycling and rainwater harvesting systems can also contribute to reducing water use in the home. Addressing water use inside the home will provide financial savings and personal rewards for your "sustainability bank account."

PART II

THE COLORS OF WATER

Blue Water

Water is the most extraordinary substance!
Practically all its properties are anomalous,
which enabled life to use it as building
material for its machinery.

— Albert Szent-Gyorgyi[1]

WITH ALL THE CONCERN the past decade about reducing water consumption in both residential and non-residential uses, you'll probably not find it surprising that the water field has begun to see considerable innovation, in freshwater supply, water conservation and water reuse. In the next seven chapters, you'll learn about these innovations, their practicality and costs and how likely they are to be a strong part of the water future in North America. Let's look first at a full spectrum of water technology innovations. In this chapter, I've used the term "blue water" for these innovations, a traditional term for water of drinkable quality. Water technology has become recognized in the past two to three years as a major new investment opportunity. According to *Inc.* magazine,

> Water managers in 36 states are predicting significant shortfalls within the next decade. Even in regions that do have sufficient supplies, aging infrastructure, inadequate treatment facilities, and contamination pose significant problems. It's no surprise, then, that new technological solutions are becoming commonplace... Analysts estimate that the world will need to invest as much as $1 trillion a year on conservation technologies, infrastructure, and sanitation to meet demand through 2030.[2]

Water Technology Innovations

There is increasing concern that water issues are becoming a strategic challenge for large businesses. For example, in early 2009, the Pacific Institute and Ceres published "Water Scarcity & Climate Change: Growing Risks for Business and Investors."[3] The key finding of this report was that leading global companies are beginning to treat water issues as a strategic challenge, to position themselves competitively for the future. The report identifies global risks to eight water-intensive industries; high-tech, beverage and agriculture head the list, but there are also potential water-supply risks to electric power production (as we've seen, it has large water needs for cooling), apparel manufacturing, biotechnology/pharmaceuticals, forest products and metals/mining activities.[4]

Large companies are beginning to look at their global water footprint (Chapter 2) to see how they can reduce water consumption. For example, Starbucks cut its daily waste of six million gallons of water by turning off faucets that had been running continuously in utensil-washing sinks (perhaps you noticed this yourself in a Starbucks store and wondered why).[5] Similarly, Walmart stores were able to cut water consumption by 30 percent across 70 locations in the Southeast by retrofitting stores with high-efficiency toilets.[6]

Laura Shenkar, executive director of the Artemis Project in San Francisco, believes that we are on the cusp of a revolution in water technology at all levels. In releasing the list of the top 50 companies working in the water field and the 10 best new products for 2009, the result of an annual international competition, Shenkar said: "The goal of this competition was to show the US venture capital community the diversity and investment potential of an international network of advanced water technology companies."[7] According to the Artemis Project, "This award distinguishes advanced water and water-related technology companies as leaders in their trade for helping to build water into one of the great high-growth industries of the 21st century. The companies were selected by a panel of experts based on an integrated matrix of four criteria: technology, intellectual property and know-how, management team and market potential."[8]

Emerging technology themes in this marketplace include:
- Desalination
- Membrane technology, including both desalination and wastewater treatment
- Stormwater management and treatment
- Water-quality monitoring
- Onsite wastewater reclamation

- Disinfection of water: drinking water, recycled water, rainwater
- Irrigation automation
- Cooling tower water-use efficiency[9]

Directly or indirectly, this book addresses each of these themes and one more that is hidden in each of these: the use of Internet "software as a service" (aka "the cloud") to monitor, meter and track water use across many users, many technologies and many applications. As you'll see below, the basic principle of HydroPoint Data Systems' irrigation control technology is to use an incredible amount of weather data to tell thousands of irrigation controllers when to turn on and off and, using the Internet, to find out if they're functioning properly. It's important that water-conserving irrigation devices be closely monitored, to guard against leaks that would defeat the purpose of the entire system.

Smart Irrigation Technology

We've already seen how much of total water use is for agriculture as well as for landscape use in cities. It stands to reason that investors and entrepreneurs, along with farmers and building owners, would be interested in water-efficient irrigation technology. Using the Internet and onsite monitoring, it's relatively straightforward to irrigate only when the soil is dry and plants need water and there's no rain in the forecast. Growing up in Los Angeles, I always wondered why sprinklers were running on many large commercial lawns during rainstorms (of course, the reason was that they were on fixed watering schedules)! One of the leading companies providing outdoor smart water management is HydroPoint Data Systems of California. I interviewed HydroPoint's Chief Strategy Officer Chris Spain about what the company has accomplished and where he sees the industry going.

> From a high level, the technology, which has been proven across our customer base of over 21,000 subscribers, can do two things: one, to ensure that no waste occurs on the application of watered landscapes and two, almost equally important as far as the adoption curve goes, to do it in an economically sustainable fashion.
>
> We ensure that the right amount of water is applied at the right time for each specific landscape. That's extraordinarily different from the status quo, which is driven by an existing technology called an irrigation controller. Currently, these irrigation controllers are nothing more than timers. There are two problems with the timers. First, they do a great job keeping time, but they do a lousy job calculating exactly how much

water the landscape specifically requires, and they also ask a huge requirement from the installer or the user, which is to guess how much [irrigation] time [is required].[10]

As water becomes more expensive and in some cases, unavailable to wasteful users, "hands-free" irrigation control will become more desirable and cost-effective. Says Spain,

> Additionally, from an ongoing operational perspective, to be able to execute on water conservation, clock-timer controllers require the user to be able to, everyday or at least weekly, go out and adjust that controller. The basic problem is really calculating how much water or how much time to irrigate based on their landscape. The American Water Works Association did a study that showed that 75 or 80 percent of all installed controllers still had the same default settings as when they left the factory. Obviously, the [irrigation] workforce is poorly equipped to calculate a specific landscape's requirements.

To make their controllers (Figure 7.1) work optimally, HydroPoint collects 19 specific parameters about each specific hydro-zone (or irrigation area), including soil type, plant types, slope, amount of sun and type of sprinkler. Once that information is entered into the controller, the controller then

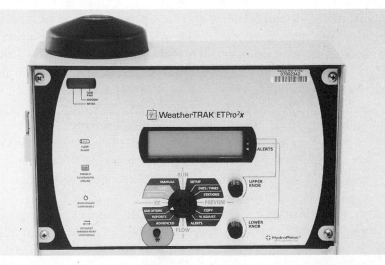

FIGURE 7.1 Internet-connected weather controllers apply only the amount of water needed for plant growth and also help troubleshoot excessive water use. Courtesy of HydroPoint Data Systems.

looks up a vast table of database values like crop water coefficients, infiltration rates and soil holding capacity, and then it calculates a baseline irrigation schedule using scientific principles. This schedule is in turn changed and adjusted based on site-specific local weather changes. The optimal amount of water to apply to a crop will maximize crop yield but minimize water use. The same principles used in agriculture can be applied to landscape plants and even lawns.

According to Spain, the gold standard for determining application rate is the weather index called *evapotranspiration* (ET).

It's really a simple idea for such a fancy word. It means how much water has evaporated from the soil or transpired from the plant during a given day. It's kind of like a gas tank model where the soil itself is the tank of gas and the evapotranspiration is how much gas or water is used up during the day. Using that value, you can figure out how much water to reapply to the root zone. But we don't just constantly run to the gas station and fill up the tank regardless of how much we've used. We watch how much water has been used, and we let it get down to the maximum allowable depletion, a well-known idea in horticulture and agriculture. We let the water table go down until it reaches the maximum depth of the roots, and then we fill the water back up. That's the best irrigation schedule, not just for water conservation and runoff reduction but also for the plant's health and productivity.

HydroPoint relies on a network of 40,000 weather stations around the US that report weather data to the National Oceanic and Atmospheric Administration (NOAA). HydroPoint downloads these data from a NOAA satellite every hour to a supercomputer. The HydroPoint system then puts the information through an advanced modeling program that can calculate ET down to every square kilometer in the US. The proper ET value is then delivered wirelessly to the irrigation controller, without each customer having to install a weather station, maintain a weather station or even verify that the weather station is working. Spain says that, in this way, HydroPoint addresses "all three key issues of having an onsite weather station, and what's amazing about the technology is that it's compatible with all 45 million irrigation controllers in the country."

Matching Water Quality and Source with Water Use

One of the key ideas for stretching our water supplies is to match end-use needs for water quality with the supply source. For example, reclaimed wastewater is often used to irrigate golf courses, highway/roadway medians and lawns on corporate campuses. Since there is little direct public contact with these large expanses of greenery, there's no need to use potable water. In the same way, constructed wetlands and large landscapes can be irrigated with stormwater runoff from parking lots and office parks.

Figure 7.2 shows how this analysis might be done even inside a home or apartment building (in the future). Potable water is needed for only about half the total use, for shower and bath, dishwashing and personal washing, cooking and drinking water. Employing 38 percent harvested rainwater (toilet and washing machine) and 12 percent graywater for garden irrigation and site cleaning (hosing down patios, cars, etc.) could supply the balance. The details of how to make the plumbing work are not that obvious to most homeowners, so eventually the ability to use graywater and to harvest rainwater will have to be built into local building codes. For example, the City of Tucson, Arizona, recently enacted a graywater ordinance that requires, starting June 1, 2010, all new single-family homes and duplexes to include plumbing for future graywater distribution.[11]

In a commercial, industrial or institutional (CII) building, non-potable water could supply even greater percentages of total use (as shown in Figure 5.3) given that 35 percent of water is used for landscaping, 16 percent for restrooms, 15 percent for cooling and very little for drinking or personal hygiene. Process water inside the building typically would remain potable water, as would kitchen and laundry water supply in institutional settings.

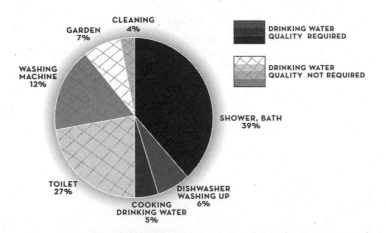

Figure 7.2 Analyzing quality requirements for specific water uses can help building owners decide on the feasibility of using lower-grade water sources. Percentages based on daily use of 129 liters per person per day in Germany.[12]

Even with these exceptions, it's likely that *non-potable water could easily supply two-thirds of total use* in CII applications.

Total Water System Analysis

The best way to minimize use of potable water and to maximize use of reclaimed or recycled water for "once-through" applications in most new projects is to perform a "total water system analysis." Engineer and Australian water expert Guenter Hauber-Davidson advocates integrated design which encompasses:

> a systems understanding where we think in terms of ecological systems, so solving a problem for a single need can also provide a solution for other needs. With industrial ecology, a waste product from one stream becomes a resource for another stream. It's not just looking at a water, energy or indoor air-quality solution in isolation, but looking at how we can holistically, through applied systems thinking, solve the entire problem with the minimum environmental impact. What we're seeing at the moment is people chasing water savings with complete disregard for the other environmental impacts associated with water use, in particular, energy use and therefore carbon emissions. To me, that is just not the right approach.[13]

In my 2008 book, *Green Building through Integrated Design*, I advocate a similar approach, taking water-related questions and goals into account at the earliest conceptual and schematic design phase, even starting with the basic question: how much water does nature supply (for free) to the project site?[14] Then the building designer attempts to match available water sources (including treated sewage, graywater, potable water) to water requirements for the project. It may even be possible to use adjoining roofs to collect and treat rainwater for use in the new building. This was done at the Tacoma police rainwater harvesting project profiled in Chapter 9, where a large roof space from an adjacent building collects water for the new police headquarters as well as for a vehicle maintenance facility on the same property.

Comprehensive Onsite Water Treatment

Some of the more advanced LEED-seeking projects are now attempting to derive all of their water use from onsite sources. This achievement constitutes part of a program called the Living Building Challenge, described in greater depth in Chapter 12. At this point, though, let's take a look at a

remarkable project in Portland, Oregon, completed in 2005, which was one
of the largest LEED Platinum-certified buildings in the world in 2009.

At a cost of $150 million, a private developer built to suit the Oregon
Health & Science University's (OHSU) Center for Health and Healing in
Portland. This project achieves a measured 51 percent savings in water use
compared with a conventional building. The building contains more than
200 exam rooms, so you can imagine how much water use there is just for
handwashing! Figure 7.3 shows how the engineering design team, Interface
Engineering, Inc. of Portland, conceived of the total water system.[15]

There are four main water flows and sources in this project:

1. Fresh water (3.3 million gallons per year [mgy]) enters the building
   from the local water mains and is used for all potable water uses, such as
   drinking, showers, sinks and kitchen.

2. Rainwater (0.5 mgy) is harvested from the roof and directed to a large

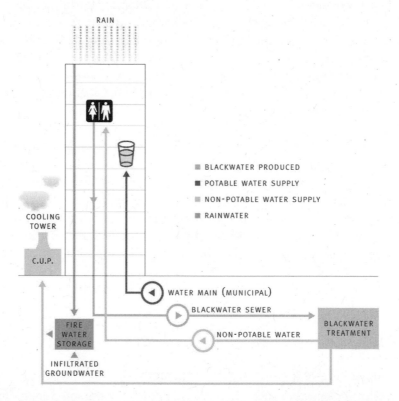

FIGURE 7.3 At the Oregon Health & Sciences University project in Portland,
designers looked at the entire water system for ways to cut use more than
50 percent through a "reduce, reuse, recycle" approach. Courtesy of Interface
Engineering.

storage tank (25,000 gallons) below the building, which doubles as the fire suppression storage tank for the project. It is then treated and used for a portion of toilet flushing, cooling tower makeup water (1.5 mgy) and irrigation (1.0 mgy) for the project's green roof and site landscaping.

3. Blackwater (sewage) from toilets, urinals and fixtures (5.0 mgy) is treated in the basement (to drinking water standards) and reused for site irrigation, cooling tower makeup and toilet/urinal flushing in the building's core restrooms. Excess treated blackwater is sent out to the stormwater management system through a bioswale (essentially a vegetated ditch). Wastewater solids, about two percent of the wastewater stream, are collected and disposed of on a regular basis, but no wastewater is sent to the city's sewer system.

4. A final source of non-potable water comes from reclaimed groundwater that must be continually removed via foundation drains, owing to a high water table. The relatively low and constant temperature of this groundwater also makes it useful for radiant cooling in various places in the building.

As you will see in Chapter 12, some smaller projects are aiming at "net-zero water use," relying on annual rainfall, conservation measures and recycled water for all of their water needs. However, as an example for others to follow, the OHSU project has the virtue of cutting water use more than 50 percent using "state of the shelf" technology (nothing exotic or particularly new) and fairly conventional economic calculations in a major commercial building with more than 2,000 daily occupants and visitors.[16]

Total Water Systems Analysis: A German Approach

The Stuttgart-based building engineering firm Transsolar is part of the Behnisch Architekten design team for a new 700,000-square-foot laboratory building complex in a new biosciences compound for Harvard University in Allston, Massachusetts. Their total water system analysis, for a building with 1,000 occupants per day, includes both water and wastewater flows and focuses on four major areas of water consumption:

- Building operations
- Special applications (laboratory, food services)
- Irrigation (indoor and outdoor)
- Utility plant (cooling towers)[17]

Part of the design idea is to *look at more alternatives than usual*. In this case, the team is investigating a number of water-saving strategies:

- Vacuum flushing technology for urinals and toilets (think about your last airplane flight)
- Hybrid cooling towers (potential 50 percent water savings)
- Closed-loop hydronic cooling throughout the building for room conditioning and equipment cooling, instead of once-through lab equipment cooling
- Reduction of the overall building mechanical cooling demand and thus cooling tower water use by energy-efficient lab equipment
- Internal heat shift between hot and cold zones and free geothermal cooling
- Eliminating unnecessary water treatment (such as softening and filtering)
- Using ozone and ultraviolet light for treating bacteria in cooling towers instead of chemicals.

A fairly equal precipitation falls in Boston each month, resulting in a favorable situation for rainwater harvesting, and requiring minimal storage volumes. A bioswale onsite captures about 60 to 75 percent of site runoff and directs it into a cistern. Rainwater is also soft and pure, meeting some of the project's key water-quality requirements. The design uses only captured water for irrigation of indoor and outdoor plants. Part of the building cooling strategy is to use a waterwall in the atrium, so having treated rainwater available for use is ideal for this approach to space conditioning, since the water in a public space needs to be quite clean.

The project team would also have liked to use condensate water from makeup air dehumidification for part of the cooling tower supply, since, like rainwater, it is also a pure water source. However, in the State of Massachusetts, condensate water is considered industrial waste because of possible antifreeze (glycol) contamination, so that option is not available. The project is also looking to reuse discharge water from the reverse osmosis water purification process.

Mathias Rudolph and Helmut Meyer spoke of Transsolar's design considerations for this very large new laboratory project:

> The big water consumers in a lab building — or in any building located in a humid environment — [come from the need for] some kind of chilled water for dehumidification and fresh air for cooling. This is the really big water consumer within a building, because to provide chilled water to cool down outside air before it enters the building, you need a compression chiller, which needs to reject the heat through a cooling tower.

For cooling towers of a project of this size and capacity, open cooling towers are used. The cooling tower sprays the cooling liquid (which is water) into the tower, and through an evaporation process, the water cools down. To produce chilled water, you have considerable evaporation (water loss) in this type of cooling tower.

In a lab building, you also have sizable demand for chilled water — not only in the summertime but also in wintertime. This leads to a really high water demand year-round that, when compared to all other water consumers, can be a factor 20 to 40 times greater than water needs for landscaping, toilets and other interior uses.

We looked at these [water demand] numbers at the very beginning to determine the [key] water consumers in the building and the water demand of each end-use. At the very beginning, we realized that if we wanted real water savings, we had to improve the way we created chilled water.[18]

This is the key approach of whole systems analysis: start with the biggest water demand and see what you can do to reduce it considerably before starting with potential sources of water supply.

So how do you improve the water demand of a cooling tower? The technology is there, and it is called a hybrid cooling tower.[19] Compared to an open cooling tower, the water used in a hybrid cooling tower is concealed within a heat exchanger, and you can run the cooling tower dry whenever the outdoor temperature is low [such as all winter long].

So your water demand for cooling is limited to the high temperature season in the summer. In the winter, spring and autumn, you can run the cooling towers without any water. *By doing so, you have the potential of reducing the water demand of your cooling towers by 50 percent.* For this project, it means you can reduce your water demand from 90,000 cubic meters (24 million gallons) per year down to 45,000 cubic meters (12 million gallons). Compared to low-flow fixtures and high-performance toilets, this represents tremendous savings. With low-flow toilets and fixtures, you can decrease water demand down to maybe 1,500 cubic meters (400,000 gallons), but there's nothing where you can save 45,000 cubic meters (except cooling towers).

This project and their approach represent an example of good engineering. The basic approach: Don't start with conventional systems and then try to work your way around the problems they create. Look for alternatives first, but be realistic: The hybrid cooling tower approach has some drawbacks. It is somewhat more complex to run; it takes more roof area, which is always in demand in most buildings; and it requires a larger initial investment (according to Meyer, as much as 30 percent over conventional cooling), one which is repaid quickly in both water savings and reduced chemical use.[20]

Total Water Systems Approach: A Canadian Approach

Dockside Green is a remarkable mixed-use urban development on a former brownfield (contaminated) industrial site next to the harbor in Victoria, British Columbia. The architects Busby Perkins + Will designed the integration of water and energy systems, along with stormwater management and blackwater treatment, into the infrastructure. Starting with a new development at Dockside Green made the job a bit easier, but one has to remember that, when the design work began, this type of integration had never before been tried on this large a scale.

When complete, the Dockside Green development will be a community of approximately 2,500 residents and will also include live/work spaces, hotel, retail, office and light industrial uses, as well as numerous public amenities. The developer pledged to achieve LEED Platinum certification for each of the project's 26 buildings.

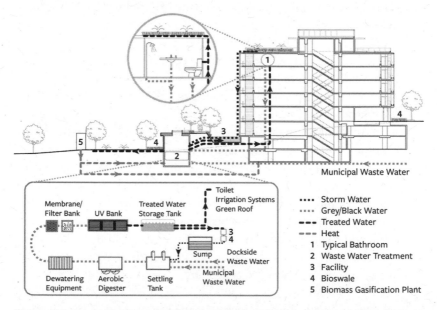

Figure 7.4 Dockside Green in Victoria, British Columbia, uses an integrated design approach that combines energy, water and drainage into a unified and cost-effective system. Courtesy Busby Perkins + Will.

Dockside Green uses an integrated energy system to ensure that the development will be greenhouse-gas neutral, while also providing the opportunity for the project to become a net-energy provider. The system includes a biomass gasification plant that converts locally sourced wood waste into clean-burning gas to produce heat and hot water. Among the development's other sustainable features are an onsite wastewater treatment plant that is expected to save more than 70 million gallons of water annually,[21] rooftop gardens and a series of ponds spread throughout Dockside's central greenway that assist in onsite stormwater storage.[22]

All of Dockside Green's sewage is treated onsite and reused primarily for toilets and irrigation, reducing the demand for potable water. Residual treated water will recharge the naturalized waterway that flows across the site and collects rainwater as it flows towards the inner harbor. Dockside Green's treatment system blends in with the naturalized setting of the community.[23]

Supplied by General Electric, the Z-MOD Membrane BioReactor (MBR) system installed at Dockside Green is designed to treat an average daily flow (ADF) of 50,000 gpd (189,000 liters per day). A future plant expansion will increase the ADF capacity to 100,000 gpd (378,000 liters per day) by simply adding more membranes and ancillary equipment. In this treatment process, all graywater and blackwater effluent first flows to a concrete bioreactor tank where bacteria consume or digest the biodegradable waste before it enters the membrane chamber where GE's Zee-Weed membranes are immersed. Water is gently drawn through billions of microscopic pores on the surface of the membrane fiber via a pump. The pores act as a filter that physically blocks suspended solids, bacteria and viruses from passing through, producing a water quality suitable for non-potable applications. Ultraviolet units further disinfect the treated water. The sanitized, finished water flows to the water storage tank for use within the community.[24]

Dockside Green's potable water use in residential and commercial buildings expects to be approximately 60 to 65 percent below conventional developments. The project achieves this level of water conservation largely by using reclaimed water for toilets and use of low-flow fixtures throughout—such as dual-flush toilets, 1.5 gpm shower heads, 0.9 gpm sinks, 0.5 gpm lavatories and water-free urinals. This approach results in some interesting water/energy synergies. For example, energy-efficient front-loading washers are gentler on clothes, use less water and require less heat for drying, thanks to a high-speed spin-cycle feature that removes more water. Similarly, the project's investment in energy- and water-efficient dishwashers, washing machines and shower heads for the residential units saves energy costs because they require less hot water. There are also individual water meters in each residence for accurate monitoring of water consumption, heat and energy, thereby promoting the behavioral changes so essential to conservation.[25]

Summary

Is water the new oil? Various media outlets are exploring the question of whether water is now becoming the kind of precious commodity that oil became in the 20th century. According to *Business Week*, among many others, billionaire oilman and financier T. Boone Pickens thinks so.[26] Therefore, even if it hasn't already arrived full-blown, a water technology revolution is imminent because of the need to get more use out of the hydrologic gifts nature gives us. Innovative companies are developing sophisticated products that reduce commercial, industrial, agricultural and residential water use, and venture capitalists are investing in them. Beyond implementing some of these new technologies, forward-thinking design teams are also looking at new ways to provide for more integrated water systems in the built environment and, as a result, are dramatically reducing water use in new buildings and developments.

Graywater

Water, taken in moderation,
cannot hurt anybody.

Mark Twain[1]

U NLIKE RAINWATER, which is highly variable both year to year and
seasonally, graywater tends to be reliably present in most commercial
environments. In a large office building, just the waste water from sinks
can be significant on a daily basis, certainly enough to flush many of the
building's toilets and urinals. In a hotel, there is almost a guaranteed flow of
water from guest showers and public bathroom faucets, so why use potable
water for flushing toilets, when there is another supply that you've already
paid for?

Graywater is generally defined as wastewater that is not combined with
toilet waste, kitchen sink waste, dishwasher waste, diaper rinse water or
similarly contaminated sources.[2] According to one source, there are eight
million graywater systems in use in the US, serving about 22 million people.[3] Many of these are likely "bootleg" installations, done without permits,
by people living in rural and water-short areas with landscape watering restrictions.

Graywater includes wastewater from bathtubs, showers, bathroom
washbasins, clothes washers and laundry tubs from both residential and
non-residential installations. From Chapter 6, you might recall that these
water sources account for nearly 40 percent of household water consumption. The capture, treatment and reuse of graywater not only produces
usable water that would otherwise be directed to the sewer, its use on the

landscape and for car washing is generally not subject to the typical watering restrictions sometimes imposed by local jurisdictions.[4]

One important caveat about toilet or urinal flushing with graywater: Toilet manufacturers are concerned and are very much involved with the development of a water-quality standard that graywater systems must meet if the water is to be used for flushing toilets or urinals. Until such a standard exists and these systems can be tested and certified by a third-party lab, many believe that the water should only be used for subsurface irrigation.[5] Even though the water is not intended for drinking, there are some legitimate health concerns about possible inhalation of water aerosols (generated during flushing) and potential skin contact. For this reason, residential graywater typically is used only in landscape irrigation and in most cases only with subsurface application.

Commercial Graywater Systems

Andy Kruse is executive vice-president of L. J. Kruse Co., a large plumbing contractor in Berkeley, California. His take on the potential for graywater systems is that there is interest, but it may be somewhat limited until code officials are more willing to cooperate.[6]

> I think there's potential with graywater, and that area is going to develop, but I think probably it will be a little bit slower. There are some issues with local code enforcements for the local authorities to approve graywater usage. In the city of Oakland, there's a group called Greywater Guerrillas,[7] a local graywater company that's trying to get a foothold in the area. They recently met with the City of Oakland to try to get approval for graywater use. That's an example of code issues — the City of Oakland is resisting the use of graywater because they say they've been working on enforcing the plumbing code, keeping everybody healthy for all these years, and they're not quite ready to make a wholesale switch. From a plumbing standpoint, graywater is an expensive system to install, and there's a limited use for that graywater — for either landscape or maybe some replacement of potable use.

Others have a more optimistic viewpoint. Water Harvesting Solutions is a Midwest-based provider of graywater ultrafiltration systems for large buildings.[8] In their view, the most important advantage of graywater over rainwater harvesting is that in a residential building — where there may be many users of showers and sinks — graywater provides a constant supply of harvested water for flushing toilets. There's enough graywater generated in a building typically to meet 100 percent of flushing requirements. Unlike rainwater, the supply is steady and predictable, so the storage requirements are dramatically less; however, graywater normally contains biological and chemical contaminants that can quickly turn to blackwater, resulting in unpleasant odors, colors and health hazards if not treated correctly.[9]

How Graywater Systems Work

Figure 8.1 shows a typical schematic of a graywater harvesting and reuse system. Graywater from bathroom sinks (not kitchen sinks, however), showers, laundry and other lightly used water sources drains to a settling bioreactor tank, where it is treated before entering a storage tank. After a disinfection stage, typically chlorine or ultraviolet light, it resupplies toilet fixtures and outdoor irrigation systems. In retrofit applications, harvested graywater is used solely for subsurface drip irrigation, since it may be costly to put in a separate line to resupply toilets in a building.

Packaged Graywater Systems

The Pontos division of German manufacturer Hansgrohe makes a product called AquaCycle that relies on biological treatment means, rather than chemical, and can accommodate varying graywater inflows, such as from

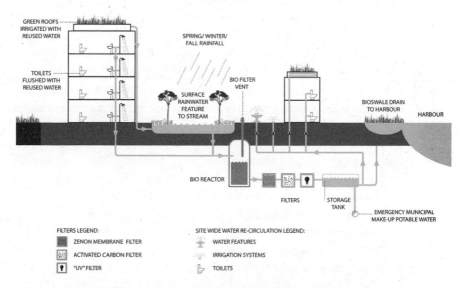

FIGURE 8.1 At Dockside Green in Victoria, British Columbia, graywater systems take water from sinks, showers, laundry and other lightly contaminated sources, clean it up and reuse it for toilet flushing or irrigation. Courtesy of Busby Perkins + Will.

office buildings and educational facilities that may have much lower water use on weekends and holidays. I saw an installation at a large office complex in Frankfurt that was plumbed to supply the bathroom sinks and seemed to be working quite well, according to the building facility manager. This system serves only showers, bathtubs and sinks.

The AquaCycle units are available from 2.0-cubic-meter and 4.5-cubic-meter (cu.m.) per day modules, about 525 and 1,200 gallons, respectively. Units can be combined to serve up to 45 cubic meters (12,000 gallons) per day. Since the storage capacity is primarily required only for one day, you can easily calculate how many gallons of storage are needed to collect graywater and return it for toilet and urinal flushing. The AquaCycle 4500 (4.5 cu.m.) is also low-energy-using, with a power demand of 5.4 kWh per day.[10] Pontos systems are used in almost all European countries, South Africa and Jordan, even at a municipal swimming pool in Yerres, France.

How Does the System Work?
The system is quite simple, consisting of four major steps (Figure 8.2):

1. **Pre-filtration.** First, the graywater enters a filter that retains coarser particles such as textile fluff, hairs, etc. The filter is cleaned automatically at regular intervals and the residues are fed into the wastewater drain.
2. **Biological treatment.** After pre-filtration, the graywater undergoes a two-stage biological treatment process. In stage 1, the water is treated with oxygen at normal atmospheric pressure. Microorganisms adhering to the surface of the carrier material introduced into the tanks at stages 1 and 2 break down the biodegradable content of the water with metabolic processes. After 3 hours, the water is pumped from stage 1 to stage 2, where it undergoes the same treatment a second time.
3. **Sediment removal.** During the biological treatment process (stages 1 and 2), surplus biologically active sludge is generated. This is automatically removed at set intervals and fed into the wastewater drain.
4. **UV disinfection.** After the sedimentation stage, the water enters a fourth stage in which it passes through a UV lamp light for sterilization purposes. After this stage, the recycled water is odorless and can be stored for a long period. It can be reused as high-quality process water, depending on local sanitation regulations.[11]

Benefits of Packaged Systems
Packaged biological treatment systems provide many benefits, including:
- No requirement for chemical additives.

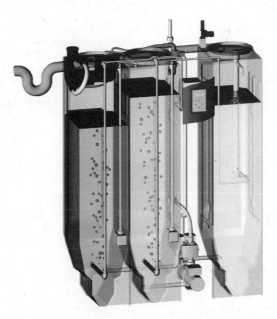

FIGURE 8.2 This graywater system provides good-water-quality effluent without chemicals, using filters, biological treatment and UV sterilization. Courtesy of Pontos/Hansgrohe AG.

- Certified water quality — the products, production and cleaning process are approved by Germany's TÜV (a product quality organization).[12]
- Consistent water quality — the treated water complies with the European Union bathing-water directive, which means it can be used for direct human contact.[13]
- Fully automatic system due to self-cleaning components — no user intervention necessary.
- Independent of weather (unlike rainwater harvesting) — shower, sink and bath water is always produced, in most installations, at about the same rate required for toilet flushing.
- Fits into a standard mechanical room in large buildings.
- Low maintenance — service is required only once a year for smaller units, twice a year for larger units.
- Low operating costs — power consumption estimated at 1.5 to 2.5 kWh per treated cubic meter of clear water (about 6 to 10 kWh per 1,000 gallons).

Graywater recovery and onsite reuse has compelling arguments and should be considered for new building installations.

TABLE 8.1 Some Examples of Packaged Commercial Graywater Systems

Company	System	Size	Notes
Brac Systems (Canada)	Brac Graywater recycling system	4,590 gallons (17,373 liters)	Provides up to 13,192 gph @ 71 psi.
ReWater Systems (US)	Models RWAF4 and RWAF5	200-gallon surge tank	For irrigation only, uses sand filter, serves up to 32 sources
Hansgrohe (Germany)	Pontos AquaCycle	4,500 to 13,500 liters per day (1,200 to 3,600 gallons)	4-phase water treatment, including UV-light sterilization, primarily commercial
Perpetual Water (Australia)	Catchment 720L	One unit produces up to 1,360 liters per day, from 1,440 liters input	Commercial system uses multiple tanks; serves toilets, garden

Types of Commercial Systems

Table 8.1 describes some of the packaged commercial graywater systems currently on the market. Although not a comprehensive listing, it can serve as an initial guide to suppliers for larger projects. For household systems, you'll have to turn to local companies that can assemble the project from components or perhaps find an imported system, such as the Perpetual Water system from Australia.[14]

Market Interest in Graywater Systems

Don Giarratano of D/K Mechanical Contractors in Anaheim, California, points out that, in water-short regions such as Southern California, the market interest in graywater and reclaimed water systems is growing dramatically.

> For us in Southern California, reclaimed water or graywater systems are where we really need to create a broader availability of use of those types of systems. It's already water that's out there. It's reprocessed water. There's no reason that it can't be delivered to the right locations. It makes sense for new construction or even retrofit construction. It's not like we get rain every month here in Southern California. In many places, water rationing is already taking place.
>
> We're doing three projects at the University of California, Irvine. They mandate that reclaimed water systems be used in all of their facilities. The City of Irvine has been at the leading edge when it comes to

reclaimed wastewater systems for commercial building applications. It's mandated within the city, and they have done a great job providing a distribution source for that. For these projects, the reclaimed system is a filter bank and pump system, and usually we buy those out as a package from companies such as Weil Aquatronics, a manufacturer's representative. These projects will save a minimum of 20 percent and possibility up to 50 percent of total water use.

We have projects at Camp Pendleton [in northern San Diego County] where there's no reclaimed water distribution currently available for use in barrack applications. There are 1,000 water closets in the barracks. We are installing a dual-water pipe system because there will be a time where Camp Pendleton will have reclaimed water available. For the buildings they're currently constructing, they're making preparations so, when that time comes, the systems will already be built into the structures. It will just be a matter of making the final connection.[15]

Seeing the interest in the commercial market, can a homeowner also use graywater for water-use reduction? In the home, it seems the best answer is for garden and landscape irrigation, preferably subsurface through drip irrigation. Let's look at the value of a home graywater system.

Residential Graywater Reuse

Residential systems are similar to commercial graywater applications but are typically smaller and more modest in end uses. If you have a basement or crawl space, you may be able to access directly the plumbing lines that can feed into a graywater system. In much of the West, where homes are built "slab on grade," it's going to be hard to catch much besides the laundry water for outdoor irrigation, since the graywater will get mixed with toilet water in pipes running through the slab, and you won't be able to use it. A rudimentary alternative, in case of a significant drought, is to fill buckets in the shower and tub and carry them outside. That approach will likely get old in a hurry for most homeowners. Figure 8.3 shows the elements of a household graywater system.

Economics of Residential Graywater Use

One supplier provided the following analysis of the value of graywater systems in San Diego County, CA, for a residential system.[17] As a source of water, at a current average mid-tier retail price of $2.47 per hundred cubic feet (CCF) for water supply, the systems would supply 3.6 acre-feet (1560 CCF) over a 20-year system life, with a total lifetime value of $3,873,

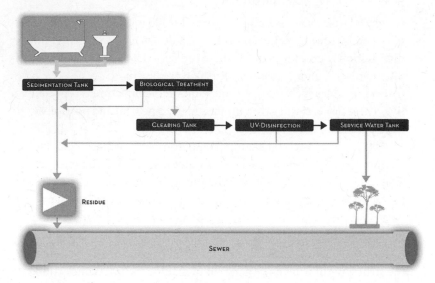

FIGURE 8.3 Residential graywater systems can be simple to design, build and operate, if your main goal is to provide some supplemental outdoor irrigation.[16]

assuming 125-gallons-per-day water use from a 3.2-person household. As a replacement for a basic drip irrigation system (controller, valves, tubing, etc.), a new graywater system installation would cost $1,500. As a method of reducing wastewater treatment charges, assuming a cost of $3.22 per CCF and a production of 3.6 acre-feet over a 20-year life, the system would save $5,050. This produces a total life-cycle value of $10,423 per system, at 2007 local water and sewer treatment rates in San Diego.

One caveat to keep in mind: as fixtures and appliances in homes and offices, schools and restaurants become more water efficient, graywater volumes will decline, so systems may need to be designed to accommodate reduced future inflows.

New Products

New products are continually being introduced for increasing water conservation and reuse. For example, the Sloan Valve Company is introducing a graywater recovery product, the Sloan® AQUS® Greywater System, that will fit under a bathroom sink and pump the graywater directly into a toilet tank for flushing.[18] This might save 5,000 gallons per year in two-person households, more than switching to a dual-flush toilet.[19]

Similarly, the Brac system, which can be used for both rainwater harvesting and graywater reuse is now being sold in the US and Canada.[20] Water from showers, sinks and clothes washers can be used to flush toilets and irrigate gardens. It's currently allowed by code in some US jurisdictions.[21]

Many household graywater systems can be easily designed by homeowners. A great source for this activity is Art Ludwig's, *Create an Oasis with Greywater*.[22] As you might have guessed, designing your own system is the best way to proceed, if you want to maximize the benefits of graywater in your own home (provided, of course, that it is legal in your community). Sometimes, as in my home, you'll only be able to access the laundry water and use it for outdoor irrigation.

Health Considerations

Public health officials express concern over graywater quality, especially about the potential of reintroducing pathogens back into households. In the early 1990s, California adopted a draconian permitting process for graywater that led many to install systems without a permit. This is not an acceptable situation from anyone's viewpoint, but is the status quo in many areas. According to one source, more than one million California households may be using graywater *illegally* for garden irrigation, and there are even "graywater guerrillas" at work around the state.[23] Arizona law provides for reuse of graywater by drip or flood irrigation only (most people are concerned that spray irrigation could release bacteria into the air that people might breathe).[24] In Arizona, systems using fewer than 400 gallons per day require no special permits.

Summary

Although the laws vary according to state and jurisdiction, there is an increased interest in recycling and reusing graywater. In the commercial sector, a good solution involves biological treatment of graywater so that it can be used for toilet flushing, cooling towers, exterior washing and landscape irrigation. Many applications for the home and business don't require potable-quality water, which provides a design opportunity for incorporating graywater reuse, especially in new homes and buildings. As a result, some people are figuring out ways to reuse this lightly contaminated water, from do-it-yourself set-ups to engineered systems for green building projects to larger packaged systems. In any case, the reuse of graywater can contribute to an overall water-reduction strategy for both the residential and commercial sectors.

Brown Water

The good rain, like the bad preacher,
does not know when to leave off.

— Ralph Waldo Emerson[1]

I'VE CALLED THIS CHAPTER "brown water" because most stormwater runoff has sediment in it and looks brown. The fact is that rainwater harvested off most roofs is almost as clear as potable water. Nevertheless, I'm using the term "brown water" to distinguish it from graywater in the previous chapter and blackwater (sewage) in the next chapter.

Rainwater Harvesting

One of my favorite green building technologies is rainwater harvesting: the capture, treatment and use of rainwater for uses inside the building, such as toilet flushing and cooling-tower makeup water (to replace water lost by evaporation and back-flushing), and for landscape irrigation outside the building. This is such a simple and obvious thing to do that one wonders why it has taken so long to be considered as a viable new water supply. Why harvest rainwater? There are many good reasons, starting with the fact that rainwater is high-quality water:[2]

- Rainwater is soft, with a near-neutral pH (acid/alkaline balance).
- Rainwater's hardness ranges from 2 to 20 parts per million (ppm), compared with municipal water sources, which may have total dissolved solids of 100 to 800 ppm.
- It's free from disinfection (chlorine) by-products, salts, minerals and human contaminants.

121

- Appliances last longer because of the lack of scale and corrosion from hard water.

Commercial (Non-residential) Rainwater Harvesting

Beyond water conservation, rainwater harvesting can help reduce storm-water runoff from building sites. One of my favorite projects is shown in Figure 9.1, a rainwater harvesting system at the Tacoma, Washington, Police Headquarters and Vehicle Maintenance Facility. Formerly a big box store, the 100,000-square-foot roof provides ample runoff from about 45 inches of annual rainfall to flush toilets in the headquarters building opposite the tanks and the vehicle maintenance facility.

Imagine even a modest half-inch rainfall on a 24,000-square-foot roof. That storm event will generate 1,000 cubic feet, or about 7,500 gallons, of clean free water. In a climate like the Pacific Northwest, or anywhere that receives light rainfall a good part of the year, this system could be quite productive. Assuming one could collect 80 percent of an annual rainfall of 35 inches, one would harvest about 420,000 gallons for reuse each year from a 24,000-square-foot roof. Basic treatment with a sand filter and ultraviolet light would make it suitable for toilet flushing and similar non-potable

FIGURE 9.1 At the LEED Silver-certified Tacoma, WA, Police Vehicle Mainte-nance Facility, two 4,800-gallon culvert tanks collect rainwater and recycle it for toilet flushing. Courtesy of TCF Architecture, Tacoma.

uses. What could be simpler? Nothing, except that you might pay $20,000 to $50,000 for such a system, an amount that's not included in most new building construction budgets.

But that may not be the end of the story. Many urban areas have quite expensive charges for storm-drain hookups. I have seen cases where the impact fees or system development charges that were avoided by a 100 percent rainwater reclamation system were greater than the total cost of the rainwater collection and treatment system. In that case, a building owner is "money ahead" to install it. In one northern California university project in which I was involved, just the cost of installing the storm drainage pipes to take water off the site and to connect to the town's storm drains was greater than the cost of installing two 20,000-gallon tanks to hold runoff from the *100-year rainfall* event and a treatment system that provides enough water for toilet flushing for a good part of the year.

Figure 9.2 shows a schematic of a typical commercial rainwater harvesting system. Note that each system needs a way to collect roof drainage, a storage tank, treatment system and then a series of pipes to points of use. An overflow valve is required on all rainwater systems, for those rare heavy rain events that more than fill the storage tank. The rainwater collection system may also decide to take water from landscape and hardscape elements, as well as parking lots. The project elements include:

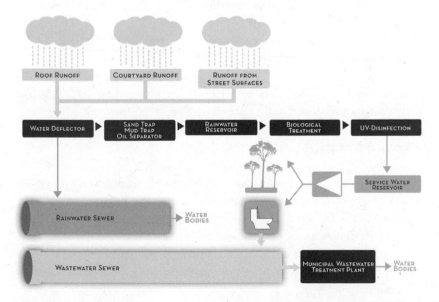

FIGURE 9.2 Commercial rainwater harvesting systems involve collection, filtration, storage, treatment, pumping and distribution to points of use.[4]

- Catchment system, typically the roof
- Conveyance system, such as piping from the roof to storage
- Pre-filtration system (first-flush diverter, roof washers, collection filters, leaf screen)
- Initial water storage tank
- Pump
- Water treatment (Sand filtration, with UV disinfection is typical for commercial uses.)
- Final water storage for daily uses (This may be a smaller tank than primary storage.)[3]

One caution: don't expect harvested rainwater to provide all of a site's needs, unless you are prepared to treat it to potable water standards and get approval for that from local code officials (see the discussion of the Tyson Center in Chapter 12, which did just that). In some jurisdictions, a code variance may be necessary to use harvested rainwater inside the building for toilet and urinal flushing. In addition, the taller the building, the lower the percentage of annual needs the system will supply, because you've only got one roof for collection purposes, but more toilet and sink fixtures for each added story. So it's useful to distinguish two things:

- Percentage of total rainwater falling on the roof that you can productively use (some will always overflow during severe storm events and some will just evaporate without runoff)
- Percentage of total building water demand supplied by harvested rainwater

One further complication: many commercial systems have flat roofs that can make gravity-sloped drain systems more difficult to install. Mike Kotubey of Midwest Mechanical Contractors, Kansas City, Missouri, says there is a new alternative, the siphonic roof drain.[5]

A conventional gravity roof drain system obviously depends upon pitch, so it takes up considerable space in the ceiling and has to be directional. You have to be selective in picking exit spots where the system is tied into the underground storm sewer system. Most designs limit the number of vertical drops from a roof drain system so plumbing runs tend to be long and requires a significant amount of space above the finished ceiling.

A siphonic system allows you more flexibility.[6] You're not as driven by pitch because it's really a non-gravity system. You route it to multiple spots within the building, and you take up much less ceiling space, so it gives you a lot more flexibility to capture rainwater from the roof and direct it to an appropriate spot, internal or external to the building.

While rainwater harvesting is a well-established technology in the residential sector, its use in the non-residential (CII) sector is fairly recent and has certainly been accelerated by the presence of the LEED system, which awards points for both stormwater management and water conservation. Table 9.1 shows some of the practical issues involved in new and retrofit onsite water reuse applications.

Jonathan Gray, a plumbing engineer in Portland, Oregon, is a fan of rainwater harvesting for commercial buildings and has been one of the innovators in this field.[8] One of Gray's early rainwater-harvesting projects was at the Stephen E. Epler Hall residential building at Portland State University, a six-story dormitory completed in 2003 that received a LEED Silver rating. In this project, collected rainwater drains into a 5,600-gallon tank. Over the course of the year, the tank is drained and refilled numerous times, and the

TABLE 9.1 Issues in New and Retrofit Applications of Onsite Water Capture and Reuse[7]

Issue	New	Retrofit
Piping	Cost-effective if built-in initially	Requires opening walls and possibly foundation changes
Codes	Built to code	May require additional updates
Systems	Integrated/working together	All separate systems with no connections
Aesthetics	Designed components	Added and may look added (not in original design)
	Components can be inside	Tanks must remain outside due to size.
Equipment	State-of-the-art	New connecting to old, which may cause leaks or breaks
	Effect on building function	May not be as efficient and equipment may not match up
	Metering and water usage available	Meters may be too expensive to install as supply lines may not be easily metered.
Environmental	Fully sustainable water savings	Adding a sustainable element to a non-sustainable building may not help much.
Maintenance	Knowledgeable manager available	Manager from existing system may have less knowledge and need more training.

captured rainwater is used without further treatment as reclaimed water for both flushing water closets and urinals in the first-floor public restrooms. As a further use of the rainwater, excess water is pumped out of the storage tank and used for onsite irrigation.[9]

While a typical rainwater harvesting system has been built from components, with collection/storage tank, treatment system, valves and pumps, Gray says: "Many manufacturers like Jay R. Smith have packaged rainwater harvesting systems.[10] That's a great thing because we won't have to 'build' a system [from scratch] anymore."

One variant of rainwater harvesting systems, particularly in LEED projects, would be to combine the rainwater collection system with a green roof application.[11] Mechanical designers and contractors interacting with green roofs also have come up with a number of innovative ways to handle roof runoff for both detention and retention purposes. An excellent resource for this purpose is the Texas Water Development Board's "Texas Guide to Rainwater Harvesting."[12] What's involved in a typical green roof system for harvesting rainwater? Some form of roof drainage, a collection and storage tank, a treatment system and a redistribution system. If you're going to flush toilets, you'll need a dual piping system, usually done only in a new building or major retrofit.[13]

Some commercial systems can be quite large. In January 2010, Major League Baseball's Minnesota Twins and Pentair announced plans to install the highest-profile sustainable water solution in professional sports.[14] Pentair will donate and install a custom-designed Rain Water Recycle System (RWRS) that will capture, conserve and reuse rainwater at the club's $425 million Target Field, the new world-class home of the Minnesota Twins (Figure 9.3). The system will reduce the need for municipal water at Target Field by more than 50 percent, qualifying it for LEED silver certification, the highest LEED rating of any ballpark in America, and saving more than two million gallons of water annually. Pentair technology will purify rainwater to a level equal to or better than potable water standards. The system is designed to allow the Minnesota Twins to conserve water used to wash down the lower decks of the stadium and irrigate the ball field.

Site-built Rainwater Harvesting Systems

Heather Kinkade is a landscape architect and one of the more experienced practitioners of the art of commercial rainwater harvesting. She says that even though the payoff from rainwater catchment is typically long-term, there are ways to save money on large projects by reducing the cost of one of

FIGURE 9.3 Target Field, the new home of the Minnesota Twins, features an advanced rainwater harvesting and reuse system, the largest to date in professional sports. Courtesy Wayne Kryduba.

the key elements, the storage tank, using an interlinked plastic lattice below ground level that can be sized to fit and be placed just about anywhere:

> In the long run, the crates are a lot cheaper than building a concrete tank onsite or bringing in a poly tank or a fiberglass tank. So there are savings to be had within the different products now, whereas formerly there weren't as many different products to chose from. I represent a manufacturer called EcoRain, which manufactures the crate-style catchment systems. The crate systems can be put under driveways or high-traffic areas, versus some tanks that can't be put in those locations. There are some tanks that are just coming on the market that are made from a plastic poly that have been lined with a food-grade emulsion. In that situation, you don't need to have tank liners. The technology is becoming more advanced, so it's cheaper because you're putting all these different products into one item, a packaged system. For a large commercial project, it's too hard to simply use a packaged system in most cases. You may start with a packaged system, but then you have to massage it to fit the site or specific catchment area.[15]

A demonstration of the effectiveness of this approach is at the US Naval Air Station in Jacksonville, Florida. (Figure 9.4) In this project, the US Navy

FIGURE 9.4 The Jacksonville Naval Air Station used a simple collection and storage approach with a "plastic crate" system to harvest rainwater from a large roof expanse to use for helicopter washing. Courtesy of Aqua Nueva.

contracted with a vendor of crate-type storage for a 100,000-gallon rain harvesting system on base in Jacksonville. Their aim was to collect rooftop rainwater from nearby naval hangars. This system will harvest more than 2.3 million gallons of usable water every year, for helicopter washing and other non-potable uses. The supplier installed this system with less than two-feet of excavation, which offered an innovative and inexpensive alternative to a storage tank solution. The project's installation took less than two weeks.[16]

Advantages, Selling Points and Benefits of Rainwater Harvesting and Reuse

Rainwater harvesting is desirable because it reduces demand on the municipal water supply systems, and reduces water utility bills. By diminishing stormwater flows, it reduces the contamination of surface water from rainwater runoff, resulting in cleaner lakes, rivers and oceans. Onsite stormwater detention can be used to recharge groundwater. Rainwater collection may also extend the life of plumbing equipment because it has low total dissolved solids and does not produce corrosion or scale like hard water found in many municipal supplies, particularly in the West.

For LEED certification projects, collecting and reusing rainwater can help achieve multiple credit points within the categories of Water Use Reduction, Water Efficient Landscaping, Heat Island Effect and Stormwater Management.[17]

Considering the "water/energy nexus," discussed in Chapter 4, recall that approximately three percent of total energy use in the US goes to drinking water and wastewater treatment. For appropriate uses, non-potable rainwater water requires less treatment than potable water, and by decreasing the distance that water is transported, it provides an energy-efficient alternative to traditional water supply. Rainwater harvesting can therefore reduce strain on an aging water supply infrastructure.[18]

What's driving the renewed interest in rainwater harvesting? One goal is to reduce stormwater flows through rainwater roof collection and cisterns in urban settings. In some designs, the cisterns hold additional alternative water resources (graywater, condensate, cooling tower blow-down, etc.) along with the rainwater for uses beyond just landscape irrigation. Various alternative water sources are collected in the cistern, filtered and sanitized for use in flushing urinals and toilets throughout the building.[19]

Rainwater harvesting may also become a rational economic response for large users to increasing water costs, coupled with erratic seasonal and annual rainfall that may lead to water rationing. Figure 9.5 shows the seasonal variation of rainfall in Los Angeles. In spite of an average annual rainfall of about 16 inches, it has a pronounced dry season, from May through October, common to the entire West Coast. This means that more rainwater storage capacity is required to supply dry-season irrigation and toilet flushing needs. By focusing on low-rise buildings that have a greater ratio of roof area (collection surface) to total water use, a larger percentage of total annual use can be supplied. For the regions east of the Mississippi River,

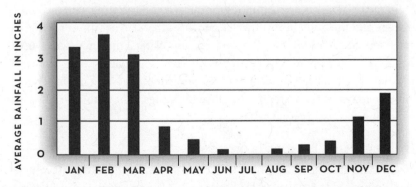

FIGURE 9.5 In the West Coast maritime climate, there are long periods without much rain, requiring both river storage and groundwater use, along with onsite sources.[20]

rainfall or snow is fairly evenly distributed by month or season, allowing rainwater harvesting for longer periods of time, with relatively smaller storage tanks.

In spite of these manifold benefits, some Western states still have 19th-century water laws that prohibit or limit capturing rainfall for private use, typically because of concern over downstream water rights. For example, Colorado recently legalized limited rainwater harvesting, but much of Utah and Washington State still have widespread rainwater harvesting restrictions.[21] Washington allows rainwater harvesting only in a few areas, including Seattle and the San Juan Islands, where some residents have spent $50,000 or more on 10,000-gallon rain storage tanks and filtration systems.[22] To understand the different state laws and regulations, consult the American Rainwater Catchment Systems Association's website as a resource.[23]

Rainwater harvesting is, of course, a worldwide phenomenon. For example, national legislation in Belgium requires all new construction to have rainwater harvesting systems for the purposes of flushing toilets and external water uses. The purpose of this legislation is twofold: to reduce demand for treated water and the expansion of the water supply infrastructure and to collect and use rainwater instead of surcharging stormwater management systems. Bangalore is the first city in India to have a policy requiring rainwater harvesting. With an average rainfall of 900 to 970 mm (36 to 39 in.) over seven months, and an elevation of 900 meters above mean sea level (MSL), water currently has to be pumped up from reservoirs at 400 meters above MSL. Water is heavy, and pumping costs are large because electric power charges are quite expensive, therefore rainwater harvesting is much more economical.[24]

In the US, market opportunities for rainwater harvesting vary by building type and the availability of water end-uses that can accept non-potable water sources. According to the Alliance for Water Efficiency, water uses that don't require potable water such as restrooms, landscape irrigation and space cooling and heating account for 87 percent of the water use in schools and 89 percent of the water use in office buildings.[25] In schools, rainwater harvesting can also be used as a teaching tool.

Challenges and Lessons Learned

Cost-benefit analysis of rainwater collection systems is not always favorable when compared to most potable water prices. Using a ten-year cost analysis for a rainy US climate, the rainwater collected over the ten years would cost approximately $4.55 per hundred cubic feet (CCF), and this assumes the water replaces potable water use. This is higher than average water rates in most US cities, so the system wouldn't quite pay for itself just with water savings. While it is true that the rainwater can be used to flush toilets, the added cost of extra plumbing to convey the water to the points of use hampers overall cost-effectiveness.[26]

Rainwater harvesting for in-the-building reuse is obviously much easier to integrate into new buildings, because the dual-piping system required is easier to install, and there is a possibility of reducing water meter size and/or avoiding fees for hooking up to the storm or sanitary sewer. Many municipal water systems charge commercial users for both the meter size (equivalent to a capacity charge on an electricity bill) and for actual water use. In addition, many utilities charge for sewage treatment based on water use, so the economics of displacing those charges may lower the payback to acceptable durations.

In existing buildings, the best use for harvested rainwater may be landscape irrigation and exterior hardscape or vehicle washing, since the rainwater is collected at ground level and can be distributed without full treatment; it can also be pumped back outside the building to use as cooling tower makeup water, often a major water user in commercial and institutional buildings. When designing systems, it's important to match rainfall patterns with use patterns to minimize storage volumes. For example, on the West Coast, the November to May rainy season closely approximates the academic year, making rainwater recovery and reuse a natural fit for K12 schools and colleges. Projects also need to find a protected location for 10,000-gallon to 50,000-gallon storage tanks, or groups of tanks. Sometimes, designers can fit tanks underneath ramps in underground parking garages or bury them under parking lots during site excavation.

Justifying the Costs of Commercial Rainwater Harvesting Systems

The key costs in a rainwater harvesting system revolve around tanks, pumps and the treatment system. Some cost estimates vary between $3.00 and $4.00 per gallon of storage for larger commercial systems, including both site-built and modular systems. These costs indicate that a large rainwater harvesting and treatment system designed with a 15,000-gallon storage tank would cost $45,000 to $60,000 for a large office building. Such a system might save 670 CCF per year (about 500,000 gallons), for a total value of $3,350 at $5.00 per CCF. The actual savings will depend on the local water utility rate structure for commercial buildings. You can see that this is a long payback, but that may not be the entire story. Avoiding the costs of hooking up to the local storm-sewer system (assuming you can capture 100 percent of rainwater falling on the site) might pay for the entire system. Again, each locality will have different rules and fees for hooking up to the storm-sewer system, so it's impossible to give a generalized answer to the question: does it pay off?

Finally, as mentioned earlier, if a project is pursuing a LEED building certification, harvested rainwater can contribute a significant number of points toward eventual certification, so that the extra cost might be incidental to the overall project goals.

Rainwater Harvesting for Schools and Universities

Schools, colleges and universities present ideal opportunities for rainwater harvesting, since they tend to use a lot of water for landscaping and also tend to have multiple low-rise buildings that produce considerable rainwater for harvesting relative to building water use. Two good examples are Yale University in New Haven, Connecticut, and the Twenhofel School in Kentucky.

Rainwater Harvesting at Yale University, New Haven, Connecticut

Certified in 2010 at the LEED Platinum level, the $34 million, 57,000-square-foot Kroon Hall at Yale University is a joint project of London's Hopkins Architects and Connecticut's Centerbrook Architects, both leading sustainable design firms. The rainwater collection system channels water from the roof and grounds to a landscape water feature in the south courtyard, where aquatic plants filter out sediment and contaminants. Treated stormwater is stored in an underground rainwater harvesting system, and then pumped back into Kroon Hall for flushing toilets and is also used for site irrigation. The system is expected to save 465,000 gallons of potable water annually (about 8.2 gallons per sq.ft.) and to reduce the burden on city sewers by retaining stormwater runoff onsite.[27]

Like many locations in the eastern US, New Haven receives between two and four inches of precipitation each month, making rainwater harvesting an ideal strategy for replacing potable water use. The rainwater harvesting and stormwater detention system is integrated with several of the campus's green spaces adjacent to the building. A 10,000-gallon underground tank for stormwater detention collects runoff from the southern part of the project site. The northern part of the site and the building rooftop is channeled through the landscape water feature. Native wetland plants remove impurities before the water is returned for reuse.[28] Treated stormwater from the landscape water feature is directed to a storage tank for reuse.[29]

The rainwater diversion system consists of an underground manhole-type structure that pipes the first inch of rain in a storm event to the water feature that includes specially selected aquatic plants serving as biofilters to clean the water. A separate pipe carries rainwater flows greater than one inch via a separate pipe to a 20,000-gallon fiberglass-reinforced underground tank, which also collects overflow from the pond. The stored water is continuously recirculated through the pond for additional cleansing. Water stored in the rainwater tank is used for landscape irrigation and can also be diverted to a separate 940-gallon "day" tank located in Kroon Hall's basement, where it is filtered and disinfected for use in toilet flushing.[30]

In combination with water conserving plumbing fixtures, the design expects to save more than 80 percent of the annual potable water use of a conventional building and also up to 100 percent of the irrigation water, according to the environmental systems designer, Atelier Ten.[31] Table 9.2 shows how Kroon Hall conserves on potable water demand.

More important to the University and the architects than water savings, however, was creating a building that would stand the test of time. According to Hopkins' principal architect, Michael Taylor:

> True sustainability, however, is about more than improved quantitative performance. We have striven to create a piece of contemporary

TABLE 9.2 Estimated Potable Water Savings at Kroon Hall[32]

Annual Water Demand/ Supply (gallons)	Conventional Building/ Site (gallons/year)	Kroon Hall and Site (gallons/year)
Demand: Building	375,763	246,236
Demand: Site	157,893 (Conventional plantings)	50,609 (107,284 saved with xeriscaping)
Savings from Efficient Fixtures	—	(129,527)
Harvested Rainwater: Building	—	(175,966)
Harvested Rainwater: Site		(50,609)
Net Potable Water Use	533,656	70,270
Total Potable Water Savings	—	463,386
Total Water Savings: Building	—	305,493
Total Water Savings: Site		157,893
Percentage Savings: Building	—	81%
Percentage Savings: Site		100%

architecture that belongs in the context of the historic Yale campus. We think it will encourage interaction among its occupants and stand up to several generations of intense use.[33]

This is the key lesson of sustainable design: unless a building is beautiful, functional in use and valued by its users, resource-conserving systems by themselves do not lead to true sustainability, a subject we expand upon in Chapter 14.

Rainwater Harvesting at Twenhofel School

Shown in Figure 9.6, Twenhofel School in Kenton County, Kentucky, is an outstanding example of rainwater harvesting in the K-12 school environment. In 2004, the county school district decided to implement sustainable design principles and resource conservation measures into its buildings, and then to integrate them into the curriculum based on the building systems.[34] Rainwater harvesting became an important means for realizing these goals. There were economic benefits as well, according to the project engineer: "Twenhofel is in rural southern Kenton County where the utility infrastructure is inconsistent and impact fees are charged for utility extensions."[35] The rainwater harvesting system has a 100,000-gallon underground tank and a piping system within the school to serve toilets and urinals. The system also irrigates the athletic field. The buildings' 120,000-square-foot roof area collects rainwater to feed into the harvesting and reuse system.

FIGURE 9.6.   Twenhofel School in Kentucky provides rainwater harvesting for flushing toilets and irrigating athletic fields. Courtesy of Kenton County School District.

Regulatory Concerns

Plumbing engineer Winston Huff of Smith Seckman Reid, Inc., based in Nashville, Tennessee, believes that the main issues are not technological but institutional:

> The issue of why rainwater, graywater or any kind of reuse water is not used in buildings is not that the technology is not available; rather, the main issue concerns national maintenance and regulation standards. Plumbing engineers design the water systems for a building and are usually involved in the building design early in the design process. For example, an owner may want to build a 20-floor office building, so they contact the design architects and engineers, including the plumbing engineer. The owner may ask the plumbing engineer to design a rainwater system. I will tell our designers not to spend time and effort designing the details of the system until they first contact the regulatory (code) agencies to verify if the rainwater system is allowed and what standards they have. Each local authority will have different design standards unique to them. Then they need to check to make sure the maintenance people can keep the systems running properly and safely. The issue is that there are no national regulatory standards to build and maintain these systems.[36]

Combining Rainwater and Graywater Harvesting

For commercial and institutional projects, it may make sense to combine rainwater and graywater harvesting systems, particularly in the western US, where rainfall is intermittent (and even non-existent in some months) while graywater is relatively constant. The same may also be true for the northern tier of the US and Alaska, where graywater volumes can be counted on, but much of the annual precipitation falls as snow and can stay on a roof for months. In high-rise buildings, the combined system represents an optimal configuration, since the amount of rainfall captured does not increase with building height (after all, there is only one roof), but the amount of graywater does (there are about the same number of fixtures on each floor). Figure 9.7 shows how such a combined system schematic would work.

What to Do With All That Rainwater?

Many green building projects set out to eliminate offsite runoff of rainfall, to eliminate the impact of stormwater runoff on overburdened municipal drainage systems. In older cities, stormwater runoff may be contaminated with sewage overflows from combined storm and sanitary sewer systems.

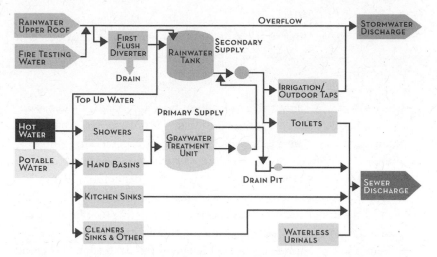

FIGURE 9.7 A combined rainwater/graywater harvesting system may make the most sense for larger commercial projects, which have considerable water demand.[37] Courtesy Guenter Hauber-Davidson, Water Conservation Group.

In many of these projects, rainfall captured that exceeds building needs is directed toward constructed wetlands or onsite infiltration in the form of bioswales, porous paving of parking lots, landscape ponds, gravel parking areas and similar approaches. In more arid areas, some projects intentionally divert excess runoff toward landscape plantings and use this water as the only irrigation source. Sometimes, the areas that are planted to absorb excess runoff are called rain gardens.[38]

Using Harvested Rainwater in Rain Gardens

Some landscape architects incorporate stormwater runoff into buildings to create attractive indoor/outdoor spaces. The German landscape architect Herbert Dreiseitl is especially known for such approaches. In the spring of 2008, I visited one such project, called Prisma Nürnberg, in Nuremberg (Nürnberg), Germany. The project sits alongside a busy street, separating a commercial block with 32 offices, 9 stores, and a coffeehouse from a residential block with 61 residential units and a kindergarten. Under about 15,000 square feet of glass is a peaceful enclave, full of plants, water and light, as shown in Figure 9.8.[39]

Completed in 1997, Prisma ("prism") Nürnberg combines the elements of managing stormwater, collecting and treating rainwater, daylight harvesting and creating a pleasing indoor environment. Stepping into the space between the commercial and residential blocks, one enters into a semitropi-

FIGURE 9.8 Prisma Nürnberg illustrates a creative approach to using water to create more livable spaces in densely populated cities. Courtesy © Atelier Dreiseitl.

cal paradise, surrounded by plants from South America and Australia, with the sound of running water from five, five-meter-high "waterwalls" placed along a city block. The 15-meter-high glass house rises over a series of water features, with 240 square meters (2,583 square feet) of water surface area.[40]

The falling water draws down fresh air pulled in from a slit in the wall, and moist air blows gently into the space at a speed of about ten feet per second. The system cools the building in summer (with the water between 64°F and 68°F) and heats it in winter. Layers of "artistic glass," lit at night, provide a backdrop for each waterwall.

Stormwater is collected from the roof of the glass building, a 65,000-square-foot catchment area, stored in a 64,000-gallon tank, pumped up to the surface where it flows along a 110-meter watercourse, never more than a foot deep. The overall effect of the flowing water inside the building is quite delightful.

Rainwater Harvesting in Germany

In June 2009, I met Dieter Sperfeld, head of the German rainwater harvesting association (FBR),[41] at his office in Darmstadt, to learn more about the German approach. The purpose of the FBR is to promote water recycling and rainwater utilization, save drinking water and reduce sewage flows. Rainwater harvesting is fairly advanced in Germany, with the rules for such systems incorporated into national building codes (specifically DIN 1989).[42] The German expert on the subject is Klaus W. König, an architect with a passion for rainwater harvesting who has written an important book on the subject.[43]

According to König,[44] about one of three detached homes in Germany installs a tank for rainwater harvesting. He says that the number of pubic and commercial buildings with rainwater harvesting is increasing in Germany, partly owing to a court case that ordered rainwater runoff into the public sewer system to be separately charged for by cities, leading to lower costs for projects that recover all of their rainwater and reuse it onsite. At this time, he says that German health authorities accept harvested rainwater for use in irrigation, toilet flushing and laundries.[45]

> In 2005, about one out of 10 new public buildings had some tank for rainwater. This is increasing. The number of industrial buildings with rainwater harvesting systems then was maybe one out of 20, and this is also strongly increasing now. The reason for this development is not the energy crisis or environmental concerns, it is just because there is now an extra fee for discharging rainwater into the public sewer.

With siphonic (vacuum) roof drains, many existing industrial facilities and distribution centers with large expanses of flat roofs can now harvest rainwater and direct it to storage tanks located quite a distance away from the roof or in more convenient locations. König says,

> Existing buildings make up the majority of German cities. A retrofit that involves rainwater harvesting is usually very difficult, but there are some inexpensive technologies used to retrofit industrial and public build-

ings. There are gravity-operated valves combined with a vacuum system that allow you to move water using pipes. There must be a load of water on the roof of about 3 centimeters (1.2-inches) and when that load is reached, then the valve will open and the water is sucked very quickly into the pipe and can be transported for hundreds of meters to a storage tank. This can be a very cheap retrofit for factories, because the pipes can be placed inside the building just below the roof.

König also believes that rainwater harvesting will lead naturally into more widespread reuse of graywater, especially if there are public subsidies.

> The next movement after rainwater harvesting in the retrofit of build-ings and the sanitation of buildings will be graywater reuse. This water, which just contains soap and shampoo, has very few bacteria, and it is not a problem to reuse in buildings. This technology has been develop-ing over the past 10 years in Germany. For example, Hamburg offers subsidies to everybody — industry and private — who installs graywater systems in retrofits and in new construction. Whenever there is a sub-sidy in Germany, the technology is developed very quickly. This is the next step, which will be very important in Europe, especially in tourist areas with many hotels.

In the German town of Mühlheim am Main, near Frankfurt, König has documented an apartment block using rainwater harvesting for domestic laundry use.[46]

> At Schillerstrasse 62–96, 176 families have an opportunity to use rain-water from the roof for their washing machines. They are saving drink-ing water charges and detergents [because of the softer water], as well as fees for sending rainwater into the public storm sewer system. In August 2006, the first half of the apartments were ready. Now the tenants have the choice of connecting their washing machines in the basement, as before, to the drinking water supply, or instead using the rainwater from the cistern, for which there is no charge. The first households have al-ready decided on the cheaper alternative offered by the landlord.

Rainwater Harvesting for Commercial Applications
The German building engineering firm, Transsolar, designed a rainwater harvesting system for a large commercial office park project in Frankfurt.[47] For an effective roof area of about 67,500 square feet (6,272 square meters)

and an annual precipitation of 24.2 inches (614 millimeters), a 26,560-gallon (100-cubic-meter) tank will provide about 2.1 million gallons per year (7,807 cubic meters) of water for designated uses.

In this building, the bulk of the water use from the tank (79.2 percent) is for cooling tower makeup water, with 14.4 percent for fixture flushing and 6.4 percent for landscaping. This system uses about 73 percent of the total annual incoming rainwater (there will always be some overflow from the tank, because of heavy rain that exceeds storage tank capacity). Looked at another way, harvested rainwater provides 674,000 gallons (2,538 cubic meters) of potable water savings, with the rainwater providing 32 percent of the total water used for the specified applications. (Of course, the office park will also have direct potable water supply connections for drinking water, food service and lavatories.)

The engineers also provided an economic analysis that indicated that this system would provide the most ecological benefit (quantity of harvested rainwater) at the lowest additional cost, considering local water rates. In this situation, the rainwater harvesting will add a *net* cost of 2,900 Euros (about $4,300) per year to the cost of water supply, taking into account amortization of the additional capital cost of 76,000 Euros (about $110,000), plus savings on water supply and sewage treatment costs.[48] In the US, if I were planning to use the LEED system to certify this project, I would consider it a fairly inexpensive way to gain a large number of LEED credit points for water efficiency at cost of less than $4,500 ($6.67 per 1,000 gallons).

Rainwater Harvesting in Australia

One of Australia's leading experts on water conservation through rainwater harvesting is Guenter Hauber-Davidson, an engineer based in Sydney. In his view, rainwater harvesting should be designed with smaller tanks than most engineers would design in the US, so that the tank is frequently emptied in time to capture each new rainfall. In this way, the system can capture and reuse a higher annual percentage of total rainfall, since there won't be much overflow from the tank to the storm sewer.[49] System sizing will also vary depending on location because, even in a high-density urban area such as Sydney, rainfall drops off quite dramatically as one moves inland. According to Hauber-Davidson,

> The key to make these projects viable is to work the tanks hard. An empty tank is a good tank. That way, sensible demand has drawn down the storage in time to capture the next rain event. Some schemes can achieve annual savings of up to 15 times their tank volume, implying

that the tank has emptied and filled 15 times per year. The trick is to connect large and ideally continuous demands to the tank. Cooling towers are a perfect example of this. They even match demand with seasonal rainfall patterns (higher temperatures and more rain in the summer in Sydney). Process water, wash water, irrigation or swimming pool top-up are other good supply points. Toilet and urinal flushing (unless waterless urinals are installed) are also suitable.[50]

He says that water reuse is almost a given in any half-decent new development in Australia nowadays and claims that, "You will not be able to sell a commercial or institutional office development or facility unless there are at least some serious water conservation measures included." Even going beyond water conservation or rainwater harvesting, Hauber-Davidson advocates a more holistic approach (see Chapter 7) not typically seen even in most green building projects, where plumbing engineers design water systems typically without much regard for the rest of the design. In one of his research projects, for example, Hauber-Davidson and his colleagues found that the energy use for some rainwater harvesting systems, in kWh per gallon of water supplied, could approach half that of desalination. In his view, the key reason was that engineers habitually oversize the pump that moves water from storage tank to point of use, so much so that it's often running at less than five percent efficiency.[51]

Rainwater Harvesting in the Home

Anyone can harvest rainwater at home, and there are many great resources to help you set up your own system. Beyond the *Texas Guide* mentioned earlier, there are books by Arizonans Heather Kinkade and Brad Lancaster. You'll find these listed in Appendix II. Millions of rainwater harvesting systems are already in place in homes across the US. Until the development of public water supplies in the mid- to late 19th century, there was very little choice for household water supply but to drill a well, to pump water by hand or harvest it in a cistern.

At my home in Tucson, Arizona, I began harvesting rainwater in 2008 by installing two 200-gallon fiberglass tanks to take water from the front half of my roof, collect it and use it for watering the garden and filling fountains. In southern Arizona, there is a summer "monsoon" season during the hot months, typically producing half or more of the annual rainfall, so planning to collect rainfall and reuse it in the garden makes good sense. The State of Arizona supports household systems with a 25 percent tax credit (up $1,000 total), so the net cost of $750 was quite reasonable. In 2010, I'm hoping to install a larger 600-gallon tank to take rain from the back roof, so hopefully I'll be able to collect about 375 gallons from each rainfall (a 0.5-inch rainfall on the 1,200-square-foot back roof would yield about 50 cubic feet, or 375 gallons) for use in the garden.

Table 9.3 shows the amount of rainwater you can harvest from a home in St. Louis, Missouri. There's enough potential rainfall in wetter regions such as St. Louis to provide a significant amount of water for lawn irrigation, garden, car washing and some household uses. You can make your own chart by taking your local rainfall data by month, applying the conversion factor of 624 gallons per inch, per 1,000 square feet of roof area, and then estimating how much you will recover, recognizing that some rainfall may be so light there is very little runoff (therefore, you won't collect all of the rain that falls). I've done some of the work for you with the table in Appendix II.

Summary

Capturing the free water falling from the sky is gaining popularity in the US and in other countries as diverse as Australia and Germany. When discussing rainwater harvesting, we usually think of the "active" variety. This combines storage with on-demand use and is an excellent way to supplement residential and commercial water supplies because rainwater is soft and free

TABLE 9.3 Rainwater Collected from a 1,000-square-foot Roof in St. Louis, Missouri[52]

Month	Rainfall (inches)	Conversion: Gallons/Inch of Rainfall	Gallons of Rain	60% Collection Efficiency (Gallons)
January	2.01	624	1,252	751
February	2.06	624	1,284	770
March	3.70	624	2,309	1,385
April	3.82	624	2,384	1,430
May	3.92	624	2,446	1,468
June	3.73	624	2,328	1,397
July	3.78	624	2,359	1,415
August	3.70	624	2,309	1,385
September	2.69	624	1,679	1,007
October	2.81	624	1,753	1,052
November	4.06	624	2,533	1,520
December	2.56	624	1,597	958
Total	38.84	624	24,236	14,542

of disinfectants, salts, minerals and human containments. The majority of
captured rainwater is used for irrigation and flushing toilets. With today's
water prices, installing a rainwater collection system typically has medium-
to long-term payoffs. However, there may be other financial benefits for
commercial projects such as reduced sewage and meter fees. "Passive" rainwater harvesting, on the other hand, is less expensive. It would typically fall
under the realm of a landscape professional and involves studying the land
and its natural water flows, with the goal of directing runoff to plant basins
or areas where it can be infiltrated into the soil or other pervious surfaces.
We're going to see a lot more of both varieties of rainwater harvesting in
the next decade, as urban water crises occur more frequently and require
designers to come up with new water-conserving approaches for building
projects.

Blackwater

*Til taught by pain, men really know not
what good water is worth.*

— Byron, "Don Juan"[1]

MOST OF US would rather not think about sewage. We've been taught since we were kids that human waste was really "icky" stuff and, as a result, we live in what I call the "flush without fear" society, where we flush and "they" take care of it somewhere downstream. That's as much as we want to be bothered to think about sewage unless we live in a rural area with septic tanks and poor soils; then it's everyone's problem. There's nothing really wrong with this system; after all, it's worked well for us for the past 100 years, especially with the more advanced forms of wastewater treatment introduced in the 1970s, as the environmental movement forced sewage treatment authorities to literally "clean up their act."

However, wastewater is also another water source; after all if you live inland along a large river, your water supply started upriver as someone else's wastewater. So, wastewater is just water that starts life as clean drinkable water and winds up polluted. Why not clean it up and reuse it onsite? With that philosophy, an enterprising project team can look for sources of blackwater, intercept it on its way out of the building, clean and reuse it at least once. In Chapter 6, I showed how that was done at the Oregon Health & Science University project in Portland, in which all sewage from the building was treated in the basement and reused for site irrigation, cooling tower makeup water and toilet flushing. There are also a few examples of onsite blackwater treatment for residential applications, with the treated water typically used for site irrigation. Later on in this chapter, I'll also present some blackwater treatment systems that don't use water.

Onsite Blackwater Treatment Systems

At the 35-story Visionaire residential tower in New York City's Battery Park City on the west side of Manhattan, a LEED Platinum-certified project treats all wastewater from the building in the basement and recycles it for site irrigation, toilet flushing and cooling tower makeup water.[2] Building sewage is collected in tanks that occupy about a quarter of the basement's footprint and is cleaned biologically to a potable water standard.[3] The building is expected to reduce potable water demand by 40 percent below the norm for a similar building.[4] This system was first used in the 27-story Solaire LEED Gold-certified apartments nearby.[5] In both cases, the elimination of sewage helps reduce the burden on the district's sewerage system, as well as provide water for onsite applications. Owing to the overburdened local infrastructure in this part of New York City, without onsite sewage treatment neither the Solaire nor the Visionaire would have received the necessary permits to be built.

The chosen solution in each of these cases was the use of a membrane bioreactor (see the discussion of Dockside Green in Chapter 7), which uses standard wastewater treatment technology coupled with a semi-permeable membrane to help with water purification. What's new in these cases is the application of sewage treatment technology at the small scale of an apartment building or office building. At the Visionaire, potable water is supplied for personal use, while rainwater and blackwater are collected and treated, then reused onsite.

Each project brings with it "lessons learned." John An, who helped design the Visionaire, says:

> This is the third building [in New York City] where the developers have done a blackwater treatment system. One of the lessons learned — and it's not specific to this building — was that initially the treated blackwater, while it is clean, has a higher salinity content. So when they were using the treated water in the cooling towers, they found that there was damage to some of the equipment over time. On this project, they changed the water balance so more of the stormwater and graywater gets mixed into the blackwater treatment system so salinity is diluted. On occasion, potable water could be put in as well. The lesson learned: you can't take treated blackwater and dump it into the cooling tower without dilution.[6]

FIGURE 10.1 The 35-story Visionaire condominium tower in New York City recycles wastewater for on-site reuse. Courtesy of Pelli Clarke Pelli Architects.

Vancouver Convention Centre

At the Vancouver, British Columbia, Convention Centre, an innovative water conservation and reuse strategy will reduce potable water use 60 to 70 percent. The Centre was significantly expanded, tripling its size, to function as the main press center for the coverage of the 2010 XXI Olympic & Paralympic Winter Games in Vancouver (Figure 10.2). Using a membrane bioreactor, similar to that used in Dockside Green (Chapter 7), the onsite

FIGURE 10.2 The Vancouver Convention Centre hosted visiting press covering the 2010 XXI Winter Olympics and Paralympics in British Columbia. Courtesy of Vancouver Convention Centre.

blackwater treatment system processes the building's sewage and provides 80 percent of the water needs for toilet flushing in the building and supplemental water for irrigation of a 6-acre (24,280-square-meter) living roof.[7] Completed in March of 2008, the system treats 20,000 gallons per day (76,000 liters) of wastewater from the building.[8]

The membrane bioreactor (MBR) system, consisting of a combined system for graywater and blackwater treatment, incorporates General Electric's ZeeWeed* MBR technology. This system combines an activated-sludge process with a physical barrier using ultrafiltration (UF) membranes.[9] Activated sludge is an aerobic biological process that separates waste from water by using micro-organisms that metabolize and transform organic and inorganic substances, "digesting" them into environmentally acceptable material.[10] (Figure 10.3) This system illustrates one of nature's key principles, "waste = food." Nutrients in the sewage nourish micro-organisms that clean it up. By creating a mini-wastewater treatment plant, the MBR system combines the activated-sludge process with pressure-driven ultrafiltration that physically separates solids, bacteria and viruses from water. An activated-carbon filter and ultraviolet (UV) disinfection are the final steps in creating high-quality effluent for recycling.[11]

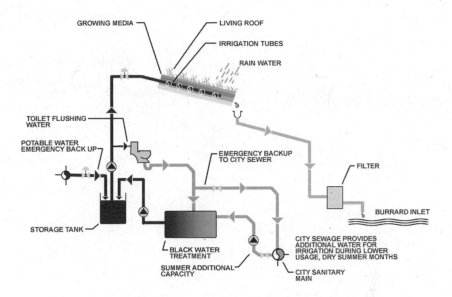

GROWING MEDIA

LIVING ROOF

IRRIGATION TUBES

RAIN WATER

TOILET FLUSHING WATER

POTABLE WATER EMERGENCY BACK UP

EMERGENCY BACKUP TO CITY SEWER

FILTER

BURRARD INLET

STORAGE TANK

BLACK WATER TREATMENT

SUMMER ADDITIONAL CAPACITY

CITY SEWAGE PROVIDES ADDITIONAL WATER FOR IRRIGATION DURING LOWER USAGE, DRY SUMMER MONTHS

CITY SANITARY MAIN

FIGURE 10.3 Treated sewage and rainwater will provide toilet flushing and irrigation of a 6-acre green roof at the Vancouver Convention Centre. Courtesy of LMN.

Community Blackwater Treatment Solutions

Of course, wastewater reuse can be practiced on a larger scale for more than just one building; it can be applied to a community of buildings. Anders Nyquist is a pioneering Swedish architect who has created ecological designs for more than 30 years. In his design philosophy, it should be possible for small rural communities to have good sanitation and still avoid both septic tanks and sewerage. Nyquist developed an approach he calls Eco-CycleDesign,[12] in which waste from small developments is treated and returned to the environment using a "split box" system, shown in Figure 10.4. SplitBox is an energy supply and sewage system designed to use modern "ecocycling" technology to supply a home's energy requirements, combined with technology to provide ventilation, heat recovery and water and wastewater management.[13] The system has been successfully applied in Sweden for vacation homes, single-family residences and apartment blocks of as many as 32 units.

At the level of the individual household, if you are really bold and in particular have a home in a rural environment or low-density suburban area, you might want to consider an alternative approach to wastewater treatment, especially if septic tanks won't work very well where you live: a composting toilet, with or without urine separation. (After all, urine is

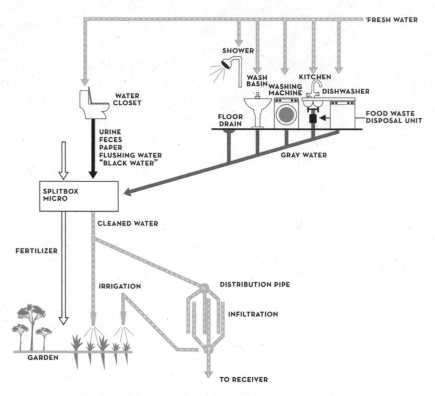

FIGURE 10.4 The Swedish EcoCycleDesign system integrates water supply, waste recycling and energy efficiency into a single system to serve a small community. Courtesy of Anders Nyquist.

mostly nitrogen, a good fertilizer, so why not reuse it?) Urine-separating toilets (Figure 10.5) now sold in Europe also function as composting toilets to eliminate the need for flushing altogether and, in combination with graywater recycling systems, to relieve the need for a septic tank and drainage field system.

Composting toilets used in commercial buildings typically require a basement or two-story building to work well. They have been sold in the US for more than 30 years by Clivus Multrum (Figure 10.6) and are used in numerous residential, recreational and other low-intensity applications. I have seen them in use at the C. K. Choi building, an early (1995) green project at the University of British Columbia in Vancouver, and at the Philip Merrill Environmental Center in Annapolis, Maryland, the first LEED Platinum-certified building in the US. Recent large building applications include installations at the Bronx Zoo and Queens Botanical Gardens in New York City.[14]

Constructed Wetlands

Constructed wetlands function to hold stormwater and use treated sewage to supply nutrients to aquatic plants and animals. As ecology students learn, wetlands are the most productive ecosystems in the world, straddling the intersection of land and water. They are also nature's kidneys, helping to transform sewage nutrients into life-giving carbon, nitrogen, phosphorus and trace minerals. Properly designed, constructed wetlands can provide wildlife habitat and open space for green building projects, as well as a place for tours and outdoor environmental education.[15]

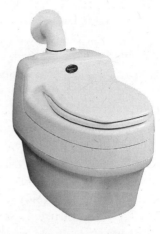

FIGURE 10.5 Urine-separating toilets can capture urine and save it for future use as a nitrogen fertilizer. Courtesy of Ecovita.

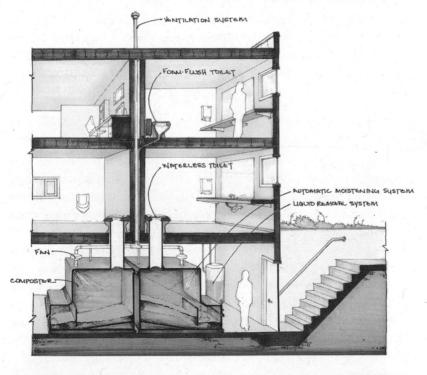

FIGURE 10.6 The composting toilet captures solid waste and composts it over time through natural bacterial action, after which it can be used as a garden fertilizer. Courtesy of Clivus Multrum.

Constructed wetlands can have either surface or subsurface flows. Surface flows resemble marshes, while subsurface flows support a wide variety of plants by supplying them with nutrients. Constructed wetlands may be cheaper to build than traditional sewage and stormwater treatment plants, have lower operating and maintenance costs and can handle widely varying volumes of wastewater.[16]

Michael Ogden is an engineer and one of the country's leading experts in onsite disposal. Many of his systems are designed for resorts, schools and other low-density developments. He specializes in using constructed wetlands to treat wastewater, thereby providing nutrients as well as water to landscaping and avoiding any runoff into surface waters. With enough land area, a constructed wetland is an excellent way to treat wastewater from a variety of developments, eliminating contaminants through natural bacteriological activity.[17] Rather than trying to eliminate water use for toilet and urinal flushing, Ogden instead puts the water back into the ground using the wetland and recycles the nutrients in the wastewater for plant growth. Ogden's approach considers the total water cycle of a place, including rainwater, stormwater, surface water and groundwater, graywater and sewage effluent, along with the various opportunities to reuse water for appropriate quality demands. Ogden helped design the wastewater treatment system at the Omega Center for Sustainable Living discussed later in this chapter.

Ecological Wastewater Treatment

The Living Machine® ecological wastewater treatment system from Worrell Water Technologies uses biological processes to break down waste products in blackwater. The process delivers clean water for site irrigation and other uses such as process water, or returns it to the building for toilet flushing. As an advanced ecological system, it requires much less hands-on maintenance than conventional technology. The Worrell Tidal Wetland Living Machine® system (Figure 10.7) incorporates a series of wetland cells, or basins, that are filled with special gravel, which provide extensive surface area for the growth of micro-ecosystems. As water moves through the system, the cells are alternately flooded and drained to simulate daily tidal cycles, resulting in high-quality treatment of domestic wastewater. This patented tidal process naturally brings oxygen to the micro-organisms that consume the wastewater, improving treatment performance and producing cleaner water using less energy. The wetland vegetation and micro-organisms, especially in the root zone, promote a complex and stable ecosystem, generating clean

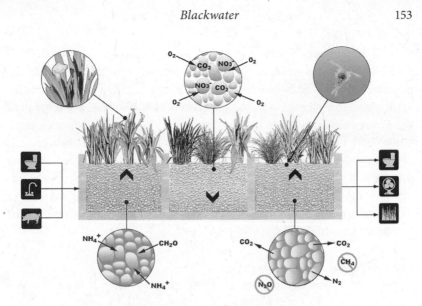

FIGURE 10.7 The Living Machine® simulates natural tidal cycles to aerobically clean wastewater and return it for beneficial reuse. Courtesy of Worrell Water Technologies.

water under a variety of conditions.[18] According to Eric Lohan and Will Kirksey of Worrell Water Technologies,

> You can think of a Living Machine as the engine for the water treatment process. We use other technologies for disinfection, and pumps, filters and other plumbing components to take that treated water and put it back into building systems for flushing toilets.[19]

Generally the installation of the system is done by a mechanical contractor. Because these biological systems straddle a number of different disciplines, sometimes irrigation contractors and general residential plumbers install them. Some firms that specialize in onsite wastewater treatment systems would do everything: electrical and mechanical contracting and the earthworks. According to Lohan and Kirksey, Living Machine systems can be built:

> with capacity as large as 200,000 gallons per day. With our current technology, you can start out small and expand the system to support increased demand. We have several installed projects applying our latest technology in the range of about 30,000 gallons per day. We could easily parlay that experience into 100,000 gallons per day or more.

Worrell Water has one of its current generation installations at North Guilford Middle School in North Carolina, a project from the architects, Innovative Design, Inc.[20] Serving the middle school and a high school, the Living Machine cleans up to 30,000 gallons of wastewater per day (all of the wastewater from toilets, kitchens, showers, sinks) and produces enough clean water to irrigate three athletic fields with subsurface irrigation. The project used this treatment strategy because there were no central sewer lines within miles of the site. By using water twice, the system saves an additional 5 million gallons per year. Guilford County schools saved over $4 million by installing the Living Machine system instead of extending the city sewer lines to the site.

Eco-machines

A hydroponic type of biological treatment process known as an Eco Machine™ was installed at the Omega Institute. Located north of New York City along the Hudson River in Rhinebeck, New York, the Omega Center for Sustainable Living (OCSL) (Figure 10.8) aims to be a LEED Platinum project and also to be the first to complete the Living Building Challenge (LBC). The Living Building Challenge facilitates changes in the green building industry by examining the best practices and knowledge available today in sustainable architecture, including design, materials sourcing, occupant health and economics, to define the highest level of sustainability currently possible in the built environment. Among its 16 prerequisites, two directly affect water supply and wastewater treatment:

- One hundred percent of occupants' water use must come from captured precipitation or closed-loop water systems that account for downstream ecosystem impacts and that are appropriately purified without use of chemicals.
- One hundred percent of stormwater and building water discharge must be managed onsite to feed the project's internal water demands or released onto adjacent sites for management through acceptable (natural time-scale) surface flow, groundwater recharge, agricultural use or adjacent building needs.[21]

The heart of OCSL's water system is the Eco Machine, a "natural wastewater treatment system that cleans water by mimicking the systems of the natural world."[22] It consists of five phases through which the wastewater flows:

1. Anaerobic digestion (much like a septic tank) that begins the wastewater treatment process

FIGURE 10.8 At the Omega Center for Sustainable Living in Rhinebeck, New York, the Eco Machine™ forms the basis for integrating the water cycle. Courtesy © 2009 Farshid Assassi.

2. Constructed wetlands, in which four cells filled with plants continue to break down the waste with micro-organisms
3. Aerated lagoons (inside a greenhouse) where the waste is further treated by plants, fungi, algae, bacteria, snails and other organisms in the tanks
4. Polishing phase in a sand filter that prepares the water for reuse
5. Dispersal phase (subsurface at this time) that reintroduces water into the environment

Omega's Eco Machine can process up to 52,000 gallons a day. Much of its natural wastewater treatment system is gravity-fed, decreasing the amount of energy needed to operate.

Design principals Steve McDowell and Laura Lesniewski were in charge of the OCSL project for BNIM Architects.[23] According to the architects, "This is fundamentally a large plumbing project using natural systems, with a building attached; it's hard to break down the costs because the [treatment] building and the water reclamation system serve more than 70 buildings, from cottages to a big dining hall on a 200-acre campus." Lesniewski talked about how the project's scope changed as both the client and the architects recognized a unique opportunity to create something larger than the original project:

The project started off as a "wastewater infiltration facility," an upgrade to an existing septic system. Now the building is called the Omega Center for Sustainable Living. With water and water education at the core of intent, the project became much more than just a septic tank upgrade. Regionally, it's having an impact on the way that people understand water, and because of adherence to the Living Building Challenge, it's being shared nationally.

The environmental requirements for the proper operation of the Eco Machine also ended up dictating much of the building form, according to McDowell:

> One of the things that happened in the design process is that the performance of the building was measured, tested and documented more than any other project that we've ever worked on. For instance, to understand how the plants would thrive in the greenhouse, we had to have very precise measurements about the amount of light, the direction of the light on both the north and south sides of the plants, along with everything else. When we really understood the requirements and how the building would perform, it caused us to change the form of the building. The roof changed slope so that, instead of the high side being on the north, it was on the south side (see Figure 10.8). It changed everything. It required us to rethink of all the things we conceived earlier [in the design process] to confirm we had made the right decisions.

In a way, one of the lessons learned is that if you're going to mimic nature with wastewater treatment systems, you need to understand that there are many subtle nuances in natural systems that make nature-inspired design inherently integrative and challenging. (The entire field of *biomimicry* offers lessons for nature-inspired design.[24])

Sewer Mining

One response to extreme water shortages is a practice first tried out in Australia called "sewer mining." Recognizing that there is plenty of water flowing in cities in the sanitary sewer system, the City of Melbourne decided to tap into it and treat it for their new building. The City of Melbourne's Council House 2 (CH2), completed in August 2006, is the new home for about 540 staff (Figure 10.9). The project received the highest "6 Star Green Star — Office Design" rating from the Green Building Council of Australia.

FIGURE 10.9 A 6-Star Green Star-rated building, Council House 2 in Melbourne, Australia, pioneered an urban innovation, "sewer mining" of blackwater for treatment and reuse in buildings. Courtesy of the City of Melbourne.

Topping the list of CH2's water-saving innovations is a unique sewer-mining system. This system processes approximately 100,000 liters (26,420 gallons) of wastewater per day, made up of blackwater and graywater produced in the building and sewage mined from a sewer main located in the street near the building. The combined wastewater is purified in the basement of CH2 using a multi-water reuse (MWR) plant. This approach helps to meet 72 percent of the building's water needs and provides an always-plentiful, non-potable water source.[25]

The system harvests water directly from the sewer and directs it into the MWR plant where it undergoes a micron-sized prescreening, ceramic ultrafiltration and finally reverse osmosis, which together purify it to a

Grade-A drinking-water-quality standard. The sewer-mining system was designed to reduce dramatically the amount of potable water required to meet the building's demand. During holiday periods when staff is reduced, the system can lower its daily production to 20,000 liters (5,280 gallons) with few adverse effects.

The estimated financial payback period for the wastewater treatment system is 15 to 20 years. The sewage treatment plant, coupled with a 20,000-liter (5,280-gallon) rainwater and fire-sprinkler-test water collection system and storage tank on site, will supply 100 percent of CH2's non-potable water for toilet flushing and for cooling, along with irrigation of the green roof and the green wall of the building. Surplus water will be directed to other nearby council (government) buildings, fountains, street cleaning and plant irrigation.

Summary

Waste treatment systems have evolved from primitive pit privies to complex installations capable of producing drinking-quality water from millions of gallons per day of incoming wastewater. Today's conventional sewage treatment is an enormous undertaking requiring intensive energy use and complex infrastructure. Forward-thinking designers looking to create a more sustainable built environment are considering and implementing onsite sewage treatment systems, both to reduce burdens on local infrastructure and to provide a new source of water for building uses. Options range from simple composting toilets to complex onsite chemical-free treatment systems that convert sewage into clean water along with beneficial by-products used by plants and micro-organisms.

Green Water

> *Water has no taste, no color, no odor;*
> *it cannot be defined, yet is relished while ever*
> *mysterious.... It fills us with a gratification*
> *that exceeds the delight of the senses.*
>
> — Antoine de Saint-Exupery,
> from *Wind, Sand, and Stars*[1]

A LARGE PORTION of urban water use in homes is for landscaping; commercial and institutional water use is also heavily influenced by landscaping requirements, so it makes sense to look at ways to cut water use for landscaping, while recognizing that we don't want to lose the positive benefits of greening the urban environment. For example, the "urban heat island" effect can be mitigated by green roofs and exterior landscape choices. Appropriately chosen vegetation can reduce the energy requirements of homes and buildings by letting the sun in during the winter and keeping it out during the summer, a process known as passive solar design. It's also possible to increase habitat in cities and promote habitat diversity with appropriate choices of native and adapted vegetation. For these reasons, there is good justification for having substantial amounts of greenery in cities, beyond the usual lawns, parks and golf courses. The key concept is to secure the benefits of a green landscape without incurring unnecessary penalties in excessive water use.

In this chapter, you'll learn about opportunities for conserving the use of potable water in landscape, ways to integrate stormwater management with landscaping and systems for reusing water in the landscape, especially

159

at the building level. In previous chapters, you learned about the attractiveness of using graywater from homes for residential landscaping and about how irrigation controllers are revolutionizing and dramatically reducing water use for landscaping and farm irrigation. Many cities supply "purple pipe" reclaimed water for commercial landscapes and industrial process water use, a subject covered in more detail in Chapter 13.[2]

A major source of water pollution of both rivers and oceans is stormwater runoff, which carries away everything from the ground: oil and grease, rubber from tires, animal waste, sediment, fertilizers, pesticides, you name it. According to the US Environmental Protection Agency (EPA) non-point-source pollution is the leading cause of water quality degradation.[3] Landscape approaches that treat stormwater onsite with green roofs, bio-swales, infiltration, detention ponds and constructed wetlands all contribute to controlling stormwater pollution by reducing the rate and quantity of runoff. While there are many best practices for controlling stormwater pollution, this chapter focuses primarily on reducing landscaping water waste and on positive measures for keeping water onsite.

Los Angeles Stormwater Management Ordinance

One of the key measures for creating green water is to redirect stormwater away from urban drainage to recharge groundwater or landscape onsite. A proposed law would require new homes, larger developments and some re-developments in Los Angeles to capture and reuse runoff generated in rain-storms. Recommended in January 2010 by the City's Department of Public Works, the ordinance would require these projects to capture, reuse or in-filtrate 100 percent of runoff generated in a three-quarter-inch rainstorm or to pay a stormwater pollution mitigation fee that would help fund off-site, low-impact development measures.

This new approach to reducing stormwater would mitigate water quality degradation from urban runoff, especially coastal pollution. By controlling runoff at its source with small, cost-effective natural systems, the City would avoid the need to construct new treatment facilities. The City estimates the new requirements would reduce polluted runoff by more than 100 million gallons annually and would also create more groundwater recharge.

Options available under the proposal include rainwater storage tanks, permeable pavement, infiltration swales or curb bump-outs to manage runoff. Builders unable to manage 100 percent of a project's runoff onsite would be required to pay a penalty of $13 per gallon of runoff. The City would also allow runoff if it were first processed through a high-efficiency bio-filtration system.

You can expect to see similar ordinances in many other cities, as urban runoff is a major source of pollution of rivers, lakes and oceans. Capturing rainwater at the source and reusing, recharging or cleaning it up makes all the sense in the world.[4]

Queens Botanical Garden

The Queens Botanical Garden in New York City is an outstanding recent example of fully integrating landscape with water runoff. The 15,831-square-foot, $14-million LEED Platinum Visitor and Administration Center (Figure 11.1) opened in 2007 and features a green roof, 16 kW of solar panels and a major water recycling and stormwater management program.[5] There are two water recycling systems: one takes rainwater to fill an engineered watercourse through the property, while the other takes graywater, cleans it in constructed wetlands and then recycles it back into the building for toilet

FIGURE 11.1 The Queens Botanical Garden's LEED Platinum Visitor Center features an integrated stormwater and graywater recycling system. © Atelier Dreiseitl.

flushing. Inside the building are two composting toilets and waterless uri-nals for garden staff.[6] Overall, fixture water use has been reduced by 82 per-cent, compared with a similar project with conventional toilets and urinals. Adding to this project in 2008, an existing parking lot was transformed into a 125-space "parking garden" as part of the Garden's overall decade-long Sustainable Landscapes and Buildings Project.[7]

Figure 11.2 shows a schematic design of the stormwater management system that recycles rainwater into the site's waterways. Rainwater falls off the roof into a "cleansing biotope," a constructed wetland, then goes into a 24,000-gallon underground tank. The stream bed through the property reflects the available water; if there's a drought or an extended period of dry weather, it will be empty. Aided by a 3,000-square-foot green roof, the stormwater management system aims to keep 100 percent of precipitation on the property throughout the year.

The site design's primary theme is the *visible expression of water*. As a cultural bridge, the awareness of water is the most critical element to sup-port life in every corner of the world.[8] Therefore water was consciously cho-sen as a combining theme both for diverse ethnic groups of the city and to celebrate the connection between people and the environment in a dense

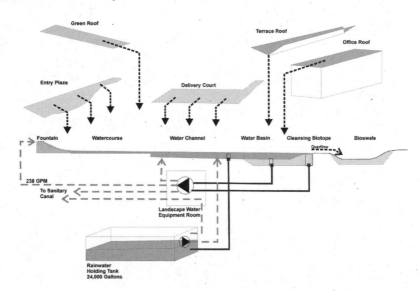

FIGURE 11.2 Rain falling on roofs and hardscape areas flows into the central stream channel and then goes to storage and treatment before it is returned for reuse. Courtesy © Atelier Dreiseitl.

urban location. Atelier Dreiseitl provided the water concept and landscape planning.

The water elements make use of harvested rainwater, rather than allowing stormwater to enter the city's combined sewer system, ultimately reducing water pollution in Long Island Sound. In lush planted gardens with open water surfaces, stormwater is cooled and filtered with bioswales (vegetated runoff channels) that mimic the function of natural ecosystems.[9] When it is raining, water cascades off a single point onto a stone dissipater, directing cooled, aerated water to the water channel in an engaging display, using only free, renewable resources: rainwater and gravity.

Beyond rainwater harvesting, the building's plumbing systems direct graywater from the Visitor and Administration Center's sinks, dishwashers and shower to a constructed wetland. The water is filtered and treated naturally through bacterial activity on the roots of plants, and returned to the building for use in toilet flushing.

In this project, both bioswales and constructed wetlands are integrated with the water supply, wastewater disposal and stormwater management systems, quite a trick for an addition to an existing project in the middle of the largest city in the US! According to the project's landscape architects, "Sustainable water resource management combines aesthetic appeal and technological transparency while making a significant 'green' space contribution to our urban environments."[10]

Zhangjiawo, Tianjin, China

Tianjin is a major port city southeast of Beijing with a current population of 10 million. After conducting an urban planning study, the City opened up land for development to provide housing for current and future urban citizens. The developer of Zhangjiawo (which means Society Hill)[11] chose the design team to deliver new urban housing specifically adapted to the site with the quality of "outstanding liveability." The first 20 hectares (48 acres), completed in 2007, showcase the design qualities at the heart of the development: transforming the site's landscape heritage into contemporary green features. Existing orchard trees, some 200 years old, have been protected and integrated into the design. Irrigation channels of the former farmland are found again as decentralized stormwater management bioswales, channels and water features that support the enjoyment of water within an urban environment, while allowing rainwater to be cleansed and infiltrated to the groundwater. A 30-meter-wide (100-foot) irrigation canal was restored as an internal "river." (Figure 11.3) The banks are shaped and planted to create a flourishing environment to help cleanse the water after years of receiving

FIGURE 11.3 Currently a 48-acre development, Zhangjiawo was built on former farmland and strives to integrate water and land into a new urban form, using an internal "river." © Atelier Dreiseitl.

industrial and agricultural pollution. (A cleansing biotope with active circulation is also integrated with the system.) Accessible by boardwalk, steps and ramps, the restored river-canal creates a community asset that serves as a focal point for leisure and socializing.[12]

Green Roofs

The green roof at the Queens Botanical Garden is part of a larger movement that has inspired thousands of green roofs on buildings in North America over the past ten years. More than three million square feet of green roofs were installed in 2008, a 35 percent increase over 2007.[13]

Green roofs can play an important role in water management in cities. They cumulatively reduce a city's need for air conditioning (and electric power generation requires considerable water), since they keep the sun off the roof and provide an extra layer of roof insulation. They are a critical component of stormwater management, decreasing the total runoff and cutting the peak runoff from a building site.[14] They also help reduce the building's energy demand. One drawback: if you're planning a rainwater harvesting system, green roofs will soak up some of that water, and the run-

FIGURE 11.4 The Chicago Transit Authority installed a large green roof on its headquarters, providing a great amenity in a dense urban area. Photo by John Herbst, courtesy of Transwestern.

off from them may be richer in organic matter, requiring additional treatment. Nevertheless, green roofs are likely to be seen in many green building projects because of their many beneficial features.

Green roofs are an increasingly popular option for both new and existing buildings. The City of Chicago has led the way in promoting green roofs in urban environments as a way to reduce the urban heat island effect — the documented tendency of cities to be hotter than the surrounding countryside and to require more energy use for air conditioning in the summers.[15] By 2006, Chicago city officials and private developers had installed more than 200 green roofs, covering 2.5 million square feet of space, the equivalent of a 60-acre park.[16]

A good example is the Chicago Transit Authority (CTA) headquarters, which installed a 29,000-square-foot green roof as part of its LEED for Existing Buildings Gold certification project. Figure 11.4 shows how attractive a green roof can be, especially in a dense urban environment.

Green roofs come in two varieties, intensive and extensive. An intensive green roof has more than four inches of soil and can support a wide variety of plants; for example, a LEED Gold apartment project in New York City, the 27-story Solaire apartment building in Battery Park City, contains a rose garden on a roof at the 19th floor.[17] However, intensive green roofs add more weight and require more irrigation and maintenance, so most projects use extensive green roof treatments, in which the soil layer is thinner (less than four inches) and typically uses lightweight materials such as perlite.

Green roofs have another drawback: they are not cheap. Typical costs range from $10 to $30 per square foot. For a 15,000-square-foot green roof, that would be $150,000 to $450,000. However, for a tall building, a green roof might represent a significant amenity at a much lower cost per square foot (since there is more area over which to spread the initial cost). For a project with high-level LEED certification goals, a green roof can help with open-space goals, thermal comfort, stormwater management, and reducing the urban heat island effect, cutting air-conditioning costs in summer and holding water from small to medium-sized storms for later use in landscape irrigation, toilet flushing or release to waterways.

Green roofs are used in many applications, including commercial, industrial, governmental and residential buildings. In Europe they are widely used for their stormwater management and energy savings, as well as their aesthetic benefits. Green roof systems may be modular, with drainage layers, filter cloth, growing media and plants already prepared in movable, interlocking grids, or each component of the system may be installed separately in layers.

A good industrial example is the Ford Motor Company's River Rouge plant. Lying at the center of the plant's revitalization project, this new assembly facility represents Ford's efforts to rethink the ecological footprint of a large manufacturing installation. The design emphasizes a safe and healthy workplace with an approach that reduces the impact of the facility on the natural environment. The keystone of the site's stormwater management system is a 10-acre living roof, the largest in the world. This green roof is expected to retain half the annual rainfall that falls on its surface. It also provides bird habitat, decreases the building's energy costs and protects the roof membrane from thermal shock and UV degradation, extending its expected life.[18]

Cutting Water Use in Shopping Centers

Smart Water Application Technologies (SWAT) is a national partnership initiative of water suppliers and the irrigation industry, created to promote landscape water use efficiency through the application of modern irrigation technologies.[19] Since outdoor water use constitutes 40 to 50 percent of all urban water use, saving on wasteful outdoor watering is critical to achieving effective water conservation in cities. One CII water user that can easily adopt efficient irrigation technologies is the shopping center industry.

Regency Centers, a large shopping center developer, owns and operates about 410 grocery-anchored shopping centers throughout the US. As part of its *greengenuity*™ sustainability initiative, Regency partnered with HydroPoint Data Systems (see Chapter 7) to install smart irrigation controllers at more than 90 of its shopping centers by the end of 2009.[20] The first year's data from 36 systems installed in a pilot program in 2008 showed a decrease of 30 percent in irrigation water use. As a result of this success, Regency Centers installed smart irrigation controllers at 54 additional shopping centers in Arizona, California, Colorado, Florida, Oregon, Texas and Washington.

The company estimates savings from the 90 systems to be about 96 million gallons per year, an average of slightly more than *one million gallons per center*. Economic payback of the original investment ranged from one to three years, according to Mark Peternell, vice president of sustainability for Regency Centers:

> Success is determined by a year-over-year decrease in water consumption while maintaining landscaping to Regency's quality standard. The "smart" systems have met our savings expectations of 30 percent and

FIGURE 11.5 Regency Centers has installed automated "smart" irrigation controllers at nearly 100 shopping centers, such as the Hilltop Village in Thornton, Colorado. Courtesy of Regency Centers.

resulted in substantially lower water bills, especially at properties with progressively tiered rate structures.[21]

Summary

The Queens Botanical Garden and Zhangjiawo projects demonstrate that water-conscious landscapes can also be beautiful. Of the numerous different techniques and devices that contribute to outdoor water conservation, many have additional benefits such as reducing water pollution, combating the urban heat island effect and maintaining healthy habitats. Green roofs are one such example that have the additional benefits of reducing energy use inside the building and increasing the roof's lifespan. Because landscape water use is such a large slice of the water use "pie" in cities, the vast array of water conservation techniques create a major opportunity to reduce water use and create productive habitat.

Zen Water

When the well's dry,
we know the worth of water

— Benjamin Franklin[1]

THERE ARE MANY WAYS to conserve water, but what about projects that use no water at all, that place no demand on urban infrastructure? I'm calling these "no water" projects "Zen Water," in answer to the koan, "How can you provide for a project's water use without really supplying any more water?"

In the green building movement, there is a "hyper-green" approach called restorative or regenerative building, which generates more water and energy than it uses and puts this excess water and energy back into the landscape and into the grid. The best-known is the Living Building Challenge, originally created by Jason McLennan of the Cascadia Region Green Building Council in the Pacific Northwest (and British Columbia).

Living Building Challenge

In contrast to the US Green Building Council's LEED rating system, which awards points that determine a project's level of "greenness," the Living Building Challenge (LBC) has only 16 prerequisites that a "living building" must meet. As we saw in Chapter 10, two of these deal with water:

- The first specifies that all occupant water use[2] must come from "captured precipitation or closed-loop water systems."[3]
- The second requires tall stormwater and building water discharge to be managed onsite.[4]

Reviewing the LBC criteria, it appears that most such projects would also qualify as LEED Platinum projects, but LBC is certainly an attempt to define a universe of green buildings "beyond LEED." At this time, several projects are vying to become the first certified Living Buildings, which must demonstrate not only that they meet the design and construction criteria, but that they continue to meet the energy and water criteria in actual operations for at least one year.

As of November 2009, about 70 projects were pursuing certification from the Living Building Challenge. Three projects have completed construction and have entered their verification phase: Tyson Living Learning Center in Eureka, Missouri; Omega Center for Sustainable Living in Rhinebeck, New York (profiled in part in Chapter 10); and Eco-Sense, a private home in Victoria, British Columbia.[5]

Tyson Living Learning Center (LLC)

Opened at Washington University's research center in Eureka, Missouri, on May 29, 2009, the Tyson LLC (Figure 12.1) aims to become the first Living Building.[6]

FIGURE 12.1 The Tyson Living Learning Center at Washington University aims to become the first Living Building certified in the US. Photography by Joe Angeles.

A south-sloping, standing-seam metal roof is covered with solar photo-voltaic panels that can produce a peak output of 20 kW of electricity. Excess energy is fed back into the grid, and the Center receives credit through a local utility program called "net metering." Even when power output is less than demand at the LLC, it can draw on its accumulated credits to maintain a "net-zero energy" demand over the year.[7]

Rainwater is also collected from this sloped roof, passing through four different types of filters and then into an underground, 3,000-gallon storage tank. Another filter, one at each faucet, will eliminate any water-borne bacteria, a health code requirement. The building has composting toilets that eliminate the need for water other than an intermittent compost misting manifold, and landscaping that does not require watering. The project estimates that the 3,000-gallon storage tank could sustain the center without any rainfall for up to 60 days. As we saw in Table 9.3, St. Louis is blessed with fairly steady precipitation throughout the year, so 60 days of supply is probably more than would ever be required.

The $1.5 million, 2,900-square-foot facility was designed by architect Dan Hellmuth of St. Louis. According to Hellmuth and engineer Matt Ford of Solutions AEC, this project posed some unique challenges for the water systems:

> The project is in a 2,000-acre field study center about 15 minutes outside of the main campus for Washington University. It was already on a well water system but they had some site-related water issues involving an old pressure tank and underground leaks. Any new building would have been on a septic system, but because none of the situations [that we were proposing] met code, we made some anonymous calls to the county asking, "Can we do this, this and this?" The answer always was, "We don't do that here." We met with the facilities team at the university; then our whole design team, the director and associate director of Tyson Research Center sat down with the code officials and said, "What we are trying to do is probably a little bit different, and it is a unique opportunity for Washington University, our design team and hopefully the country. How can we work with you during the design process to figure how we can do this rather than go through the process and discover why we can't do it?"[8]

Hellmuth and Ford said their approach was purposefully non-confrontational, and that seemed to help the situation with St. Louis County code officials. From the beginning, said Ford,

The challenge wasn't just the drinking-water side; just as big and per-haps larger was the wastewater side, with the composting toilets [black-water] system and collection of graywater. They needed to understand what was happening there. For example, we originally had building-wide UV filtration, but the County requested some additional filtration at the point of use for the potable sinks.

From the 3,000-gallon rainwater collection and storage tank, water is pres-surized and pushed through a series of four filtration devices: a UV filter, a large-sediment filter, a fine-sediment filter and an activated-carbon fil-ter. Then the water goes to the individual fixtures where there is a small 0.45-micron bacteria barrier that is located at each of three potable sinks. Water in the rainwater tank is also recirculated five to eight hours a day to provide adequate turnover rates in the tank, to filter and clean the water and give it run-time through the UV filter.

Graywater is also collected and infiltrated through a special soil mound that is planted with species that help with filtration and purification. The base system was designed by Clivus Multrum and then site-adapted by Solutions AEC. The system collects graywater from the potable and non-potable sinks into a collection tank or "dosing basin" and then pumps it out to the graywater infiltration garden. The basin is calibrated so when the graywater reaches a certain level in the tank, it's distributed to a manifold underneath the mound of engineered soil. This engineered graywater treat-ment system also recharges the groundwater at the same time.

Architect Hellmuth reflects on what it means to run a project with a "closed-loop" water cycle. In the real world, some accommodations have to be made:

The concept of net-zero water and the Living Building Challenge is an interesting one. What does that mean? It means something differ-ent when you're not on water from the city mains. We took the strict-est interpretation of it, in reality because any water that we're capturing and not using for drinking is directly recharged in the groundwater. We talked to the Challenge people about this, so even though we designed it to have 100 percent rainwater used for drinking water, we can take water out of the well and use that. That is recharged from the conservation stormwater system into the groundwater and still meets the net-zero test. So it's interesting to ask, "What is the real water cycle?" because you're mixing many [different] things. It's a little different when you're on a potable water system with water coming out of pipe. But what does

The 23-story Twelve I West residential/office/retail tower in Portland, OR, completed in 2009, provides a comprehensive approach to stormwater management and was designed to receive two LEED Platinum certifications. Courtesy of ZGF Architects LLP.

Top: The Plumbing Industry Climate Action Centre in Brunswick, Victoria, Australia, is one of the world leaders in training working plumbers in new green technologies. (Chapter 3) Courtesy of Plumbing Industry Climate Action Centre.

Bottom: The Green Streets program in Portland, OR, converts impervious surfaces into attractive urban green spaces that capture and filter stormwater, returning it to groundwater supply, reducing sewer system volume, and improving pedestrian and bicycle safety.(Chapter 11) © Environmental Services, City of Portland, OR.

At Dockside Green, this three-story retail/office building reduces water and energy use so dramatically that it's the highest-rated LEED for Core + Shell project in the world. Specifically selected plants help scrub rainwater to clean it for reuse in site irrigation. (Chapter 7) Courtesy of Busby Perkins + Will.

Top: Swedish architect Anders Nyquist designed this apartment block of 32 units around a central interior courtyard in Nydala, Umea, Sweden. Built in 2006 and illustrating his "split box" concept, there is no connection to the sewer or district heating system, since the water and energy cycles are completely integrated with the building design. (Chapter 10) Courtesy of Anders Nyquist.

Bottom: The Tampa Bay Desalination Plant produces 25 million gallons per day of fresh water from seawater using 9,600 of these reverse osmosis membranes. (Chapter 13) Courtesy of Poseidon Resources.

Originally constructed in 1979 and renovated in 2000, the 18-story Park Tower office building at South Coast Plaza in Costa Mesa, CA, remodeled its restrooms over several years and installed efficient flush fixtures to replace all the original toilets. Along with other measures, indoor water use was reduced 31 percent from the LEED-EBOM baseline levels. (Chapter 5) Courtesy of The Offices of South Coast Plaza.

Top: The Vancouver Convention Centre hosted visiting press covering the 2010 XXI Winter Olympics and Paralympics in British Columbia. All wastewater is treated and recycled onsite. (Chapter 10) Courtesy of Vancouver Convention Centre.

Bottom: The Lady Bird Johnson Wildflower Center in Austin, TX, was one of the first US projects to incorporate a green roof with native plants for stormwater management. Courtesy of Overland Partners.

Prisma Nürnberg illustrates a creative approach to using water to create more livable spaces in densely populated cities. (Chapter 9) © Atelier Dreiseitl.

Top: At this apartment block in Mühlheim am Main in Germany, residents can choose to wash their clothes with harvested rainwater at no cost. (Chapter 9) Courtesy of Buettner and Loeffler.

Bottom: At the €2 million DEUS 21 research project in Knittlingen near Pforzheim, Germany, the Water House not only cleans rainwater and recycles wastewater from the connected households, but it also produces biogas and electrical power. Courtesy of Klaus König.

it mean when you're off of that type of system? It's a different situation. For example, stormwater onsite that doesn't go into a tank for reuse goes into a rainwater garden, a constructed stream bank. It's all absorbed on-site. We have pervious pavement in the parking area and the pathways. Basically, everything falling onsite is recharged into the groundwater. That's another part of the water cycle. It's part of the bigger picture as far as mitigating the fact that you developed the site and put a building on it. The building was built on an old parking lot. This project turned a nasty old parking lot into a conservation stormwater garden.

To meet the net-zero water test is challenging enough, but to meet a larger test of creating a beautiful, useful building that has no ongoing demand on the power or water grid is even more of a stretch. Yet, this project illustrates that it can be done.

Omega Center for Sustainable Living, Rhinebeck, New York

The $2.8-million Omega Center for Sustainable Living (OCSL), which officially opened in the summer of 2009, is at the leading edge of green building.[9] (Figure 12.2) It's located on the 195-acre campus of the Omega Institute in Rhinebeck, New York, an education and retreat center. A 48.5 kW solar photovoltaic system provides electric power.[10] The center has indoor and outdoor classroom areas, but at the core of the 6,250-square-foot building is a 4,500-square-foot greenhouse containing a water filtration system called the Eco Machine. Compared with the Tyson Center's much smaller staff and visitor numbers, the Omega Center's systems have to accommodate

FIGURE 12.2 The Omega Center for Sustainable Living aims at net-zero water use on an annual basis, one of the key requirements of the Living Building Challenge. Courtesy © 2009 Farshid Assassi.

23,000 annual visitors and an estimated five million gallons of wastewater annually.[11] Systems have been designed for a maximum 52,000 gallons per day (gpd) flow (based on 700 campus guests), with measured maximum daily flow of approximately 38,000 gpd through the fall of 2009. Rainwater use for toilet flushing is estimated at an average of 40 gallons per day; therefore, the 1,800-gallon cistern stores enough water for at least 45 days of typical toilet flushing demand.

Chapter 10 profiled the Omega Center's water treatment and recycling systems, especially the greenhouse. Yet there is more to the project. Architects Laura Lesniewski and Steve McDowell pointed out the driving vision of the Omega Center's CEO, Skip Backus:

> It's amazing to think about where the building is located, the watershed it is in, the proximity to New York City — one of the most important settlements in the world — and about this relatively small organization. It was actually a single person in that organization, Skip Backus, who decided to be brave and to go way beyond his responsibilities — [to set an example] for treating water respectfully on their campus and in their local watershed. They wanted to create a building and a water cleaning process that is experimental — a laboratory for how our whole society can start to think differently about how we use water. I think the building is extraordinary because of the client's vision and willingness to set an example for how we all should be thinking about taking care of a precious resource. From an architectural point of view, it's extraordinary that this same person was willing to trust that a Living Building could be achieved. We talk about intuition — intuitive design, scientific design and experiential aspects — and in a way, Skip Backus knew enough about the science of water, about the issues to accept that this project could make a difference. He allowed the team to proceed along this road of the Living Building Challenge. Because of that level of trust and because of the commitment and passion that was put into it by the whole team, we ended up with a building that is interesting [in itself], beautiful and important in the long-term scheme of sustainability.[12]

Lesniewski says that the Omega Center already is operating in a closed loop regarding water supply because it gets all of its water from wells, not from a municipal system.

> Any water use is being pulled from the wells, if they are not collecting rainwater and using it somehow. Any water that the building is using

is doing the same thing: pulling from the well, using it and sending it into the system which then puts it back into the groundwater as clean or cleaner than it originated. There's no metering of the water use. There's nothing that's recording how much comes out of a faucet or anything like that, which is unusual for us. The net-zero water prerequisite for the Living Building Challenge allows you to have a closed-loop system, which is the situation with this project.[13]

The architects also brought a much broader perspective to the project, as evidenced by some of the explicit project goals:

Beyond the wastewater filtration system, the Omega Center for Sustainable Living also acts as a pedagogical tool in teaching sustainable design and construction. Early in the design process, Omega and the design team adopted the Living Building Challenge as a guide towards achieving true sustainability in the design and construction of the facility. Educational workshops will be designed around the ecological effect of the filtration system as well as our profound relationship with water. As part of its educational mission, Omega plans to invite:

- area school children to learn about water purification and wetland composition during field trips and onsite classes;
- university students to use the facility as an eco-lab, modeling alternative wastewater treatment solutions; and
- visitors from surrounding communities to view a working model that demonstrates improved wastewater treatment efforts.[14]

Summary

While most of us are not immediately going to be designing, building and living or working in Living Buildings, we can all ask passionate questions about the long-term sustainability of whatever project or activity we undertake or of the places where we live and work. Fortunately, a few innovative owners, architects and developers are paving the way to introduce net-zero water and Living Buildings into our building stock. Let's hope that the wisdom of what works and what doesn't, along with the enlightened insights from these pioneering projects, will be incorporated into many more projects.

New Water

The tides are in our veins,
we still mirror the stars...

— Robinson Jeffers[1]

IN THIS CHAPTER, we'll learn more about two sources of "new water" from technologies not typically in widespread use today throughout the US, desalination of seawater and expanded use of reclaimed wastewater from sewage treatment plants. Both of these sources are likely to find their way into mainstream water-supply planning in the next two decades, as we saw in the San Diego County case study in Chapter 3. For most of history, Americans have been blessed with abundant water resources, and the political will (and capital) to develop them.

Some countries don't have the luxury of relying on conservation and water recycling to meet future water needs or of building dams on previously untapped rivers; they simply don't have enough. Many Mediterranean, Caribbean and Middle Eastern countries must rely on desalination of seawater or brackish water (or rainwater capture) for all or most of their freshwater needs. It may be that in future decades of this century, if global warming consequences are as severe as many fear, more of the coastal populations in these regions will have to turn to the ocean for their water supplies (Figure 13.1). Because of the high energy requirements per gallon of water produced (at least with today's technology), it's likely to be much more expensive water as well.

Figure 13.2 shows the production capacity of freshwater from seawater for various countries. Worldwide, 13,080 desalination plants produced more

FIGURE 13.1 To many, the sea is the ultimate source of drinking water.

than 12 billion gallons of water a day in 2008.[2] The total production capacity in the US is about 1.6 billion gallons per day (6 million cubic meters).[3] Except for the US and Japan, countries with high desalination production capacity have extreme water shortages, or high population density and/or large and growing populations. We saw in the Australia case study that each large city is committed to providing some of its future water supply from seawater, even though the expense is high, since all are coastal, except for the capital, Canberra.

The world's largest desalination plant is the $550 million Jebel Ali Desalination Plant in Dubai, United Arab Emirates. Built for the Dubai Electricity and Water Authority, Phase 2 of Jebel Ali is a dual-purpose facility that uses multistage flash distillation technology and is capable of produc-

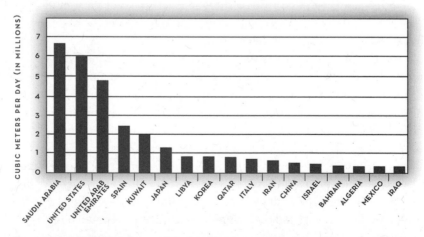

FIGURE 13.2 Much of the world's desalination capacity in 2006 was in countries that are extremely hot and dry, but the US is rapidly developing its own capacities.[4]

ing 140 million gallons per day from eight treatment units.[5] The project will also produce 2,000 megawatts of power from steam, about the output of two large coal-fired power plants.

Desalination Plants in the US

In Tampa Bay, Florida, the largest desalination plant in the US began producing 25 million gallons of water per day in December 2007.[6] The $158 million plant runs at about 12 percent of the output of both phases of the Jebel Ali Desalination Plants.

The San Diego County plant in Carlsbad, California, will be the second major plant for Poseidon Resources, developers of the Tampa Bay project. A third such plant is planned by the same firm for a location in Huntington Beach, California, about 60 miles north of Carlsbad. At about $900 to $1,100 per acre-foot, costs for desalinated water are running 30 percent or more than conventional sources in California (including water imported from far away, when such sources are available), with electricity to produce 1,000 gallons running about $1.10, according to recent estimates. A number of such plants will likely be built in the next decade or two, since they represent one of the few drought-proof water resources, outside of wastewater reclamation and recycling.[7]

Shown in Figure 13.3, the Carlsbad project is being built, and will be owned and operated by Poseidon, a private company, provided that it can sell $530 million in tax-exempt bonds to finance the construction.[8] In November 2009, the regional water wholesaler, the Metropolitan Water District of Southern California (MWD), agreed to provide a subsidy of $250 per acre-foot of water delivered by the project,[9] more than a 30 percent premium over the current cost of water MWD gets from the Colorado River Aqueduct or the State Water Project. However, since these supplies are under pressure from climate change and may be restricted by environmental protection lawsuits, MWD and its customers are likely to face supply constraints within a few years, so new sources must be found.

From Figure 3.4, you can see that the San Diego County Water District expects supplies from the MWD to decrease from 71 to 29 percent of its total water supply between 2008 and 2020. Desalination would make up a quarter of the shortfall, with conservation and recycling picking up the rest.

The project has been controversial because of the MWD subsidy for a private company and because the plant would be one of the largest ever built in the US, so critics argue that desalination technology at this scale is not proven. California-based water expert Peter Gleick claims, "In practice, desalination in California is an idea whose time has not yet come. It remains

FIGURE 13.3 The $350-million Carlsbad desalination plant near San Diego, California, broke ground late in 2009. Courtesy of Poseidon Resources.

too expensive, compared to untapped conservation and efficiency, recycled water, capturing stormwater and smart trades with agriculture."[10] As in past battles over the costs of nuclear power or current criticisms of vast subsidies for (currently uneconomic) solar power, critics argue that we should not be giving public money to the most expensive form of new water supply. Certainly, we should not fund this source, they argue, before we have exhausted all feasible demand-reduction strategies that are available, at often considerably lower cost to achieve the same supply result.

Nevertheless, I think it's hard to argue that desalination plants aren't going to be part of our 21st-century water future, if current demand growth continues and supply constraints escalate. In that case, it may make sense for public subsidies to be given for actual water deliveries as MWD has done, instead of plant capital costs. That approach forces operators to find cheaper methods for desalination. Indeed, Chapter 7 pointed out that private equity investors, not only in the US but worldwide, are quite eager to fund desalination technology development.

Peter Gleick also believes that desalination plants will become more common in the future, but has major reservations. In 2009, he argued:

Compared to most water alternatives facing us, desalination is very expensive, environmentally and economically. But there are places where we are willing to pay a lot for water. It is also possible to build a bad desalination plant that harms marine systems — we've built plenty of them around the world. [Yet], it is possible to build them in ways that don't harm them, and I just think that ought to be mandated. It makes the water more expensive, but so be it. Too much of the 20th century was built while ignoring the environmental impacts. That's why we have a climate problem — these externalities have been ignored.[11]

Desalination Technology

There are two basic ways to remove the salt from seawater: either distill it as steam from brine or separate the salts from the freshwater through a reverse osmosis or electrical process. For cleaning up brackish water with concentrations of up to 5,000 parts per million of salt and minerals (seawater is about 35,000 parts per million, or 3.5 percent salt), other microfiltration or ultrafiltration technologies may also be suitable. Cleaning up blackwater from buildings for reuse onsite, another form of brackish water treatment, also relies on membrane technology, as we learned in Chapters 7 and 12.

In a desalination process, salt water is separated into two parts: one that has a low concentration of salt, essentially drinkable (treated water or product water), and the other with a much higher concentration than the original feed water, usually referred to simply as "concentrate."

The two major types of technologies used around the world for desalination are either thermal or membrane. Thermal technologies work like a steam iron: put in tap water (that may be high in dissolved solids) and get out steam, which then condenses into pure water. Membrane technologies work like the water purifier under your sink: force tap water through a reverse osmosis membrane at city water pressure and get out pure water from a separate faucet. Both technologies need energy to operate, and both produce freshwater. Within those two broad types, there are subcategories (processes) using different techniques, identified in Table 13.1.[12] Thermal and membrane capacity on a worldwide basis is split almost evenly between thermal processes and membrane technologies.

TABLE 13.1 Desalination Technologies[13]

Thermal Technology	Membrane Technology
Multi-stage flash distillation (15 mgd limit)	Reverse osmosis (RO)
Multi-effect distillation	Electrodialysis (mostly brackish water)
Vapor compression distillation (small systems)	Electrodialysis reversal (brackish)

The National Academy of Sciences prepared a "Technology Roadmap" in 2004 that concluded that substantial cost reductions in reverse osmosis (RO) technology are less likely to occur in the future, but that

> while thermal desalination is not expected to displace membrane-based desalination in the United States, thermal technologies have substantial potential and should be more seriously considered, especially when combined with other industrial applications, such as electric power generating facilities (cogeneration), to use waste heat and improve flexibility and economics.[14]

In other words, by using waste heat from power plants located along the coast, it might be possible to cut the cost of thermal desalination technologies significantly. However, for the long run, the Academy study concluded that "dramatic cost reductions will require novel technologies, perhaps based on entirely different desalination processes or powered by entirely new energy sources. Specific areas that could benefit from alternative technologies for cost reduction include energy [efficiency], capital costs, and brine disposal."[15] Other than energy use, brine disposal is often cited as one of the key environmental impacts (and critiques) of desalination projects.[16]

Economics of Desalination

Table 13.2 shows the relative economics of desalination compared with traditional water supplies for coastal communities in the US, as of 2003. The cost comparison for desalination is likely to become more favorable as costs decrease with experience, while the cost of adding new water supplies will continue to increase. (This table does *not* include the costs of water conservation programs and incentives, which are even less expensive than *current* water supplies.) The same report estimated that energy represented 44 percent of the costs of reverse osmosis and 50 percent of the costs of thermal

TABLE 13.2 Water costs to consumer, including treatment and delivery, for existing traditional supplies and desalinated water[18]

Thermal Technology	Water cost delivered to consumer, $ per 1,000 gallons (2003)
Existing traditional supply	$0.90–$2.50
New Desalted Water	
Brackish	$1.50–$3.00
Seawater	$3.00–$8.00

technology, so methods that recover energy and access complementary sources such as power production are critical to long-term cost reduction.[17]

Wastewater Recycling

The same National Academy study added that, "aside from the desalination of seawater or brackish aquifers, one potential solution to the nation's water supply problem is to utilize increasingly impaired waters, such as municipal wastewater, by applying desalination treatment technologies for contaminant removal."[19] Reclaimed wastewater is a plentiful water resource that is far cheaper than ocean desalting, though not without its own set of issues, particularly potential public health concerns. Nonetheless, use of reclaimed wastewater is increasing throughout the US. It is in a sense a steady source of supply, unaffected much by weather, and of reasonable quality once it leaves the treatment plant. Continued public concern over "toilet to tap" water recycling represents a persistent political problem. Therefore, uses such as crop irrigation, groundwater recharge, landscaping, golf course watering and industrial cooling make considerable sense, to avoid attempts by concerned citizens to overturn at the ballot box decisions to reuse wastewater. Another good use for wastewater is to return water to the environment, where it will supplement local streamflows, provide stream-side habitat and undergo additional cleaning.

Figure 13.4 shows the current uses for wastewater in California. Agriculture and landscaping use more than 50 percent of the total recycled effluent. Another 25 percent is used for direct groundwater recharge, which cleans the water so it can be pumped out later and used as potable water. In Southern California, treated effluent is also injected into aquifers up to 700 feet deep along the ocean as a barrier against seawater intrusion into freshwater supplies. Currently, the recharge system uses both potable water and recycled municipal wastewater treated by microfiltration, reverse osmosis and (in some cases) advanced oxidation (ultraviolet light and hydrogen peroxide).[20]

Habitat Restoration

Interestingly, one of the best uses I've come across for habitat restoration is in the desert near Phoenix, where treated effluent from one of the city's treatment plants supplies water to constructed wetlands, not only cleaning up the effluent but creating a desirable riparian habitat, shown in Figure 13.5. The Tres Rios wetlands eventually will create a 7-mile, 480-acre corridor in southwestern Phoenix, at the conjunction of the Salt, Aqua Fria and Gila rivers.[22] As a wildlife sanctuary and place of repose in an increasingly

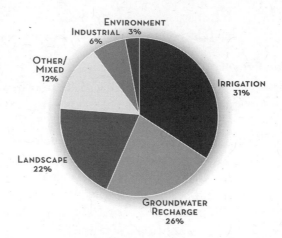

Figure 13.4 More than 50 percent of recycled wastewater in California is used in agriculture and landscaping, including golf courses.[21]

dense urban area, Tres Rios not only treats 153 million gallons (580 million liters) per day of effluent from the 91st Avenue treatment plant, but provides many public use benefits for the Phoenix metropolitan area.[23] The project's long-term goal is to see whether the riparian habitat can clean up the wastewater enough to meet federal water quality standards.

Wastewater Recycling in Australia

Given its severe decade-long drought, you would be correct to expect that Australia is one of the leaders in wastewater recycling for beneficial use. Currently, the greater Sydney metro area recycles about 25 billion liters (6.6 billion gallons) of wastewater a year. By 2015, the area expects to be recycling 70 billion liters (18.5 billion gallons) of wastewater a year, up to 12 percent of Sydney's water needs.[24] Initiated in 2001, Australia's largest residential recycling scheme in the Rouse Hill suburb of northwest Sydney provides recycled water to about 18,000 homes, currently using 1.7 billion liters (450 million gallons) per year. This will double to around 36,000 homes by 2015. Recycled water is used for toilet flushing.[25] Sydney Water supplies about 3.8 billion liters (1 billion gallons) of recycled water a year for irrigating farms, golf courses (Figure 13.6), sports grounds, parks and a race track. About 25 percent of the recycled wastewater is returned to the environment: according to Sydney Water, a new water recycling plant at St. Marys will produce up to 18 billion liters (4.75 billion gallons) a year of highly treated recycled water to help maintain the flow of the Hawkesbury-Nepean River system.

FIGURE 13.5 The Tres Rios plant uses treated wastewater to create seven miles of riparian habitat to clean up effluent to federal standards. Courtesy of the City of Phoenix Water Services Department.

South East Queensland, especially the large metro area of Brisbane, has been extremely hard hit by Australia's long drought. Currently, the AUD$2.5 billion Western Corridor Recycled Water Project is Australia's largest recycled water scheme and the third-largest advanced water treatment project in the world. It uses secondary treated wastewater from Brisbane and Ipswich to produce clean recycled water for Southeast Queensland. The network of pipelines, storage tanks, reservoirs and pumping stations transports recycled water to various customers. The project will deliver up to 232 megaliters (ML) per day (61 million gallons) of recycled water to power stations, industry and agriculture. A key element was the construction of more than 200 kilometers (120 miles) of underground pipelines and three advanced water treatment plants.[26]

Wastewater Recycling in the Arizona Desert

The Tucson, Arizona, metropolitan area has about one million residents living in the Sonoran Desert, which receives less than 12 inches per year of

FIGURE 13.6 Most golf courses in desert areas are irrigated using reclaimed wastewater.

rainfall. The local water utility, Tucson Water, has been delivering reclaimed wastewater since the 1980s. Its approximately 950 customers, include 18 golf courses (Figure 13.6); 39 parks; 52 schools (the University of Arizona and Pima Community College included) and more than 700 single-family homes.

Reclaimed water production facilities in Tucson have been filtering and disinfecting treated wastewater for 25 years. Tucson Water maintains that using reclaimed water for irrigation saves groundwater for drinking. For example, in 2005, reclaimed water customers saved 4.2 billion gallons of drinking water; enough to supply 39,000 families for a year.[27] According to Jeff Biggs, director of Tucson Water:

> Our reclaimed water use for the past decade is about 9 to 10 percent of our total demand, which saves us more than 4 billion gallons of potable water a year. We always have a goal of reducing our gallons per capita per day water use. That has dropped more than 25 percent in the past decade. On the residential side (individual homeowners), we're down to about 96 gallons per day per person, which is fantastic. The efforts our customers have put in over the past 30 years are really paying off [in reducing potable water demand].[28]

Like many water utilities, Tucson Water maintains a distribution system for reclaimed wastewater that is separate from the potable water supply system. In 2004, it had 4,000 miles of water mains in the drinking-water system, but only 156 miles of piping in the reclaimed water system.[29]

Summary

The desalination of seawater and the reuse of treated sewage are two options for new water supplies that have been proven in a large number of cities under a variety of circumstances. The vast quantity of these two resources makes them a viable option for future supply; however, they certainly don't come without a price. In the case of desalination, not only is the technology expensive, but there are environmental costs as well, such as increased energy use and disposal of concentrated brine. With recycled wastewater, there is still widespread public aversion to "toilet to tap" solutions, as well as legitimate public health concerns with reusing wastewater effluent. Taking advantage of reclaimed water and ocean water sources will also require a mindset shift. What we now consider waste is a potential reserve of fresh-water for every city, and the ocean is a vast and relatively untapped resource that offers many opportunities for technological innovation.

PART III

PREVENTING THE NEXT URBAN WATER CRISIS

Responding to Water Crises: A Tale of Four Cities

Eventually, all things merge into one,
and a river runs through it.

— Norman Maclean, *A River Runs Through It*[1]

IN CHAPTER 3, we looked at contemporary water crises in Australia, Atlanta and San Diego. Water crises have plagued many American cities during the past five years, and there have been many different responses. In California, a major drought in 2009 brought water crises to almost every city. In this chapter, we'll look at how four cities, two in Texas and two in California, responded to varying degrees of drought. We'll learn what their successes can teach us about how to create effective water conservation programs to reduce urban water use with full citizen participation and without undue hardship. In the next chapter, I'll show how you can take these lessons and become an activist for water conservation in your own community.

San Antonio Water System: Drought Management

San Antonio Water System (SAWS) serves over one million people in the urban area in and around San Antonio, America's seventh-largest city. (Figure 14.1) Established in 1992, SAWS currently has approximately 326,000 water and 354,000 wastewater customer accounts.[2]

FIGURE 14.1 The San Antonio River Walk shows the integration of water resources as a scenic, cultural and recreation amenity in the middle of a large urban area.

The Edwards Aquifer is the primary source of water for SAWS. As one of the largest artesian groundwater systems in the world, the Edwards Aquifer stretches for more than 8,000 square miles just 500 feet below the surface and supplies more than two million people with water for agricultural, industrial and domestic use throughout south-central Texas. In 1993, a successful endangered species lawsuit by the Sierra Club required the Texas legislature to establish water-pumping regulations governing use of the Edwards Aquifer. These forced San Antonio to initiate an aggressive conservation program that has steadily reduced the city's average per capita water use from a pre-regulation average of 200 gallons per day to currently around 135 gallons per day, about a one-third decrease in use.[3]

Aquifer Water Level Determines Drought Restrictions

Water security of the growing San Antonio region depends on careful water management of the Edwards Aquifer. SAWS' drought restrictions tie the level of required water conservation to the groundwater level of the Edwards Aquifer. The lower its water level, the more stringent the drought restrictions become, particularly relating to the amount and frequency of allowable outdoor water use. Drought-level triggers approved by the San Antonio City Council in 2009 were as follows:

- **Stage One Alert** begins when the Aquifer level reaches 660 feet above mean sea level.
- **Stage Two Alert** begins when the Aquifer level drops to 650 feet above mean sea level.
- **Stage Three Alert** begins when the Aquifer level declines to 640 feet above mean sea level.
- **Stage Four Alert** may be declared at the discretion of the city manager — as the most severe drought alert — after a Stage Three Alert has been issued.[4]

By July 2009, San Antonio had experienced the driest 22-month period on record. In April and June of 2009, declining Edwards Aquifer levels triggered Stage One and then Stage Two Drought Alerts. Owing to customers' compliance with water use restrictions, SAWS withdrew 23 percent less water from the Edwards Aquifer in June 2009 than in June 2008.[5] By linking the level of the Edwards Aquifer to the level of drought restrictions, San Antonio clearly conveys — an obvious but often obscured fact — that people's current water use choices directly influence the future availability of water resources. The good news: major rains ended the drought in September, 2009.

Commercial Water Conservation Programs

SAWS estimates that commercial customers account for 10 percent of its client base and 40 percent of its annual water sales. Beyond widely practiced commercial building toilet rebates and large-scale retrofit rebates, SAWS pioneered a number of unique water conservation services and programs designed for commercial customers.

- **Commercial Cooling Tower Audit:**[6] SAWS cooling tower audit is free for customers with cooling towers and chilled-water systems. The auditor conducts an onsite evaluation of the condition and performance of the overall building cooling system, prepares a written audit report and holds a follow-up meeting with the property owner to review the audit results.
- **Certified WaterSaver Program — Car Washes:**[7] In 1997, SAWS created the country's first certified car-wash program that defined new water conservation standards for existing and proposed car-wash facilities. Beyond saving and reusing potable water, the SAWS WaterSaver Car Wash Program provides community recognition and financial incentives for program participants.

- **Certified WaterSaver Program — Restaurants:**[8] This restaurant certification program has three basic requirements: all pre-rinse spray valves must use no more than 1.6 gallons per minute, all toilets must use no more than 1.6 gallons per flush and all ice machines must be air-cooled. SAWS aggressively markets the business case for this WaterSaver program to restaurant owners by emphasizing the ongoing water utility savings, along with entirely free equipment upgrades and positive publicity.

By labeling and certifying water conservation within the commercial sector, SAWS seeks to promote water conservation as a credible business activity and means of brand development among San Antonio's increasingly water-conscious populace. Karen Guz is the conservation director for SAWS. She emphasizes what it takes to achieve permanent conservation practices in a very large and diverse city.

> There isn't any one program that drives the collective community to lower its consumption. There are programs that in any given year account for what I call secure or permanent savings. In the mix of programs every year, we always have retrofits. There's always a secure savings you can get by doing retrofits of older appliances. We can be fairly confident of the quantity of savings from those efforts because it's not hard to manage that data. So we always have those programs in our mix, but we recognize that a huge quantity of the water that is used within our customer base is behavior-dependent and always will be. If we neglect that behavior component, we may incrementally drop the indoor consumption by a steady amount, but then, as the weather gets hot and dry, the amount of water that would be used in outdoor consumption [for irrigation] would overwhelm the savings that we had gained from indoor savings.[9]

One strategy people often recommend is to have a conservation pricing structure, which SAWS has adopted. Guz says that approach is not always the primary motivation for conservation:

> We think the pricing structure motivates people to change their behavior somewhat. *You can motivate some people on price and not others.* We have a fairly progressive price structure already, and we'd like to make it more progressive. We already have a four-tier residential price system that charges quite a bit more at the top tier than the first tier. That is an

influence on some people, in that if you can stay under the top tier or even in the first two tiers, your water bill will be significantly cheaper. For other people the opportunity to do the right thing by conserving is more influential than the cost of their water.

SAWS also recognizes that the cost of getting new water supplies is vastly more expensive than conservation. Guz says,

> Saving water is the cheapest water we're going to get as a water system. We know that we're going to grow. More people are coming to San Antonio. Our primary supply is an aquifer that's highly regulated, so all other additional supplies we can add are very expensive. We will be adding some supplies, but to minimize those extreme costs and keep our rates reasonable, we know we have to maximize what we already have. That's where those ambitious conservation goals come from.

One final note is that cities need to move beyond crisis management into long-term conservation programs. According to Guz,

> *There's a very clear distinction between drought management and conservation.* We were in the throes of a drought this past summer and had to very firmly require customers to do certain things, so that we could cut our discretionary water use by quite a bit in a short time. When we do water conservation programs, it's long-term and not just targeted at discretionary water use. It's targeted at every water use, and we're hoping that the vast majority of it is proactive and positive and leads to improved efficiencies.

San Antonio's experience shows that a multiyear drought can be successfully managed by employing a full range of conservation tools, including regulations, pricing and public education.

Los Angeles

Los Angeles, the nation's second-largest city, is located in a semi-arid region with about 16 inches of annual rainfall. (Figure 14.2) The Los Angeles Department of Water and Power (LADWP), the largest municipal utility in the nation, delivers water and electricity to more than 3.8 million residents and businesses.[10] This revenue-producing agency receives no tax support and redirects five percent of its annual water revenues to the City's general fund.

Figure 14.2 Los Angeles is the largest urban area in the country dependent on extremely variable rainfall and long-distance water transfers.

During the 2007–2008 fiscal year, LADWP customers bought approximately 199 billion gallons of water and used an average of 144 gallons per person per day. LADWP's water supply is divided among four water sources: The Los Angeles Aqueduct (water from the Owens Valley in the eastern Sierra Nevada Mountains) supplies 35 percent of the city's water; the Metropolitan Water District of Southern California supplies 53 percent; groundwater supplies 11 percent, and recycled water (for irrigation) supplies 1 percent.[11]

Los Angeles Annual Rainfall Varies Dramatically

Rainfall in Los Angeles is highly seasonal and quite variable from year to year.[12] Even though Los Angeles relies upon imported water from Northern California and the Colorado River for 88 percent of its needs, these sources are also subject to the same variability. This is typical of most cities in the West and Southwest and complicates the job of planning for long-term water supply.

Current Water Conservation Builds upon Past Success

Owing to sustained drought conditions over the past 20 years and the introduction of water conservation measures in the 1990s, Los Angeles uses the same amount of water today as 25 years ago, despite a population increase of more than one million people. This is a huge achievement for a city this size. LADWP estimates that the city has saved more than 670 billion gallons since 1990 (more than two million acre-feet) through its water conservation programs, including the use of subsidies to encourage the installation of more than 1.27 million ultra-low-flush toilets.[13]

In 2009, Los Angeles continued to face serious drought and water-supply challenges from below average rainfall and reduced water storage supply throughout California. On June 1, 2009, the LADWP introduced a mandatory water conservation ordinance, shortage-year water rates and a Water Conservation Team as part of an aggressive conservation strategy to promote near-term water savings.

Water Conservation Ordinance

The following water-related activities are banned under Los Angeles' 2009 Phase III Water Conservation Ordinance:

- Use of sprinklers on any day other than Monday and Thursday.
- Use of water to wash any hard surfaces such as sidewalks, walkways, driveways or parking areas, unless flushing is needed to protect health and safety.
- Use of water to clean, fill or maintain decorative fountains unless the water is part of a recirculation system.
- Serving water to customers in restaurants unless requested.
- Allowing leaks from any pipe or fixture to go unrepaired.
- Washing a vehicle without a self-closing, shutoff device.
- Watering during periods of rain.
- Irrigating landscaping between the hours of 9 AM and 4 PM.
- Watering outdoors for more than 15 minutes per watering station.
- Allowing runoff onto streets and gutters from excessive watering.
- Using single-pass cooling systems in new buildings.
- Installing systems without water recirculation in new car wash and commercial laundry systems.
- Landscaping large areas without rain sensors that shut off irrigation systems during wet weather.[14]

Water Rates

The LADWP has a two-tier water rate structure that applies to all customer classes. The first includes pass-through costs (or adjustment factors) for water procurement, quality assurance and security that result in a baseline water rate that is then applied to the customer's first-tier usage block, a formula-driven water budget based on historic use patterns.

Unlike residential customers, whose usage is rather consistent, commercial customers vary tremendously in how much water they use. Accordingly, the methods used to promote water conservation in the commercial sector must account for those differences. A traditional commercial customer's first-tier water rate is $1.421 per hundred cubic feet (HCF, the same as CCF), and the usage block is 125 percent of their average consumption for the preceding winter (December through March).[15] If a commercial customer's water consumption surpasses the first-tier usage block, their second-tier water rate remains $1.421/HCF during the low-use season between November 1 and May 31; but spikes to $3.280/HCF during the high-demand season between June 1 and October 31, an increase of 130 percent.[16]

Under *Shortage Year Water Rates*, first-tier allotments are reduced by 15 percent for all LADWP customers. For multifamily, commercial and industrial customers, the first-tier water budget is based on a percentage of the customer's maximum daily average during winter (December through March) over the past three years, reduced by 15 percent. The reduced allocation is applied year-round.

The Water Conservation Team
The Water Conservation Team made its debut in Los Angeles as the "Drought Busters" in 1990, as a means for the City to enforce the Water Conservation Ordinance. The program was very successful contributing to the city's 34 percent decrease in water usage during the early 1990s. Beginning June, 2009, the Water Conservation Team patrolled the city's neighborhoods to identify wasteful uses of water, educate customers about the importance of water conservation and distribute devices such as low-flow shower heads and faucet aerators. The Water Conservation Team may be tasked with citing offenders under the Water Conservation Ordinance if drought conditions persist or worsen.[17]

Permanent Water Conservation Measures
for the Commercial and Industry Sector
Through building ordinances and sustained incentive programs, the LADWP strives to make water conservation an industry standard within the commercial built environment. The following ordinances and programs in Los Angeles illustrate the broadening scope and scale of water conservation measures being implemented in cities around the country.

Water-Efficient Fixture, New and Upgraded Building Ordinance: In July 2009, the Los Angeles City Council unanimously approved a building ordinance requiring all new buildings to have low-flow faucets, toilets, urinals and shower heads as part of the city's Green Building program. Water-efficient devices also will be required when property owners replace their plumbing fixtures. LADWP officials estimate that this water conservation ordinance will reduce water consumption in new buildings by 20 percent.[18] The specific requirements of this ordinance are as follows:

- Maximum flush volume of toilets may not exceed 1.28 gallons per flush (current requirement is 1.6 gallons per flush).
- Urinals may not exceed 0.5 gallons per flush (current requirement is 1.0 gallons per flush); beginning October 1, 2010, requirement changes to 0.125 gallons (one pint) per flush.
- All faucets in public restrooms must be self-closing. The flow rate for all indoor faucets shall be 2.2 gallons per minute except as follows:
  - The maximum flow rate for private or private use lavatory faucets shall be 1.5 gallons per minute.
  - The maximum flow rate for public or public use lavatory faucets, other than metering faucets, shall be 0.5 gallons per minute. Metering faucets shall deliver not more than 0.25 gallons of water per cycle.
  - The maximum flow rate for a pre-rinse spray valve installed in a commercial kitchen shall not exceed 1.6 gallons per minute.
- Shower heads shall not exceed 2.0 gallons per minute.
- Cooling towers must be operated at a minimum of 5.5 cycles of concentration and use of single-pass cooling towers for air conditioning is prohibited.
- All residential dishwashers shall not use more than 5.8 gallons per cycle, and must be ENERGY STAR rated.
- All high-efficiency plumbing fixtures shall be listed or labeled by a listing agency such as International Association of Plumbing and Mechanical Officials (IAPMO).[19]

Technical Assistance Program (TAP): TAP is a financial incentive program offering commercial customers in Los Angeles up to $250,000 for the installation of pre-approved equipment and products that demonstrate water savings. The incentive is calculated at $1.75 per 1,000 gallons of water saved during a two-year period, not to exceed the installation cost of the project. Eligible projects must save a minimum of 150,000 gallons of potable water during a two-year period.[20]

Retrofit on Resale Ordinance and Compliance: Since January 1999, all properties sold in Los Angeles have had to complete and file a Certification of Compliance (COC) with the LADWP verifying that the property owners:

- Replaced all non-water-conserving shower heads with low-flow models;
- Installed flush-reduction devices in all non-water conserving toilets.[21]

Save-A-Buck, Commercial Water Conservation Rebate Program: In partnership with the Metropolitan Water District, the LADWP offers cash rebates for a variety of water-saving technologies including high-efficiency toilets and urinals, weather-based irrigation controllers and cooling-tower conductivity controllers. However, owing to budgetary challenges, the program's commercial rebates were not available for much of 2009.[22] (See Table 14.1 for specific products and rebate values.)

Mandatory water conservation restrictions, changes in rate structures and replacement of older water-inefficient devices have all played key roles in helping Los Angeles meet its most recent water shortage challenges.

TABLE 14.1 Los Angeles Water Rebate Program[23]

Description	Retrofit Rebate Amount	New Construction Rebate Amount
High-efficiency (1.28 gpf) Toilet: replacing ULF* Toilet	$50	$50
High-efficiency Toilet: replacing non-ULF Toilet (≥3.5 gpf)	$300	N/A
Ultra-low-water (0.0–0.25 gpf) Urinal: retrofit replacing ≥1.5 gpf	$500	N/A
Ultra-low-water (0.0–0.25 gpf) Urinal: retrofit replacing <1.5 gpf	$250	$250
Cooling Tower pH/Conductivity Controller	$3,000	$3,000
Cooling Tower Conductivity Controller	$625	$625
High-efficiency Commercial Clothes Washer	$430	$430
Air-cooled Ice Machine	$300	$300
Steam Sterilizer Retrofit	$2,300/ Device	$2,300/ Device
Connectionless Food Steamer	$600/ Compartment	$600/ Compartment
Pre-rinse Self-closing Spray Head	$60	N/A
Dry Vacuum Pump	$125/ Horsepower	$125/ Horsepower
Large Rotary Nozzle Retrofit	$13/Head	$13/Head
Weather-based Irrigation Controller	$25/Station	$25/Station
Rotating Sprinkler Nozzle for Irrigation	$5/Nozzle	$5/Nozzle
Synthetic Turf	$1.00 per square foot	$1.00 per square foot
Pressurized Waterbrooms	$150	$150

* ultra-low-flow

Austin Water Utility

Austin Water Utility (AWU) provides water to 850,000 retail and whole-sale customers in central Texas, drawing its water from the Lower Colorado River (Texas) watershed and reservoirs managed by the Lower Colorado River Authority (LCRA). Owned by the City of Austin, AWU is widely regarded as a leader in utility-scale water conservation owing to its *combined use of rebates, education and regulation* to reduce per capita water usage. The City of Austin's Water Conservation Program, first developed in 1984, has been refined by initiatives such as the Water Conservation Task Force, a group established in 2006 to reduce the city's water use by one percent per year over ten years.[24] In Austin, water conservation has evolved from a crisis response to rapid growth and water infrastructure limitations, to a critical, long-term strategy to meet the region's future water needs.[25]

Worsening Drought Conditions
and Regional Comparisons

In 2008 and 2009, Austin's main source of water — the Highland Lakes (Lake Travis and Lake Buchanan) — lost roughly half of their water supply, prompting some City officials to challenge the modest ten percent per decade water conservation target established in 2006. Water conservation advocates point to the more aggressive water conservation measures and results in San Antonio, just 80 miles south of Austin, where the average resident uses nearly one-third less water. A proposed $500 million water treatment plant, which AWU officials claim is necessary to avoid water storages as early as 2014, has also spurred questions about the City's near-term allocation of resources and commitment to water conservation.[26]

Commercial Process and Equipment Improvements

Approximately 35 percent of all AWU water sales are to customers in the Commercial, Industrial and Institutional (CII) sectors. CII customers are eligible for a free water conservation analysis for all their buildings and facilities, including inspection of cooling towers and a review of water use in production processes and building cooling systems.[27] AWU offers rebates of up to $100,000 to CII customers for installing new equipment and processes that conserve water at existing facilities.

Eligible projects that may also qualify for city property or sales tax exemptions and Energy Conservation Rebates from Austin Energy include:

- Capturing onsite sources of water such as air-conditioner condensate, rainwater or foundation drain water to use for landscape irrigation or cooling tower makeup,

- Reuse of high-quality rinse water and
- Installing water-saving equipment or processes.[28]

CII projects qualifying for this rebate must generate documentable water savings of at least 300 gallons per day, and users must agree to keep them in place for at least five years. Participants must also seek pre-approval of the project and agree to a post-installation inspection by City staff to verify proper installation and operation.[29] This type of performance-based incentive will become more important in the future for all water utilities needing to promote water conservation.

Commercial Toilet and Urinal Rebates Programs

AWU offers a range of commercial rebates for installing efficient plumbing fixtures such as high-efficiency toilets (HETs) and low-water-using urinals.

- *Commercial Toilet Rebate Program* offers rebates for qualifying tank-type and flush-valve toilet combinations. Rebate amounts vary based on the age of existing toilets and the type of replacement toilet installed.[30] For instance, replacing pre-1994 toilets with qualifying HET models can earn a rebate up to $200 per toilet.
- *Urinal Replacement Program* provides rebates for replacing "blowout" type urinals using at least 3.0 gallons per flush (gpf) that cannot be converted to 1.6 gpf or lower by changing the flush valve or flush valve diaphragm. Up to $175 is available to replace both the urinal and flush valve with a urinal using 0.5 gpf or less.[31] Austin's plumbing code currently does not allow the installation of water-free urinals.[32]
- *Commercial Free Toilet Program* offers water-efficient round-bowl tank-type toilets (Niagara EcoLogic) and Sloan Crown flush valves on qualifying projects.[33]

Water IQ: Know Your Water Campaign

The LCRA and the City of Austin were the first Central Texas public agencies to implement the "Water IQ: Know Your Water" campaign, developed by EnviroMedia Social Marketing.[34] It features an online water IQ test, experiential marketing and printed, billboard, radio and television advertising that promote clever water-conservation slogans. This ongoing water education campaign is based on research that revealed that the more people know about their water source, the more compelled they are to conserve.[35] Another water conservation campaign in North Texas helped curb projected peak-day water consumption by about 200 million gallons per day in 2006, with a three-month average decrease of 19 percent. Austin's campaign also doubled the number of people who could accurately identify their natural source of water.[36]

Epilogue: Commercial Toilet Rebates

In December 2009, Austin Water Utility halted a program of rebates, with an average of $200, for replacing older toilets in apartments and businesses with water-efficient models, after tens of thousands of applications were filed in a matter of weeks. The Austin City Council feared that the popularity of the toilet replacement program would crowd out all other programs, including water-efficient washing machines, efficient irrigation systems, rainwater collection barrels and low-flow toilets for single-family homes, so it "closed the lid" on the toilet rebate program.[37] The success of the rebate program shows that "free," or nearly free, is still a very good way to motivate people to replace older water-using devices with more efficient alternatives.

East Bay Municipal Utility District, Oakland, California

East Bay Municipal Utility District (EBMUD), a public water agency in the San Francisco Bay area, serves approximately 1.3 million people in a 325-square-mile area that includes the cities of Oakland, Berkeley and Alameda. Average water use is about 170 gallons per capita per day (gpcd). The utility's water is drawn from the 577-square-mile protected watershed of the Mokelumne River, which flows from the western slopes of the Sierra Nevada toward San Francisco Bay.[38]

A Tradition of Water Conservation Leadership

In 1994, EBMUD was the first water utility in the US to develop a water conservation master plan. The plan established the framework for the water conservation programs and supplemental supply initiatives in place today. Even earlier, beginning in 1974, EBMUD produced water conservation resources for teachers and students through Project WATER (Water Awareness Through Education and Research).[39]

Water Conservation Services and Rebates

Today EBMUD offers a range of water conservation rebates and services to its customers, including free onsite water audits conducted by EBMUD staff to evaluate property water use and recommend specific water-efficiency strategies. Free self-survey kits are also available to customers. EBMUD water conservation rebates include:

- *High Efficiency Toilets (HET) Rebate Program:* As of July 2009, EBMUD customers could receive a $50 rebate for replacing an older toilet using

3.5 gpf or higher with a qualifying WaterSmart HET using less than 1.28 gpf. Residential customers are limited to two HET rebates per living unit. There is no rebate limit for commercial water users.

- *WaterSmart Commercial Clothes Washer Rebate Program:* EBMUD offers $150 per qualifying WaterSmart washer for multifamily properties and other businesses and $250 per qualifying washer for coin-operated laundromats. EBMUD has found that replacing conventional commercial clothes washers with high-efficiency washers can reduce water use by 30 to 50 percent and energy use by 50 percent.[40]
- *Generic Commercial Rebates:* Water-efficiency improvements such as retrofitting cooling towers and replacing water-cooled with air-cooled equipment are also eligible for rebates of up to 50 percent of the installation cost. The main prerequisite for this rebate is that the contractor or property owner demonstrate the predictable and measurable future water savings that will result from the project.[41]

2008 Drought Management Program

In response to record drought conditions, in May 2008 EBMUD customers were tasked with improving their water conservation and recycling efforts. During the drought, EBMUD sought a 15 percent overall reduction in water use, with specific goals for different types of customers.[42,43] Table 14.2 shows the reduction goals and actual performance during the first five months of the drought emergency. You can see that irrigation and commercial users were the laggards at that point.

The drought program approved by EBMUD's Board of Directors prohibited the following:

- Using water for decorative ponds, lakes and fountains except those that recycle the water.
- Washing vehicles with hoses, unless they have shutoff nozzles.
- Washing sidewalks, patios and similar hardscape surfaces.
- Irrigating outdoors on consecutive days or more than three days a week (with recommended watering in the evening or before dawn).
- Lawn or garden watering resulting in excessive runoff.
- Sewer and hydrant flushing and washing streets with potable (drinking) water.
- Use of potable water for construction activities if alternatives are available.

Other EBMUD Drought Management Program measures included:
- Water conservation advertising and media campaign.

- New staff for water conservation educational outreach and onsite water audits.
- A new online drought help center for customers.
- Rebates for residential and commercial plumbing fixture upgrades.[45]

Water Rate Adjustments Encourage Conservation

Drought water rates included a ten percent increase in volume charges for all customers (except recycled water customers) and a $2 surcharge for each unit (748 gallons or 100 cubic feet, CCF) of water used above a customer's individual allocation. Allocations were based on use in each billing period (bimonthly for most customers) over the previous three years, when available.[46]

The Drought Management Program established a 15 percent overall conservation goal (Table 14.2), and by September of 2008, EBMUD customers had reduced water use by about 11 percent. EBMUD declared an end to the drought emergency and mandatory rationing effective July 1, 2009, with drought rates phased out during July and August. The District asked all of its customers to voluntarily conserve by 10 percent compared to normal years to help keep its supply reservoirs full.[47]

Best Practices: The California Urban Water Conservation Council

The California Urban Water Conservation Council (CUWCC) is a partnership of water suppliers, environmental groups and other interested parties focused on conserving California's water resources. In 1991, the CUWCC's Memorandum of Understanding (MOU) was signed by 100 urban water agencies and environmental groups. It is intended to "expedite implementation of reasonable water conservation measures in urban areas; and

TABLE 14.2 EBMUD Water Conservation Goals and Actual Performance[44]

Customer Group	Water Use Reduction Goal	October 2008 Actual Reduction (after 5 months)
Single-family Residential	19%	18%
Multifamily Residential	11%	11%
Irrigation	30%	21%
Commercial	12%	8%
Institutional	9%	8%
Industrial	5%	13%

establish assumptions for use in calculating estimates of reliable future
water conservation savings resulting from proven and reasonable conservation measures."[48]

CUWCC has since developed and implemented a list of Best Management Practices (BMP) for water conservation. To account for new technologies and trends, these water best practices are reviewed and updated
on a regular basis by representatives of the organization's membership base
comprising more than 400 members. Most of the major water utilities in
California, such as the cities of Los Angeles and San Francisco, and large
water-related environmental groups, manufacturers and trade associates
are CUWCC signatories.

Chris Brown, executive director of the CUWCC, recounts how the list
of BMPs came about:

> The original list of BMPs was 16 long, and it was just a list: ultra-low-
> flush toilets, shower heads, outdoor water audits, landscape water
> audits, etc. In 1997, the BMPs were further fleshed out, and this is the
> structure that is currently used today, and that became the template now
> used by planning agencies around the world. Essentially it starts with
> an implementation section, which is really just a description of what
> goes into the particular practice. It has a list of elements that go into a
> particular practice. For example, if it's water loss control for a utility,
> then that will include doing an annual water audit of that utility, the leak
> detection and repair programs, and it will include the way it evaluates
> water losses financially, to determine the economic value of the water
> loss. It will include customer assistance as some sort of information pro-
> gram that alerts customers if the utility personnel discover a leak on the
> customer side of the meter. Even though the utility would be making
> money off of that leak, it's the responsibility of the utility in reducing
> water waste to notify customers when they notice a leak.[49]

Upon signing the MOU, water suppliers agree to implement the CUWCC's
Best Management Practices and to state their performance on the BMP reporting website. The structure of each BMP includes an implementation
schedule, documentation requirements and pre-established water-saving
calculation assumptions. The CII BMP calls for water savings of ten percent
from baseline water use over a ten-year period by implementing a combination of locally appropriate water conservation measures. A water agency
may also choose to implement an alternative water-savings measure under
the Flex Track Menu as long as the agency demonstrates the measure's sus-

tained benefits.[50] CUWCC represents the leading edge of water conservation coordination in the US. Beyond the comprehensive water conservation BMPs and documentation systems, CUWCC provides training, technical resources, product information, publications and a means for water stakeholders to help shape the water conservations measures they themselves must follow.

Comparative Water Policies

Table 14.3 shows comparative water policies across the various jurisdictions profiled in this book: Atlanta, San Diego, Los Angeles, Austin, East Bay (California), Las Vegas and San Antonio. These include a range of representative programs, including regulatory, tax, economic and financial incentives for water conservation practices in the non-residential sector. These are often supplemented with public education and technical incentives. Many of these programs have been tested in various droughts and water shortages and are "ready for prime time" at other water utilities.

Summary

In earlier chapters, we reviewed Australia's drought experience to show that remarkable water use reductions in cities are possible, and we have seen the same percentage reductions under crisis conditions in a number of cities and states in the US. Chris Brown of the CUWCC says that there are common features of those that seem to be ahead of the pack:

> They have a least three elements that are in place that are mutually reinforcing. There is a price structure that clearly has a reward for conservation, so it's tiered, or there's some sort of structure that says: The more water you use, the more you pay for it. They have a clear communication program that tells customers both what the financial rewards are for using less water and about the overarching water conservation goals. And three, the conservation message ties the rate structure and the financial reward together with the utility's program — the specific things that customers can do. Typically that will include indoor programs like converting clothes washers and toilets and fixing leaks. It will also include an outdoor component which will either be converting the landscape or using the least amount of water necessary for a turf or traditional landscape.[51]

TABLE 14.3 Water Conservation Programs at Seven Major US Utilities

	Water Utilities and Districts						
Commercial Industrial and Institutional (CII): Water Conservation Strategies	Austin Water Utility (AWU)	East Bay Municipal Utility District (EBMUD)	Los Angeles Dept. of Water and Power (LADWP)	City of Atlanta and Metro Water District	San Antonio Water System (SAWS)	City of San Diego and SDCWA	Southern Nevada Water Authority (SNWA)
Rebates and Incentives							
Water-efficient Fixtures (Including: Toilets, Shower heads, Faucet Aerators)	X	X	X	X	X	X	X
Water-efficient Urinals	X		X			X	X
Major Equipment Replacement or Retrofit (Including: Cooling Towers)	X	X	X		X	X	X
Irrigation Equipment (Including: Weather-based Controllers)	X	X	X	No Incentive; Req by law		X	X (Plus: lawn removal rebate)
Commercial Clothes Washers	X	X	X			X	
Water-efficient Cleaning Equipment (Including: Water Brooms and Rinse Nozzles)		X	X	No Incentive; Req by law		X	
Rainwater Harvesting Equipment	X						
Regulations							
Outdoor Watering Schedule and Restrictions (Drought or Permanent)	Permanent	Drought	Drought	Permanent	Permanent	Drought	Permanent
Retrofit Upon Resale Ordinance			X			X	
New Landscaping Limits							X
Water Waste Ordinance	X	X	X	X	X	X	X
Technical Assistance							
Cooling Tower Audits	X	X	X	X	X		
Landscape Water Use Audits	X	X		X	X	X	
Education							
Workshops for Commercial Properties	X	X	X	X	X	X	X
Business Certificates and Labeling					X		X
Rainwater Harvesting	X			X	X	X	
Conservation-Driven Water Pricing							
Block Rate Structure			X	X	X		X
Peak and Off Peak	X		X				

Ten Steps
to Preventing
the Next Urban
Water Crisis

Thousands have lived without love,
not one without water.

— W.H. Auden[1]

PREVENTING THE NEXT urban water crisis will take a combination of measures that include introducing new technology, changes in water pricing, environmental considerations, financing infrastructure upgrades, new institutional arrangements (about who controls water supply) and inducing behavioral changes in people who use water — you and me. In this chapter, I propose a *10-step program* of measures that water activists can unite behind, from the immediately possible to long-term fixes that will depend on the water issues in a specific region, as well as local politics. Many of these measures will lead to "green jobs" in the water industry: doing home and building water audits and renovations, installing rainwater and graywater harvesting systems, etc. The 10-step program (Table 15.1) encompasses actions that can be taken by individuals, companies, non-profits, government and the design and construction community, with each action leading to water and energy savings.

Table 15.1 The 10-Step Program

Measure	Potential Savings*
1. Reduce water use in non-residential buildings	20 to 40 percent
2. Reduce home water use	20 to 40 percent
3. Recycle and reuse graywater, rainwater and blackwater	10 to 30 percent
4. Reduce landscaping water use, both residential and CII	20 to 40 percent
5. Build water conservation pricing into rate structures	20 to 35 percent
6. Rebates and incentives for conservation retrofits	5 to 15 percent
7. Change building codes to allow water recycling	5 to 30 percent
8. Train green plumbers to identify and install water-efficient fixtures and strategies	N/A
9. Use WaterSense homes, fixtures and appliances	5 to 20 percent
10. Meter and measure water use, eliminate water loss in distribution	5 to 30 percent

* Not all savings are cumulative, as each reduces demand.

Understanding and Implementing the 10-Step Program

1. The first step is to design, construct and operate non-residential buildings to reduce water use, including reducing energy use (in large buildings, this reduces water use in cooling towers). The US Green Building Council's LEED program, the "gold standard' for green buildings, requires at least 20 percent water savings to get a project certification from its various rating systems. The LEED for Existing Buildings Operations and Maintenance (LEED-EBOM) program specifically rewards water metering, cooling tower water alternatives, fixture change-outs and water use reduction in landscaping.[2]

2. Reduce water use in the home, starting with water audits, installing efficient technologies and changes in behavior. This is the most important thing you can do as an individual. Learn how much water you use and how you are billed for it; compare your water use with local averages; find out what fixtures you can replace to reduce water use and take advantage of local water utility incentives. Do the easy stuff first: shower heads, faucets and toilets. Then look at dishwashers and laundry water use. Finally, look at graywater and rainwater reuse for irrigation. Home water audits include an analysis of your behavior as well as the fixtures and appliances in the home.[3]

3. Recycle, capture and reuse water more than once, the basic principle behind graywater, rainwater and blackwater recycling technology and

practice. In Chapters 7 and 13, there are examples of "whole systems" thinking in examining the entire water cycle for opportunities to reduce, reuse and recycle water. The key is to match water quality of the supply source with required water quality at the point of demand.[4]

4. Reduce water use in landscaping both homes and buildings, with effective irrigation technology and revised plant choices, which emphasize native and adapted vegetation. I treated this subject extensively in Chapter 11. For more information on home landscaping water conservation, contact any local Extension Service, typically associated in each state with a land-grant public university.

5. Water pricing should be structured so that rates are steeply tiered, resulting in significant economic penalties for water waste and excessive water use. This brings the marketplace into the picture and avoids having to institute severe restrictions on individual choice and employ "water cops" during drought emergencies.

6. Water agencies should focus on conservation measures first; these usually reduce water use by 15 percent or more. Water agencies should provide cash rebates for efficient technologies and continue public education to shift behavior.[5] Amy Vickers, an engineer and author of a widely cited treatise on efficient water use,[6] has been a leading US water expert for the past two decades. She believes amazing amounts of conservation are possible with relatively straightforward approaches:

> Overall for most urban US water systems, through reducing infrastructure leakage, imposing reasonable outdoor watering restrictions and other conservation measures, most urban systems potentially could reduce their total demand anywhere from 25 to 45 percent today. For example, look at the metropolitan Boston system, the Massachusetts Water Resource Authority (MWRA) [Vickers worked there early in her career], which serves over 40 cities and towns and the metropolitan Boston area with water and sewer services. In the late 1980s, the MWRA system was using over 300 million gallons a day. Now they're using about 200 million gallons per day. They've reduced their total demand by over 35 percent.[7]

7. To accommodate new water technologies, building codes need to be changed, without losing their essential focus on protecting public health and safety.

8. The entire plumbing industry, more than 40,000 plumbers in the US,[8] needs to be trained in green plumbing practices. By working with water agencies and community colleges, many new jobs can be created by

retrofitting tens of millions of inefficient fixtures across the country and introducing new efficiency technologies.

9. Rapid adoption of new WaterSense home labels and other green build-ing labels such as LEED and ENERGY STAR will directly and indirectly reduce water use. This means every new home and building should se-cure a rating from a nationally accepted third-party certification pro-gram.

10. Meter and measure every aspect of water use. "What gets measured, gets managed." As technology becomes available, plan to use the Internet to get real-time data about your water use. Knowing your daily, even hourly water use, in a simple readout format, can affect behavior, so that water use practices can change quickly without waiting for monthly (or in some cases, even quarterly) water bills to provide the data. According to Troy Aichele, an experienced mechanical contractor,

> Sloan Valve is working on point-of-use measurement systems, to measure how often a shower, a water closet or a sink is used, along with other things like soap dispensers. They'll tie that in with the building management system, and that way you'll know when a faucet is leaking, or you'll know when a faucet is left on, or you'll know exactly how often a fixture is used, instead of using some [general] sort of guide. With that data, you can manage water use much better. Also you'll see where your high-use areas are, so you can concentrate on these areas and figure out ways to minimize that water use.[9]

Let's look at a few of these issues in more detail, beginning with water pric-ing and continuing with water-efficiency audits, green plumbing codes, green plumbers and WaterSense labels for appliances, fixtures and homes. The subject of water is vast, and the level of interest in water matters is rising rapidly, so the available information is very fluid and in a state of rapid flux. Appendix II presents a number of resources you can use to stay informed.

Water Conservation and Water Pricing

Water agencies need to employ incentives for installing more water-efficient equipment, but they can cut the costs of incentives by adopting rate struc-tures that reward conservation behavior. Every study of adoption of new technology shows that the relative economic advantage is the primary driv-ing force for adopting new products and services.[10] In my own experience, there has to be an economic gain of about 25 percent to really jump-start

conservation efforts. Up to this point, water prices have been too low to encourage conservation, especially without steeply graduated water pricing.

In 1998, I studied this phenomenon in depth in Portland, Oregon, a
metropolitan area of about 1.5 million people that had undergone a significant water crisis during the spring and summer of 1992.[11] I concluded that
the standard drought response of water rationing was an inefficient way to
deal with pending long-term water shortages.

A fundamental tenet of economics is that the more something costs,
the fewer units of it are likely to be demanded. This basic law of supply and
demand is taught in every beginning economics class. From the standpoint
of water supply, this law means there is no such thing as an absolute demand for water (beyond basic physiological requirements); rather, there is
an economic level of demand at various prices. Therefore, water demand
can, within wide ranges, be controlled through the simple mechanism of
raising prices to the largest or most inefficient users, and effectively communicating the increased prices. Increased costs for water should then lead
to changes in the behavior of water users, such as reductions in "careless"
consumption and increases in investments in water-conserving technologies. Decreases in water use per capita depend heavily upon the relative
cost of water consumption, the available alternatives for changing use patterns, the ease of implementing new technology and the perceived benefits,
both economic and social, of reducing usage. The Australian examples in
this book clearly indicate that urban consumers can meet their basic water
needs with less than half of current US usage levels.

European and North American water consumption research clearly
demonstrates the influence of price on water use. Studies show that the demand for water will decrease a certain percentage based on a certain percentage increase in price, a "price elasticity" of −0.10 to −0.35.[12] That means
a 10 percent increase in water prices (in real terms) would decrease water
use by 1.0 percent to 3.5 percent. (Similarly, a 100 percent price increase
would reduce water use by 10 percent to 35 percent.) Other studies verify
these findings; a 1992 analysis of the history of Portland area water demand
found a 34 percent decrease in per capita use for each 100 percent increase
in water prices.[13]

Beginning in the early 1990s, water customers of the Irvine Ranch Water
District (IRWD) in Southern California showed similar results. Responding
to a drought with an aggressive tiered-rate water structure, the District was
able to reduce water demand significantly without rationing.[14] It successfully implemented an allocation-based conservation rate structure.[15] Since
then, per-acre water consumption dropped significantly while the quality of

landscapes within IRWD's service area improved, according to the District. Between 1992 and 2005, the average landscape water use decreased from 4.2 acre-feet per acre per year to 1.9 acre-feet per acre per year — a 55 percent reduction. From 2001 to 2006, irrigated areas in the district increased 280 percent, but total landscape water usage only increased 70 percent. Today, the average water use in Orange County is 190 gallons per person per day while the average use in IRWD's service area is only 90 gallons per person per day — 52 percent less.[16]

Why mention rate structures so many times? As long as it has a social equity dimension, in which the lowest water user essentially pays very little for basic household water use, *pricing is a much fairer, faster, more efficient and more effective way to ration supply than imposing equal restrictions on everyone.* However, it takes planning to induce conservation behavior over many years, but planning is something water agencies are typically very good at, since it takes years, even decades to bring new water supplies to the tap. The planning efforts and programs should include education, technical assistance, effective rebates and financial incentives, which are all more effective when they complement a well-designed rate structure.

Some economists want to go beyond steeply tiered rate structures, with a "some for free, pay for more" approach, with free allocations based strictly on the number of people in a home or apartment, not how much land someone owns.[17] This system might even be an improvement on the block rate structure, but it doesn't deal effectively with non-residential water users. Setting good rate structures is a complicated business, because utilities must receive enough revenue to cover their operating costs, and yet revenue (water use) is influenced by prices!

Water-efficiency Audits

Perhaps the most important measure that a home or business owner can take is to have a water audit performed. Before you can take corrective measures to reduce water consumption, you need to know how much water is being used, how much is being wasted and specifically by which fixtures, processes or appliances. That information allows you to set realistic goals for water consumption and to prepare a management and investment plan to reduce water use to meet your goals.

In January 2010, I had a water audit done for my home by a company called The Arizona Green Plumbers, trained and licensed by the Green-*Plumbers* USA organization.[18] The results were enlightening. First, there was a 50-question survey to analyze water use and develop some quantitative information. Then, the auditors surveyed plumbing equipment, measured flow rates and installed a recirculating hot water system for immediate savings. In many homes, they would change out toilets and install faucet aerators. The audit looked in detail at water use in the following areas:

- Outdoor water use, including any use of sprinklers or drip irrigation
- Behavioral water use, such as a swimming pool or car washing
- Interior water use, including kitchen, dishwashers, laundry, and bathrooms

A short time later, they presented the audit results, with a recommended set of measures that would result in an overall 12.5 percent savings, or $110 per year. These included: installing a front-loading ENERGY STAR washing machine, a graywater system for laundry wastewater and an ENERGY STAR dishwasher and replacing shower heads and faucet aerators. A key recommendation was to install a second water meter at the street, so I could separate irrigation water use from household consumption. In this way, I wouldn't be paying sewer charges (150% of the water costs) for irrigation water use, about two-thirds of my overall use in the southern Arizona desert.

Commercial Water Audits

Sydney Water, the municipal supplier in Australia's largest city, has been a global leader in efficient water management. Their publication on best practices outlines how water-efficiency audits should be conducted.[19] In my view, such audits represent an outstanding new business opportunity for entrepreneurs. In addition, by knowing more about your client's water usage than anyone else, you are in an excellent position to present investment opportunities that can lead to more work.

What's involved in a commercial water-efficiency audit? Typically it has six key objectives:

- Identify water use patterns
- Understand a building's water supply system
- Identify deficiencies in the system, including leaks and wastage (leaks can account for 20 to 30 percent of an older building's total water use)
- Identify water and energy conservation opportunities, including water reuse
- Benchmark water and energy use
- Develop water and energy use targets[20]

The ultimate purpose of a commercial water audit is to identify Key Performance Indicators (KPIs) for the building and to set specific water use reduction targets. KPIs might be based on water use per square foot per year (as shown in Table 5.1) or per employee per day. Water use targets can also be set for each major piece of equipment or each key activity, e.g., for cooling towers and for a commercial kitchen or restaurant in a building.

To reach KPI targets, a building owner or facility manager will probably have to invest in upgrades, considering costs, benefits, possible rebates and tenant support. As part of overall sustainability planning and reporting, a business or facility can report each year on progress toward meeting KPI targets, along with costs and benefits. As part of a process of continual improvement, you'll want to repeat the water audit on an annual or biennial basis.

Identifying leaks is especially important. In Sydney (with a climate similar to Los Angeles),[21] leaks are about 28 percent of an office building's total water consumption. The building is not only wasting water, it's also getting charged for sewage treatment that it doesn't need. In this case, the most sensible thing for a water agency to do, long before it even considers investing in new supply sources, is to go in and fix the leaks, perhaps sharing the cost with the building owner, on either a voluntary or mandatory basis.

Greening the Plumbing Code

Code issues often underlie failures to get approval for innovative approaches to reducing water use in buildings. This is not the case so much in the household sector, since many homeowners install graywater irrigation or rainwater reuse systems without securing a building permit, so the code never comes into play. Perhaps the most detailed study of code issues for green buildings was done by David Eisenberg and Sonja Persram for the Living Building Challenge.[22] Their study concluded:

> A classic example of conflicting regulatory goals relates to the regulations governing water and wastewater services for buildings. Though this is beginning to change, in most places all water entering a building is required to be potable water (drinking water quality) regardless of its intended use, and once used, it must be treated as blackwater (raw sewage) regardless of the quality. If there is an available sewer system, typically there is a legal requirement to connect to it, and if not, a requirement to install a water-based septic system. In most jurisdictions, toilet flushing using rainwater or graywater is prohibited. The result is that *in most places there is a legal requirement to intentionally pollute drinking water with human excrement.* Water pollution is clearly not a public good. The costs of dealing with this legally polluted water include

the creation of entire wastewater conveyance and treatment systems and reduced availability of clean, uncontaminated water. Yet, projects pursuing the Living Building Challenge prerequisite of net-zero water often find their desired solutions in conflict with the whole set of regulations governing water and wastewater.

Changing the codes is a time-consuming and often thankless task, yet it must be done. Jonathan Gray serves as vice chair of the Oregon State Plumbing Board, which has done more to advance the practice of commercial rainwater harvesting than just about any other state. He says,

> Here in Oregon, we've changed the graywater reuse code and methods. You can drink your rainwater in Oregon in your private house. The state plumbing board has worked really hard to change these things to make it easier. You can harvest graywater in a commercial project, treat it and use it to flush toilets. There's no [code] appeal necessary — all you have to do is follow the requirements for the alternative method.[23]

Gray says that sometimes code officials in local city and county jurisdictions may not choose to follow the state code on such things as graywater and water-free urinals. In that case, he says:

> Oregon also has a system where if you run into an official that is just being really stubborn about something you can file a claim with the state building codes division. It'll cost you $20, and you send it to the head plumbing guy and to the code official that you're having trouble with. He has ten days to respond, and then the state plumbing official will provide an interpretation, and then it's done. So we don't have to kowtow to every little "dictator" out there in the state who runs a plumbing division and wants it his way. That's where Oregon has really moved forward.

Oregon has moved ahead with permitting graywater and other alternatives to potable water use in buildings, and other states need to implement similar approaches so that there is uniformity across the country in code rulings and interpretations. In this way, plumbing product manufacturers, engineers, system designers and installers can bring innovative technologies to market and design systems without fear of code official rejections or requirements for costly (and unnecessary) changes.

The plumbing industry is also wrestling with how to address these issues, because, until the code situation is clarified, it's hard to justify spending millions of dollars to bring new products into the marketplace. Shawn Martin of the International Code Council (ICC)[24] describes it as a classic chicken-and-egg problem, because the codes and standards people don't want to go to the effort to write new rules unless there are products that will be certified to those rules. According to Martin,

> As for codes and regulations, we are seeing a few problems with the pro-cess of integrating some water-efficient systems and products into the building and regulatory process. What we don't have right now are firm universal standards for the quality of the water used for various applica-tions. Potable water quality is well-defined and regulated, but quality of non-potable water varies widely throughout the country. On top of that, water quality provisions that do exist for non-potable applications typi-cally only address health and safety, and do not address suitability for that application. Knowing suitability for use is essential to ensure proper and durable operation of devices connected to non-potable sources. For example, we know what the quality of water probably should look like to protect health and safety for toilet flushing, but what we don't encom-pass within that is appropriate water quality to prevent damage to the toilets themselves. For example, water must be of sufficient quality to avoid eroding or degrading the flappers or seals on flush valves at the bottom of the toilet tanks. This is critical to avoid leaks that can waste significant amounts of water. There is no standard that covers all aspects of non-potable water quality right now, and the lack of a standard is discouraging the use and acceptance of non-potable water for various applications in many areas of the country.[25]

The Green Plumbing and Mechanical Code

One of the two major building code bodies in the US, the International Association of Plumbing and Mechanical Officials (IAPMO), in 2010 pub-lished the *Green Plumbing and Mechanical Code Supplement* to its 2009 Uniform Plumbing & Mechanical Codes.[26] Seemingly arcane code issues may make your eyes glaze over, but they are critical to opening up a new world of possibilities for the use of reclaimed water from both onsite and off-site resources. The new *IAPMO Supplement* covers five key issues that needed resolution:

- Using alternative water sources correctly, including graywater
- Properly using high-efficiency plumbing products, such as water-free urinals

- Conserving hot water by changing piping layouts to reduce length of runs
- Conserving energy in HVAC systems, by integrating plumbing codes with leading energy conservation into the building codes
- Training and education in green plumbing systems[27]

Russ Chaney, executive director of IAPMO, speaks of the challenges of green plumbing:

> IAPMO produced what we're calling a *Green Plumbing & Mechanical Code Supplement*, published in February 2010, that includes greatly enhanced requirements for water efficiency including graywater recycling, high-efficiency plumbing fixtures — not just toilets but lavatories, sinks, showers, bathtubs and urinals. There's appreciable debate in the plumbing industry right now about water-free urinals as opposed to very-low-flow urinals. There's a bit of conflict because we walk a fine line in the plumbing industry. Our paramount concern is not water conservation; it's public health and safety. Water conservation is a secondary concern. That's not to belittle the fact that energy and water conservation are important. Plumbing regulators have long known that priority must be to protect against the spread of viruses by ensuring that adequate plumbing systems are made available. To date, public health and safety has taken priority though there is now a renewed sense of importance of water and energy conservation.[28]

The biggest hurdle for any onsite treatment and/or recycling of treated wastewater is to ensure long-term adequate protection of health and safety. Anything that requires maintenance may get shortchanged over the long run as companies try to cut costs, so it's wise to ensure that there is adequate support for reuse of treated water, perhaps through service contracts with outside mechanical or plumbing contractors.

Green Plumbing and Purple Pipe

The controversy over "purple pipe" is whether it should be used strictly for municipally supplied treated wastewater or be used also to identify any non-potable source in a building. While some may hesitate to display purple pipe inside a building, one project owner viewed it differently. Winston Huff, a plumbing engineer who has worked on many rainwater harvesting projects, recounts how one project in Nashville, Tennessee, went out of its way to display the purple pipe carrying reused rainwater inside the building.

> We're working on renovating an existing office building in Nashville. They are considering installing a system that collects rainwater and uses it in their flush fixtures. They're in the old part of the city that has a combination sewer/stormwater system in the street. A combined system uses one piping system to carry wastewater and stormwater. As a result, during periods of heavy rainfall, untreated wastewater can go into the river. (Nashville is not unique in this situation. Many cities have these combined systems.)
>
> The project in Nashville is a large office building that was a warehouse when first built. A few years ago, the city started revitalizing this area and the owners changed the building to office space.
>
> The owners said, "We are renovating our public toilet rooms, and we would like to install a rainwater system that will use the water to supply to the plumbing flush fixtures. This system can show we're being a good neighbor by reducing the amount of stormwater that we're putting in the old combined system that has been a problem for the city for many years."
>
> They want to show the public what they are doing so they are installing the piping exposed in the toilet rooms and not hidden in the walls. The piping will be painted purple and signage will tell the toilet user about the benefits of the system. The building has an industrial feel in all the public spaces, with exposed ductwork, structure and piping. When a person walks into the toilet room, the purple pipe supplying the toilets and urinals will be exposed and marked "rainwater reuse." People will see there's a difference with this building and the owners are making a difference. It also helps with safety concerns and lets maintenance staff know, for example, not to connect a drinking fountain to the purple pipe system.[29]

This seems like a really good idea: if you're going to use rainwater or graywater, or some other sources of non-potable water in a building, tell people about it through pipe color, signage and other means of public education.

Training Green Plumbers

There is a growing movement toward training the plumbing industry in "green plumbing" techniques. The Green*Plumbers*® training program originated in Australia and migrated to the US a few years ago. In the Australian state of Victoria, for example, in 2009 the government opened a new AUD$9 million training center to help grow the Victorian green plumbing sector. The Plumbing Industry Climate Action Centre in Brunswick, Victoria, provides training to practicing plumbers with a focus on sustainability, energy saving, waste reduction and water conservation.[30] According to one expert, in the US, Green*Plumbers* USA is also training out-of-work and under-skilled plumbers and other individuals to be water auditors, using money earmarked for the green jobs sector with 2009 Federal stimulus funds.[31]

Tara Reynaud, a plumbing expert and a trainer with Green*Plumbers* USA,[32] talks about what it takes to retrain an entire industry. For Green-*Plumbers* USA, the retraining involves a culture change as well, so that plumbers expand their sense of their role to be a "champion of conservation."

> The technologies that we teach and that the plumbers are starting to employ include graywater, rainwater and onsite wastewater treatment — treating the water onsite to save the energy of moving it through the sanitation system. We encourage them to stress behavioral changes like "shorter showers," and we train them in such simple things as efficient irrigation. We also train them in solar thermal systems installation.[33]

There is also plenty to teach plumbers on the health risks involved in new methods of water conservation and reuse. Of course, most plumbers are already sensitive to these issues, because of their concern over preventing cross-connecting wastewater lines with potable water lines. Reynaud says,

> The thing that should be stressed is that the codes weren't written to prevent us from being able to use alternative sources of water. The health risk is serious and needs to be respected. There are some groups that promote these sorts of jury-rigged systems, which is great, and maybe people don't get sick and maybe they have lived like that for years. But there are serious health risks if there are bacteria or viruses in the water. Green*Plumbers* USA promotes healthy and safe systems. We're serious, we respect codes, we explain the potential health risks and the potential outcomes if the risk is run.

The key point is that all of these new water conservation and reuse systems eventually have to be installed by plumbers, and they need to know how to do it right. The entire course ends with plumbers learning how to do water audits, to calculate economic returns on plumbing investments and to explain all the alternatives to homeowners and building owners. A green plumber's indoor water audit will usually consist of a careful look at laundry, kitchen, bathroom and toilet, plus water softeners and water filters.[34] If you're looking for a certified green plumber in your area, you can go to the Green*Plumbers* USA website and enter your postal code.[35]

Green*Plumbers* USA developed an approach to identify residential and commercial water- and energy-savings goals, called the Urban Dam Project, a three-phase program for building your own Urban Dam inside your property boundaries.[36] In Phase One, a homeowner gets a comprehensive 50-point audit, as I did, along with an installation of devices, such as faucet aerators that provide immediate water and energy savings. The consumer can then proceed to Phase Two (appliance and fixture change-outs) and Phase Three (solar, graywater and rainwater alternative technologies). The result: lower utility bills for both energy and water, along with a greater sense of well being and environmental responsibility. For a school, the entire facility can be considered an Urban Dam, with the whole campus evaluated for water use efficiency.

Bringing WaterSense into Your Home

Following the lead of its very successful ENERGY STAR program for appliances, buildings and new homes, the US Environmental Protection Agency (EPA) has been working since 2006 to produce WaterSense labels for plumbing fixtures, appliances and, most recently, new homes. It seems like a small thing, but a federal label requires considerable work to get consensus among all affected parties, to develop criteria that will work on a national level, to devise the rules for participation, to solicit industry partners and then to get you and I, the consumer, to pay attention so that the program results in market transformation.

The basic WaterSense criterion is that labeled fixtures, appliances and homes save 20 percent of the water use of an average non-labeled unit (Figure 6.2). In addition, products bearing the WaterSense label must demonstrate that they will perform as well or better than their less-efficient counterparts, will realize water savings on a national level, achieve water efficiency through several technology options and be independently tested and certified to meet the criteria in the WaterSense specification for water efficiency and performance.[37]

For WaterSense appliances, EPA provides WaterSense labels for hundreds of models of toilets, bathroom sink faucets and flushing urinals. In 2010, the WaterSense label will add shower heads, pre-rinse spray valves in

FIGURE 15.1 The Briar Chapel Community in North Carolina by Vanguard Homes includes the first certified WaterSense homes.[40] Courtesy of the US Environmental Protection Agency.

commercial kitchens and weather-based or sensor-based irrigation control technologies.

WaterSense Homes

On December 9, 2009, EPA announced the final rules for labeling a new home as a WaterSense home (see also Chapter 6).[38] According to the program specification, "EPA's goal is that WaterSense labeled new homes will use approximately 20 percent less water than a standard new home by using a combination of prescriptive and performance-based approaches." The three criteria cover indoor water use, outdoor water use (primarily front-yard landscaping) and homeowner education. For indoor water use, the program requires installation of any devices for which a WaterSense label exists; it also requires dishwashers and clothes washers to have ENERGY STAR labels.[39] For outdoor water use, EPA requires use of a proper irrigation controller and limits turf grass (lawn) to 40 percent of the total landscaped area. This is a good program, and one can expect many builders selling green homes to strive to achieve the WaterSense home label.

In late 2009, ENERGY STAR announced it had certified one million homes over the past 15 years.[41] It's likely that WaterSense homes will also require a decade or more to achieve similar market penetration, but if you're shopping for a new home in 2010 or 2011, you might want to see local builders offering any homes with the WaterSense label. To understand the broader picture of green homes and water conservation in new housing, with a special focus on flush appliances and landscaping choices, see my 2008 book *Choosing Green: The Homebuyer's Guide to Good Green Homes.*[42] While the focus is on controlling garden and lawn water use in the Water-Sense program, landscaping also helps save energy by shading windows and walls and creating a cooler microclimate.[43]

Monitoring and Public Education

The Valencia Water Company in the Los Angeles metro area created the Water SMART Allocation program in December 2009 that provides a monthly graphic to customers, allowing them to benchmark their water use against a formula unique to each property.[44] The utility serves about 94,000 people with 25,000 individual accounts. To allocate indoor water use, the company uses national surveys to determine need, but for outdoor allocations, it uses aerial surveys coupled with daily water readings. The result is a monthly chart comparing actual use with predicted water need, placing the customer on this five-point scale:

- Super-efficient (0 to 40 percent of allocation)
- Efficient (41 to 100 percent)
- Inefficient (101 to 150 percent)
- Excessive (151 to 200 percent)
- Wasteful (above 200 percent)

SMART stands for "Saving Money and Resources Today," and the program should give most customers an accurate picture of their water use, compared with local norms. In a way, this program aims to do what the HydroPoint Data irrigation controller does: measure and control actual use by assessing need. The president of Valencia Water, Bob DiPrimio, stated, "Utilities have found that customers respond with 20 to 30 percent reductions in water use," simply by having accurate information about their water use compared with a standard.[45]

In 2011, Valencia Water plans to combine the Water SMART program with a tiered rate structure to further emphasize the conservation message. According to the company, customers will begin to see Water SMART information on water bills this year, but with no cost impact. This will give customers plenty of time to become acquainted with the program and take steps to become more water efficient as needed.[46] Hopefully the Water SMART program results will be available online and in real time, so that water use adjustments can be made more frequently.

Small Changes Can Have Large Impacts

In 2010, the Pacific Institute analyzed how California could easily and cheaply save one million acre-feet per year, one-sixth of the state's goal of reducing total water use 20 percent by 2020, "based on sound science and economics."[47] According to study author, Peter Gleick, 400,000 acre-feet of water per year could be replaced with just partial fixture change-outs from toilets, shower heads, washing machines and pre-rinse spray nozzles in commercial kitchens at a cost of less than \$2 billion, a ten-year amortized cost of about \$500 per acre-foot. By contrast a new water supply dam in the Sierra Nevada would cost at least \$3.3 billion and produce less than 200,000 acre-feet of water annually, at a considerable environmental cost. Another 600,000 acre-feet of water each year could be saved in agriculture with smart irrigation practices, at a cost of about \$100 per acre-foot. The conservation measures would also produce considerable energy savings, since so much of California's water supply has to be pumped long distances.

Summary

To prevent the next urban water crisis in your area, start by getting cities and water agencies to embrace the 10-step program outlined above. Individuals can start at home with a water audit, a series of low-cost and no-cost measures that can reduce water use 15 percent right away and installing WaterSense appliances as they come available; this is my personal plan. To reduce both residential and commercial water consumption, water agencies will have to work on reducing landscape water use. This can be done by increasing water rates steeply for uses above an indoor-consumption baseline, so that people will be incentivized to use native or adapted plantings, xeriscaping, rainwater harvesting and sophisticated irrigation controllers. The key to reducing urban water consumption is to work on all fronts at once, yet in a coordinated manner, with retrofit incentives, technological and process changes, rate structures, code modifications, public education and technical assistance. The last thing anyone wants is to go through a cycle of "ration, relax, ration" that typically characterizes responses during and after periods of drought.

Epilogue: Water and Sustainability

Blue is the new Green.

SUSTAINABILITY IS THE watchword of our times, the strongest social US movement in decades. We can expect that the pace of global warming will accelerate, as most forecasts show increasing use of fossil fuels over the next decade or two. Despite the best efforts of government, industry and individuals, fossil fuel use is just too ingrained in our technology, economy and behavior to undergo rapid deceleration. Today's carbon emissions will stay in the atmosphere for a long time, so we're going to have to live with the consequences of our fossil fuel use for many decades. We know that water supply over the next few decades will be significantly affected not only by population growth, but by global warming. We know now that water and energy are inextricably intertwined. That's one reason why sustainable buildings and homes, zero-net-carbon buildings, sustainable urban development and sustainable products and practices are all critical to addressing water scarcity.

Climate Change and Water Sustainability

Water is linked to climate change, but it is not seen as a crucially intersecting issue by most people focused on "zero-carbon" buildings and cities. According to Jon Devine, attorney for a national environmental non-profit,

I see water conservation intersecting with climate change policy in a couple of ways. First, obviously in areas where water is constrained and where droughts are worsened because of climate change, using less water to achieve the same ends is an important adaptation strategy to deal with global warming. Beyond that, the collection, distribution and treatment of drinking water and wastewater itself consume tremendous amounts of energy and therefore contribute to global warming pollution. That water/energy connection is particularly strong in places where significant amounts of energy are used to transport water and wastewater like the Southwest. So saving water in turn saves energy and reduces global warming pollution.[1]

In 2009, the World Water Council stated to delegates at the COP 15 global warming conference in Copenhagen, that "Copenhagen is a key opportunity to remind the global community that sensible water infrastructure investments can help adaptation to climate change for a minor fraction of the costs of long-term mitigation actions."[2] In other words, climate change adaptation is unavoidable, and improving water infrastructure must be a critical investment priority, before considering more exotic or unproven carbon mitigation strategies that achieve the same results as water use reduction.

In a similar vein, the Global Public Policy Network on Water Management stated:

> The failure to recognize the role of water management in adapting to climate change has numerous and multifaceted repercussions for people's lives; it means that national water suppliers will not have access to sanitation systems that are resilient to flooding or unexpected weather events. It means that farmers will not have adequate information or resources to ensure that they can cope with diminishing rainfall. It means that new pressures will be put on already-strained relations between neighboring states who depend on shared water resources.[3]

Ensuring that water management is included in carbon mitigation and adaptation strategies will help a community prepare for the future to manage climate change and avoid enduring even worse consequences for water supply availability.

Triple Bottom Line Sustainability

Many people have heard that sustainability involves the "triple bottom line" of the Three Es — economy, ethics and ecology — or the Three Ps — profits,

FIGURE 16.1 The Triple Bottom Line aligns sustainability programs along three axes: economics, environment and (social) ethics.

people and planet (Figure 16.1). More recently, thinking about sustainability has recognized that this mode of analysis can also create a "triple top line" of new products and revenue growth, new green jobs and environmental improvements. A recent influential article even argued that sustainability is now the key driver of business innovation and represents an indispensable strategic initiative for every company and institution.[4]

How will sustainability interact with water conservation in cities? In this epilogue, I profile three significant connections, based on the triple bottom line: Green jobs, social equity and environmental restoration. These are the three legs of the sustainability stool.

Water and Green Jobs

I find the words of accomplished business people more interesting than those of politicians or green advocates when it comes to the potential for green jobs, the first leg of the sustainability stool. Certainly the "new water" sector is going to generate tens of thousands of green jobs in plumbing retrofits, desalination plants and recycling and reuse of rainwater and graywater. Anthony Pratt is executive chairman of Pratt Industries USA and the Australian company Visy, both large business enterprises. He believes that we are on the cusp of a huge growth in green jobs worldwide.

> Global investments in renewable energy companies and projects totaled $155 billion in 2008, overtaking similar investments in fossil fuels for the first time. Some estimates have put the global value of green products and services worldwide at more than $3 trillion and rising. We have already seen the kind of progress that can be made. By the middle of

2008, Germany, a country hardly celebrated for endlessly sunny days, had managed to create 40,000 jobs in its solar industry alone. *Israel, a country not long in water resources, enjoys a disproportionate share of the hi-tech water efficiency market.*[5] (Italics added)

Based on US patents per capita, Israel ranks behind only the US, Japan and Taiwan,[6] demonstrating how a clear focus on technology investments can benefit a country or region. In specific industries, such as life sciences, Israel ranks easily in the top countries in per capita patents granted.[7]

My company, Pratt Industries USA, has grown from scratch to become a billion-dollar business based on recycling, as well as the largest Australian-owned employer of US citizens. Recently we commissioned a $60 million plant in Atlanta that gasifies waste from the recycling process and timber construction waste, turning it into clean energy, which then drives our recycling mills and reduces our energy costs.

The coming focus on reducing the carbon intensity of each country is going to wind up with a strong emphasis on water conservation, as the water/energy nexus becomes better recognized.

My faith in the economic potential of the low-carbon economy is not an untested prediction. In Australia and in the US, Visy has built a multibillion-dollar business based around a closed loop of packaging and recycling. In so doing, we have turned waste into jobs, creating 5,500 green-collar jobs in Australia and 3,500 in the US.

Certainly the combination of desalination plants and water rights transfer schemes powered by renewable energy is going to be a political winner in most cases. In countries where desalination plants are located, there are usually abundant solar resources to power desalination plants, either through concentrating solar thermal collectors or photovoltaics. This is certainly true in the Middle East, although, according to Pratt, the current preference is still to use cheap fossil fuels to deliver cheaper water from desalination processes:

This is just a small part of the global green picture. The international race to win a share of the new green markets and opportunities is already well under way. The international non-government organization the Climate Group[8] recently reported on the extent to which green businesses and technology development have become a mainstream element of China's growth strategy. The country is already the world leader in solar energy, supplying 40 percent of the world's photovoltaic panels. It is doubling its wind generation capacity every year. Chinese companies are leading the way with electric vehicles, creating the first car that can travel 400 km (240 miles) on a single charge, as well as starting mass production of such vehicles.

Pratt's viewpoint is remarkably global, ranging from his own base in Australia to the US, Europe and China. There is no doubt also that China will soon become a world leader in new water technologies, as well as transportation and renewable energy, since much of that country is water-stressed already. For the US and other developed countries to keep up, major new investments are needed in water technologies, along with changes in institutional arrangements that make it a profitable business opportunity.

Water and Social Equity

The second leg of the sustainability stool is social equity. Many people in the world lack access to clean water, and the pace of industrial growth, coupled with ongoing deforestation, continues to reduce the number of unpolluted water resources available to people. Many estimate that nearly one-third of the world's population cannot easily access clean water for everyday needs.[9] How to address this situation globally is the source of considerable debate. The private sector has the technology, financial resources and skilled people to attack this problem but will not do so without guaranteed profits and long-term contracts. Water activists at the global level argue for an approach led and run by government to ensure that access to clean water at affordable prices is recognized as a fundamental human right.[10] They point to many instances of private sector malfeasance, while the business sector rightly questions why governments haven't done the job to date, despite huge amounts of foreign aid.

For me, the dispute is largely ideological: Assuming the mantle representing the "public interest," the left prefers public ownership of vital resources and scores the evils of profit-making capitalism. By contrast, the right, citing the "invisible hand" of the marketplace, prefers private ownership and points out the inefficiencies and (in many countries) outright corruption of the government sector. Practical people usually meet in the middle; many opt for hybrid approaches that keep public ownership of the basic resource but contract supply and maintenance to the private sector, in a regulated fashion.

The debate is ironic in other ways: food is just as essential as water for life and health, yet we readily allow the private sector to fulfill this vital role in almost every country, even those with socialist governments. In the 20th century, wherever food production had been collectivized, it was a dismal failure. Electricity is vital for life and health, but electric power is supplied mainly by the private sector functioning as regulated utilities in many countries. The same is true for gasoline, fuel oil, health care and dozens of other vital products and services. Why is water such a special commodity that it should be supplied only by the public sector?

The US and Canada are fortunate to have a vibrant public water and wastewater sector that provides clean, affordable water supply and wastewater treatment to about 85 percent of the population, with the balance coming from private companies. However, we also have a strong private sector that delivers the technology for the public sector to deploy. Some cities have privatized their water and wastewater utilities, with mixed results. In the Atlanta case study, we saw that the city eliminated its contract with United Water after five years, complaining of poor service and poor quality water. Indianapolis, a poster child for privatization of public services under Mayor Stephen Goldsmith, in 2003 hired US Filter (now Veolia Water) under a 20-year, $1.5 billion contract to operate its water system with positive results reported thus far.[11]

What are the opportunities for public/private engagement in new water supply technologies? There are three basic models: outsourcing (private operation of public assets); design/build/operate (DBO) new, expanded or upgraded facilities; and sale of public water/wastewater assets to private companies.[12] Of these, the DBO model is likely to see the greatest use in the future, because it brings capital to the table, along with new technologies and operating expertise. Contracting of water and wastewater plant operations and maintenance (O&M) has also become an increasingly popular DBO approach. Asset sales have been less common in recent years, although the current pressure on state and municipal budgets is leading some agencies to consider this step.

One reason I like steeply tiered rate structures for water supply, such as in Irvine or Las Vegas, especially when they provide for even cheaper water at the lowest-use tier, is that they can be used to cut water costs to lower-income residents, which is a valuable social welfare measure. This is especially the case when water utilities provide no-cost programs or financial incentives to replace inefficient fixtures, such as toilets, and charge more to higher-income residents who can afford to pay for the water needed to support extensive gardens and greenery. Additional fixture and appliance retrofit programs can provide jobs for semi-skilled workers who can benefit from local green jobs training programs.

Water and the Environment

The third leg of the sustainability stool is the environment. One of the looming issues in water supply is the need to replenish groundwater levels, so that streams in the drier regions can flow freely again, and to avoid draining existing rivers, bays and deltas for urban water supply. Often overlooked in the water supply debate is where the water comes from; it all comes from nature, directly or indirectly, and nature already has plenty of good uses for water. The prevailing mindset in the first half of the twentieth century was that water that reached the sea unused by people was somehow "wasted." We have begun to move past that way of thinking, but still haven't moved to restore our watersheds to their previous vibrant health. That is one singularly good reason to support onsite water recycling and waste treatment — to reduce the pressure of urban growth on water supplies.

Sharon Megdal, at the University of Arizona, who prepared the foreword to this book, is a strong advocate for considering the environment in any discussion of water issues. She and her colleagues have developed a unique voluntary municipal water conservation approach to support environmental restoration, particularly in arid areas.[13] In a recent article, Megdal and a co-author describe the program Conserve to Enhance that "aims to develop a source of water for environmental restoration projects by connecting residential water conservation and environmental enhancement." In Conserve to Enhance, residential customers who reduce consumption would agree to pay at their previous higher level, and the extra money would pay for environmental improvement projects. In this way, you or I, as individuals, can directly connect our own water use behavior with our interests in environmental restoration. As a practical example, the authors cite a property owned by the Nature Conservancy, which used funds from such a program to buy and retire groundwater pumping rights, which increased flows in a small creek that supported important riparian habitat.[14]

Water and Green Buildings

One example of water savings is the rapid growth of the green building movement. By the end of 2009, 27,000 projects had registered for eventual certification under the US Green Building Council's LEED rating system, and 4,500 had been certified. During 2009 alone, more than 400 million square feet of existing buildings registered to participate in the LEED for Existing Buildings Operations & Maintenance program, which requires a minimum of 20 percent water savings (against a baseline calculation). The green building movement continues to grow rapidly, with a 75 percent increase in the *cumulative* number project registrations in 2009, in the teeth of the Great Recession, while commercial and residential building declined 30 percent or more in most urban areas.[15]

The Living Building Challenge

Earlier I presented the Living Building Challenge and its requirement for net-zero-water use after an initial fill-up of a storage tank. Logically, there is always the chance that the water tank will run dry, in a run of low rainfall years. To me, a bigger problem is who's going to be responsible for long-term maintenance of the system, as the building changes ownership or management. Nonetheless, there is a strong argument for cutting energy use by replacing centralized water supply and sewage treatment with decentralized onsite systems. I expect that most green buildings will begin to aim at 50 percent water savings (compared with prevailing codes) and will start incorporating graywater and rainwater into toilet flushing, landscape watering and cooling tower makeup water.

Water in the Built Environment

People need water for psychological health. The well-known 23rd Psalm, "He leads me beside still waters," shows the shepherd's concern for his flock. We all want to walk along rivers, be near the ocean, go out to the lake, have fountains in our gardens and observe the flow of water in nature. In the Sonoran Desert, where I live, rivers flow only intermittently, and many people flock to bridges and creek banks during a rainstorm just to see water flowing by.

Chapter 11 presented two projects by Atelier Dreiseitl, one of the world's leading landscape architecture firms, the Queens Botanical Garden and Zhangjiawo. What has always attracted me to Dreiseitl's work is the use of water as an ecological, cultural and healing element. I lived in Portland, Oregon, the first half of the 2000s and would often visit one of the firm's projects, Tanner Springs Park, a constructed wetland designed mostly for passive viewing. Of this project, Herbert Dreiseitl writes,

> With surgical artistry, the urban skin of one urban block is peeled back. Time is reversed and the story of land development wound back to pre-development days. The park is like a view port to the past. The long forgotten wetland habitat is restored to the full glory of its plants and animals.[16]

It's perhaps no accident that Dreiseitl was originally trained as an art therapist and that he brings the therapist's sensibility to integrating water features
and functions into landscape projects. In his view, the way we handle water
says a lot about how we are:

> The way water is handled in towns shows more than the technical inge-
> nuity of its citizens; it reflects myth and religion and shows the spiritual
> constitution of people living in a water culture.[17]

As for water themes today, Dreiseitl stresses the need to link to other functions, rather than just design isolated water features.

> Water influences our sense of well-being in towns and in buildings, it af-
> fects the humidity, the temperature, the cleanness of the air, the climate.
> Water can be used in such a way that it filters, cools or warms the out-
> side air and regulates humidity.... The sounds of water are soothing and
> compensate for urban stress.... Water creates atmosphere, something
> that is vital to our towns and cities if they are to be individual, unmistak-
> able and easily recognized, with a sense of being home.... it has to do
> with the spiritual quality of a place, defining life and movement, some-
> thing that water can convey directly like no other element.[18]

More than any other element, water defines the essential experience of life.
As one commentator expressed it:

> Wherever there is water, life can become active in the material world;
> where there is no water this possibility ceases. Water is essentially the el-
> ement of life, wherever possible it wrests life from death...water forever
> strives after balance, a living balance, never a static one.... It is every-
> where a mediator between contrasts, which grow sharper where it is
> absent.[19]

The late economist and psychologist Kenneth E. Boulding summed up
water's amazing qualities well:

> Water is politics, water's religion,
> Water is just about anyone's pigeon.
> Water is frightening, water's endearing,
> Water's a lot more than mere engineering.[20]

We've come to the end of this book, but not the end of the journey. Now that you've read this book, here's what you can do. If you live in a city, become a water activist, starting by cutting water use at home. If you work in design, engineering or building construction, cut the water demand of your projects. If you manage or own buildings, cut your water use. If you work with plants, use native varieties and xeriscaping techniques to cut water use. If you work for a water utility, enhance your conservation programs. If you're a teacher, educate your students about water crises. If you're a politician, look for new ways to engage everyone in cutting urban water use. Let's not let our precious water resources become a Dry Run.

Appendix I: Glossary

Acre-foot: 43,560 cubic feet of water, about 326,000 gallons (1.23 mega-liters); 3 acre feet = about one million gallons. An acre-foot would fill one acre with water one foot deep. Used primarily in the United States as a unit of large-scale regional water supply.

Aerobic digestion: Sewage treatment in the presence of oxygen

Anaerobic digestion: Sewage treatment in the absence of oxygen

Aqua-vore: Someone who tries to get most of his water supply from onsite resources (the author's neologism).

ASME: American Society of Mechanical Engineers have established codes and standards that regulate such water-related items like effective flushing volume for toilets.

AWE: Alliance for Water Efficiency

Blackwater: Water from septic sources such as toilets, urinals and sinks

Bleed-off, blowdown: Water used in cooling towers to flush out salts that build up as water is evaporated

Block rate: A form of water rate structure in which per unit charges increase or (less commonly now) decrease with increasing use; typically in units of 100 CCF

Blue water: Treated water, typically from a municipal source

BMP: Best Management Practices

Carbon footprint: The amount of equivalent carbon dioxide emissions from energy-using activities, both directly and indirectly. See also water footprint.

CCF: Units of 100 cubic feet (748 gallons; 2,831 liters); typical measurement unit for water bills

CII: Commercial, Industrial, Institutional (i.e., non-residential)

Cooling tower: A mechanical device that cools a circulating stream of water by evaporating a portion of it. A cooling tower is part of a system that provides air conditioning or equipment cooling. It usually includes a heat exchanger, recirculating water system, fans, drains and makeup water supply.[1]

Cost-effective: If NPV exceeds capital costs, an investment is cost-effective.

CUWCC: California Urban Water Conservation Council, cuwcc.org

CWSRF: Clean Water State Revolving Fund, the primary funding vehicle for clean water investments that received funding from the 2009 American Recovery and Reinvestment Act (ARRA)

Demand-side management: Controlling water use by reducing end-use demands; programs that encourage customers to modify the amount or timing of water use. These measures may include encouraging customers to implement hardware or behavior changes, or reduce their use, depending on the time of day or time of year.[2]

Desalination: Removing salts from brackish or sea water, to make it drinkable

DHW: Domestic hot water, used both for homes or buildings, by people for hand washing and bathing purposes, or by processes for laundry, dishwashing or food preparation

Drip irrigation: Adding water directly to plant root zones usually under reduced pressure, using small-diameter hoses and emitters

DWSRF: Drinking Water State Revolving Fund; a funding vehicle for drinking water investments that received funding from the 2009 American Recovery and Reinvestment Act (ARRA)

EPACT: Federal Energy Policy Acts (1992, 2005) define the minimum acceptable water use of various fixtures

Evapotranspiration: Water demand for irrigation to overcome natural losses from plants through evaporation and transpiration

Flow rate: Volume of water per unit time, in gallons per minute or gallons per day (gpm or gpd), typically used for flow in pipes; or cubic feet per second (cfs), typically used for streamflow; or gallons per flush (gpf), used for toilets and urinals.

Flushometer: A commercial/institutional type toilet, which generates a flush by the opening of a valve directly connected to the pressurized building water system.[3]

Gpf: Gallons per flush, flow rate of a toilet or urinal; metric users employ the term, "liters per flush"

GPCD: Gallons per capita per day, used for measuring urban water use by relating demand to population.

Gpm: Gallons per minute, flow rate of a faucet or shower head; metric users employ the term, "liters per minute"

Graywater: Water reused from non-septic sources such as lavatory sinks, showers and clothes washing machines.

Green buildings: Buildings certified by a third-party rating system such as LEED

HET: High-efficiency toilet

Hydrologic cycle: Movement of water from the oceans by evaporation, onto land as fog, dew or rainfall and back to the oceans again through runoff; driven by solar energy, this eternal cycle makes possible all life on earth.

IAPMO: International Association of Plumbing and Mechanical Officials promulgates the Uniform Plumbing Code (UPC) used in 22 western states.

Infiltration rate: The speed at which water will enter the soil by gravity drainage, typically expressed in inches per hour (in/hr).

International Plumbing Code: Provides comprehensive minimum regulations for plumbing systems such as provisions for fixtures, piping, fittings and devices, as well as design and installation methods for water supply, sanitary drainage and storm drainage, published by the International Code Council.

LEED: A green building rating system from the US Green Building Council, Leadership in Energy and Environmental Design

Life-cycle assessment: The net environmental benefits over the life cycle

Life-cycle-cost: The net cost of a water-saving device over its entire lifetime, comparing annual savings with initial cost.

Living Machine®: A blackwater treatment system relying on natural biological processes to treat contaminants

Low-flow faucet: Meets 1992 EPACT standards, 2.2 gpm at 80 psi pressure

Makeup water: In a cooling tower, water used to replace water lost to evaporation and blowdown; can be treated rainwater, graywater, etc., as well as fresh water

MaP: The Maximum Performance (MaP) testing project was undertaken in 2003 in order to identify how well popular toilet models perform using a realistic test media. A new testing protocol, cooperatively developed by water-efficiency and plumbing fixture specialists in the US and Canada, incorporated the use of soybean paste as a test media, closely replicating the "real-world demand" upon fixtures. Initial performance testing of 80 different toilet models was completed and summarized in the Final Report (December 2003).

Master meter: A single meter for an entire building or facility; see sub-meter

Mgd/MGD: Million gallons per day, typically applied to municipal water or wastewater supplies or treatment plant capacity

Municipal water: Water treated to drinking water standards and supplied by a local water supplier, in the US typically a public agency

Nega-gallons: The amount of water that doesn't have to be provided, as a result of conservation and efficiency measures (the author's neologism)

NOI: Net Operating Income, in commercial real estate, equals the gross rents and other income from a building minus all operating costs that an owner must pay.

Non-potable water: Water that doesn't meet drinking water standards for quality or health

NPV: Net present value

Payback: The time (in years) for annual savings to equal the initial investment cost

Permeability: Voids in a given volume expressed as a percentage; affects infiltration rate

Psi: Standard unit of water pressure; pounds per square inch; 1 atmosphere = 14.7 psi, about 30 feet of water elevation. City water pressures typically range from 50 to 80 psi.

Potable water: Water that meets federal or state drinking water standards; in LEED, the definition includes well water that can easily be treated to such standards.

Purple pipe: Pipe containing municipally-treated wastewater suitable for irrigation and other non-contact uses; some public officials consider this a trademarked term.

Rainwater: Natural precipitation

Reclaimed water: Usually refers to treated municipal waste water distributed for further use, such as in irrigation of golf courses or parks (a good reason not to kiss your golf ball for good luck); see also Purple pipe.

Recycle/reuse: Use of water more than once, typically after some treatment

Reverse osmosis: A process to remove dissolved solids, usually salts, from water. Salt water or brine is forced through membranes at high pressure, producing fresh water and a highly concentrated brine.[4]

ROI: Return on investment, usually a percentage annual or net return divided by investment cost

SWAT: Smart water application technology (typically for irrigation)

Storage: Any form of onsite storage, typically in a tank or vault, usually measured in gallons or liters

Stormwater: Water running off a site after a rainstorm

Sub-meter: Meters to measure the individual use of a person, apartment, portion of a building or a specific activity such as irrigation, process water, fixtures or cooling tower; typically used in demand-side management programs

TDS: Total dissolved solids, usually expressed in mg/liter (equivalent to parts per million)

Ultra-low-flow: Typically applied to urinals that use one pint per flush; sometimes applied to low-flow toilets

UPC: Uniform Plumbing Code; see also IAPMO.

Water conservation: All efforts to reduce water use; may include water efficiency, but measures the overall reduction in water use

Water efficiency: Anything that decreases the amount of water used to accomplish a specific purpose, for a given amount of incoming water; sometimes confused with water conservation

Water/energy nexus: The realization that water supply and treatment are large consumers of energy and that both water and energy production and conservation are inextricably intertwined; a frequently cited figure is: 1 kWh of electricity is required to treat and distribute 1 gallon of water.

Water footprint: The amount of fresh water used by a manufacturer or food producer, typically expressed in total gallons or liters per year, or else per unit of product produced, usually reported as part of a sustainability report, waterfootprint.org.

WaterSense™: A voluntary partnership program launched by the US Environmental Protection Agency (EPA) to designate product and services that conserve water and perform as intended. WaterSense is a registered trade/service mark of the EPA. The WaterSense label is used on toilets and fixtures that are certified by independent laboratory testing to meet rigorous criteria for both performance and efficiency. EPA also plans to certify WaterSense homes beginning in 2010.

Water-free urinals: Typically applied to urinals that do not use water to flush away urine, but employ various media to keep the urine odors at bay

Xeriscape: Approach to landscaping that employs native or adapted plant species that use less water than ornamentals and that can rely on natural rainfall once established

Zero footprint: The complete reduction and/or offset of the potable water demand of a proposed urban development project by conservation, use of recycled or reclaimed water, or other measures.[5]

Appendix II: Resources

Annual Rainfall Yield in Gallons for Various Roof Sizes[1]

Water use estimates may be based on the following averages:

1. Average water use is 60 gallons per person per day.
2. For a family of four, annual use would be about 87,600 gallons.
3. To include garden or lawn watering at the rate of 1 inch per 1000 square foot, add an additional requirement of 625 gallons per day.

To estimate potential rainwater harvest from a roof, calculate the monthly or yearly rainfall in inches and multiply by 0.624 times the square footage of the roof catchment area. Remember that you may not be able to catch all of the rain, so adjust your estimates of collectable rainwater downward by 20 percent.

TABLE A.1 Estimated Annual Rainwater Catchment (Gallons)[2]

Roof Area or Rainwater Catchment Area (Sq. Ft.)	Average Annual Rainfall (Inches)			
	12	24	36	48
1,000	6,742	13,483	20,225	26,966
1,500	10,112	20,225	30,337	40,450
2,000	13,483	26,966	40,450	53,933
2,500	16,854	33,708	50,562	67,416

Books

Terry L. Anderson and Pamela Snyder. *Water Markets: Priming the Invisible Pump*, Washington, DC: Cato Institute, 1997.

Maude Barlow. *Blue Covenant: The Global Water Crisis and the Coming Battle for the Right to Water*, New York: The New Press, 2007.

Harvey M. Bernstein and Michele A. Russo. *McGraw-Hill Construction Smart-Market Report, Water Use in Buildings: Achieving Business Performance Benefits through Efficiency*, New York: McGraw-Hill Construction, 2009.

Julian Caldecott. *Water: The Causes, Costs and Future of a Global Crisis*, London: Virgin Books, 2008.

Herbert Dreiseitl and Dieter Grau. *New Waterscapes: Planning, Building, and Designing with Water*, Berlin: Birkhäuser, Publishers for Architecture, 2005.

Herbert Dreiseitl and Dieter Grau. *Recent Waterscapes: Planning, Building, and Designing with Water*, Berlin: Birkhäuser, 2009.

Peter H. Gleick. et al. *The World's Water 2004–2005: The Biennial Report on Freshwater Resources*, Washington, DC: Island Press, 2005.

Peter H. Gleick. et al. *The World's Water 2006–2007: The Biennial Report on Freshwater Resources*, Washington, DC: Island Press, 2007.

Peter H. Gleick. et al. *The World's Water 2008–2009: The Biennial Report on Freshwater Resources*, Washington, DC: Island Press, 2009.

Robert Glennon. *Unquenchable: America's Water Crisis and What To Do About It*, Washington, DC: Island Press, 2009.

Liv Haselbach. *The Engineering Guide to New Construction: Sustainable Construction for Engineers*, New York: McGraw-Hill, 2008.

Heather Kinkade-Levario. *Design for Water*, Gabriola Island, BC: New Society Publishers, 2007.

Klaus W. König. *The Rainwater Technology Handbook*, Dortmund, Germany: Wilo-Brain, 2001.

Brad Lancaster. *Rainwater Harvesting for Drylands and Beyond: Volumes 1 & 2*, Tucson, AZ: Rainsource Press, 2008.

Art Ludwig. *The New Create an Oasis with Greywater*, Denver, Colorado: Oasis Design, 2006

Ken Midkiff. *Not a Drop to Drink: America's Water Crisis (and what you can do)*, Novato, CA: New World Library, 2007.

Fred Pearce. *When the Rivers Run Dry: Water — the Defining Crisis of the Twenty-First Century*, Boston: Beacon Press, 2006.

Texas Water Development Board. *The Texas Manual on Rainwater Harvesting*, Austin, Texas, 2005.

Theodor Schwenk. *Sensitive Chaos*, London: Rudolf Steiner Press, 1965.

Sydney Water. *Best Practice Guidelines for Water Conservation in Commercial Office Buildings and Shopping Centers*, Sydney, Australia: Sydney Water, 2007.

Amy Vickers. *Handbook of Water Use and Conservation*, Amherst, MA: WaterPlow Press, 2001.

Chris Wood. *Dry Spring: The Coming Water Crisis of North America*, Vancouver, BC: Raincoast Books, 2008.

Jerry Yudelson. *Green Building through Integrated Design*, New York: McGraw-Hill, 2008.

Jerry Yudelson. *Greening Existing Buildings*, New York: McGraw-Hill, 2009.

Jerry Yudelson. *Choosing Green: The Homebuyer's Guide to Good Green Homes*, Gabriola Island, B.C., New Society Publishers, 2008

Websites

Alliance for Water Efficiency: allianceforwaterefficiency.org.

Artemis Project: artemisproject.org.

California Urban Water Conservation Council: cuwcc.org.

Pacific Institute: pacinst.org.

U.S. Environmental Protection Agency, WaterSense Program: epa.gov/watersense/.

World Business Council for Sustainable Development, Global Water Tool: wbcsd.org/templates/TemplateWBCSD5/layout.asp?type=p&MenuId=MTUxNQ&doOpen=1&ClickMenu=LeftMenu.

Water Footprint Network: waterfootprint.org.

Appendix III: List of Interviews

Sajjad Ahmad, University of Nevada, Las Vegas, 45–47
Troy Aichele, Stirrett-Johnsen, Inc., 212
Doug Bennett, Southern Nevada Water Authority, 51–52
Jeff Biggs, Tucson Water, 186
Chris Brown, California Urban Water Conservation Council, 206, 207
Ike Casey, Plumbing-Heating-Cooling Contractors Association, 66
Russ Chaney, International Association of Plumbing & Mechanical Officials,
    77, 219
Jon Devine, National Resources Defense Council, 227–228
Matt Ford, Solutions AEC, 171–172
Don Giarratano, D/K Mechanical Contractors, 116–117
Jonathan Gray, Interface Engineering, 125–126, 217
Karen Guz, San Antonio Water System, 194–195
Guenter Hauber-Davidson, Water Conservation Group, 103, 140–141
Dan Hellmuth, Hellmuth & Bicknese, 171, 172–173
Mike Hightower, Sandia National Laboratories, 53–54, 55
Bill Hoffman, H. W. (Bill) Hoffman & Associates, 74–75
Winston Huff, Smith Seckman Reid, Inc., 135, 219–220
Heather Kinkade, Forgotten Rain, LLC, 126–127, 141
Will Kirksey, Worrell Water Technologies, 153
John Koeller, Alliance for Water Efficiency, 65
Klaus W. König, Architectural Office of Klaus W. König, 138–139
Mike Kotubey, Midwest Mechanical Contractors, 124–125
Andy Kruse, L. J. Kruse Co., 112
Wade Lange, Ashforth Pacific, 73
Laura Lesniewski, BNIM, 155–156, 174–175
Eric Lohan, Worrell Water Technologies, 153
Shawn Martin, International Code Council, 218
Steve McDowell, BNIM, 155, 156, 174
Helmut Meyer, Transsolar, 106–107, 108
Mark Morello, Infinity Water Management, 72–73
Tara Reynaud, Green*Plumbers* USA, 221
Matthias Rudolph, Transsolar, 106–107
Chris Spain, HydroPoint Data Systems, 99–100, 101
Amy Vickers, Amy Vickers and Associates, 211

Endnotes

Chapter 1

1. Anonymous quotation, often attributed to Mark Twain, twainquotes.com/WaterWhiskey.html, accessed November 22, 2009.
2. ga.water.usgs.gov/edu/watercyclefreshstorage.html, accessed December 15, 2009.
3. By some estimates, the amount of solar energy reaching the Earth's surface in one hour is enough for our needs for an entire year, or about 8,760 times our requirements! nature.com/nature/journal/v443/n7107/full/443019a.html, accessed November 22, 2009.
4. See for example, the situation near El Paso, Texas, springerlink.com/index/5N3D9WGGHKTD2WAQ.pdf, accessed November 23, 2009.
5. Fossil water is water sealed off from further recharging by geologic activity. See, for example, azocleantech.com/details.asp?ArticleID=167, accessed November 23, 2009.
6. Edward Hyams, *Soil and Civilization*, 1952, London: Thames and Hudson, 55–73.
7. livinghistoryfarm.org/farminginthe30s/water_01.html, accessed November 22, 2009.
8. geography.about.com/od/learnabouttheearth/a/100thmeridian.htm, accessed November 23, 2009.
9. In Arizona and New Mexico, most of the annual rainfall comes in the summer months, although there is some winter precipitation.
10. See Char Miller, *Fluid Arguments: Five Centuries of Western Water Conflict*, 2001, Tucson: University of Arizona Press.
11. An acre-foot, about one-third of a million gallons, is defined as the volume of water that would cover one acre (43,560 sq. ft.) to a depth of one foot. See Appendix I, Glossary.
12. ibwc.state.gov/Water_Data/Colorado/Index.html, accessed November 23, 2009.
13. www1.american.edu/TED/ice/TIGRIS.HTM, accessed November 22, 2009.
14. According to a 2009 article in the *New York Times*, "The Euphrates is drying up. Strangled by the water policies of Iraq's neighbors, Turkey and Syria; a two-year drought; and years of misuse by Iraq and its farmers, the river is significantly smaller than it was just a few years ago. Some officials worry that it could soon be half of what it is now." nytimes.com/2009/07/14/world/middleeast/14euphrates.html?_r=2&ref=global-home.

15. knowledgerush.com/kr/encyclopedia/Dune_%28novel%29, accessed November 22, 2009.
16. etext.virginia.edu/stc/Coleridge/poems/Rime_Ancient_Mariner.html, Part II, accessed November 22, 2009.
17. west.stanford.edu/cgi-bin/pager.php?id=61, accessed November 22, 2009.
18. lnweb90.worldbank.org/oed/oeddoclib.nsf/DocUNIDViewForJavaSearch/A906D0BC1761938B852567F5005D596A?opendocument, accessed November 22, 2009.
19. ltrr.arizona.edu/research.html, accessed November 22, 2009.
20. georgiaencyclopedia.org/nge/Article.jsp?id=h-950, accessed November 22, 2009.
21. westcas.org/PDF/Atlanta_Journal_Constitution17Aug09.pdf, accessed November 22, 2009.
22. Myron Fiering, *Streamflow Synthesis*, 1967, Cambridge, MA: Harvard University Press.
23. Nassim Nicholas Taleb, *The Black Swan: The Impact of the Highly Improbable*, 2007, New York: Random House, provides excellent examples of these same phenomena in the financial world.
24. quickfacts.census.gov/qfd/states/06/0644000.html, accessed November 22, 2009.
25. lwf.ncdc.noaa.gov/oa/climate/online/ccd/nrmlprcp.html, accessed December 15, 2009.
26. wsoweb.ladwp.com/Aqueduct/historyoflaa/, accessed November 22, 2009.
27. filmsite.org/chin.html, accessed November 22, 2009.
28. aguanomics.com/2009/11/california-water-legislation-moves.html, accessed November 22, 2009.
29. samueljohnson.com/mortalit.html, #383, accessed November 22, 2009.
30. sacbee.com/capitolandcalifornia/story/2316172.html, accessed November 22, 2009.
31. sangres.com/arizona/blm/san-pedro-nca.htm, accessed January 17, 2010.
32. npg.org/facts/world_pop_year.htm, based on US Census Bureau data, accessed November 22, 2009.
33. census.gov/population/www/projections/usinterimproj/, Table 1a, accessed November 22, 2009.
34. World Wildlife Fund, *Living Planet Report*, 2004, p. 18.

Chapter 2

1. jperret.tripod.com/water.html, accessed December 15, 2009.
2. pubs.usgs.gov/circ/1344/, accessed November 23, 2009.
3. water.usgs.gov/watuse/data/2000/index.html, accessed December 15, 2009.
4. watertechonline.com/news.asp?N_ID=24877, accessed December 15, 2009.
5. Source: Tucson Water, author's personal water bill for September 2009.
6. californiaagriculture.ucanr.org/landingpage.cfm?article=ca.v054n02p56&fulltext=yes, accessed November 23, 2009.

7. waterfootprint.org/?page=files/NationalWaterAccountingFramework, accessed November 23, 2009.

8. waterfootprint.org/?page=files/CorporateWaterFootprints, accessed November 24, 2009.

9. panda.org/?172161/Water-footprint-of-beer-more-on-the-farm-than-in-the -brewery, accessed December 15, 2009.

10. locavores.com, accessed December 14, 2009.

11. "Agriculture, Food and Water," 2003, p. 24. Available at ftp://ftp.fao.org/agl/ aglw/docs/agricfoodwater.pdf, accessed December 15, 2009.

Chapter 3

1. thinkexist.com/quotations/water/, accessed December 15, 2009.

2. About two-thirds of Australia receives less than 20 inches of rain a year, and only 10 percent of the continent receives more than 40 inches, according to one source, bigsiteofamazingfacts.com/what-is-the-most-arid-continent-on-earth, accessed January 17, 2010.

3. independent.co.uk/news/world/australasia/australias-epic-drought-the -situation-is-grim-445450.html, accessed January 17, 2010.

4. ngm.nationalgeographic.com/2009/04/murray-darling/draper-text.html, accessed October 18, 2009.

5. Toni O'Loughlin and John Vidal, "Adelaide Latest Victim of Global Warming Water Shortages," guardian.co.uk, accessed September 28, 2009.

6. Dr. Jim Gill, presentation at WaterSmart Innovations conference, Las Vegas, October 7, 2009.

7. "Efficiency the Key to Slaking Our Thirst," *Weekly Times Now*, January 25, 2009.

8. Rachel Nowak, "Water Conservation Is Storing Up Health Problems," *New Scientist*, January 29, 2009.

9. Australian Trade Commission, *The Australian Water Industry: Market Intelligence Report 2009*, p. 7.

10. nwc.gov.au/www/html/117-national-water-initiative.asp, accessed October 19, 2009.

11. Australian Trade Commission, p. 7.

12. National Water Commission, *National Performance Report 2007–2008 Urban Water Utilities*, March 2009, p. 18.

13. Ibid., p. 13.

14. John Kanawati, "Australia Water and Wastewater Treatment," May, 5, 2007.

15. National Water Commission, *National Performance Report 2007–2008 Urban Water Utilities*, March 2009, p. 18.

16. smartwatermark.info, accessed October 18, 2009.

17. smartwatermark.info/home/inner.asp?pageID=3&snav=0, accessed January 17, 2010.

18. smartwatermark.info, accessed October 18, 2009.

19. westender.com.au/news/378, accessed January 30, 2009.

20. pic.vic.gov.au/www/html/310-introduction.asp, accessed January 27, 2010.
21. Plumbing Industry Commission, "PlumbSmarter: The Path to a Greener Plumbing Industry," June 2008.
22. Australian Trade Commission, p. 18.
23. Ibid., p. 17.
24. sfgate.com/cgi-bin/blogs/gleick/detail?entry_id=48164, accessed September 28, 2009.
25. Queensland Water Commission, *The 2008 Water Report*, 2009, p. 11.
26. Committee for Economic Development of Australia, *Water That Works: Sustainable Water Management in the Commercial Sector*, February 2007, pp. 12–16.
27. Romilly Madew, "Water Journal: The Worth of Water in Green Building."
28. Kerry Schott, "The Urban Water Strategic Context Going Forward," March 17, 2009, p. 8.
29. *The Age*, "Desalination plant 'on time, on budget,'" news.theage.com.au/breaking-news-national/desalination-plant-on-time-on-budget-20090907-fe2q.html, accessed October 19, 2009.
30. goldcoastwater.com.au/t_gcw.aspx?PID=5154, accessed January 22, 2010.
31. Australian Trade Commission, p. 16.
32. Ibid., p. 17.
33. Ibid., p. 19.
34. northgeorgiawater.com/html/207.htm, accessed August 8, 2009.
35. Ibid.
36. atlanta.bizjournals.com/atlanta/stories/2009/06/08/daily44.html?q=Georgia%20drought%20restrictions%20lifted, accessed August 8, 2009.
37. gov.georgia.gov/00/press/detail/0,2668,78006749_78013037_143196762,00.html, accessed August 8, 2009.
38. conservewatergeorgia.net/documents/wcip.html, accessed August 8, 2009.
39. northgeorgiawater.com/html/206.htm, accessed August 8, 2009.
40. northgeorgiawater.com/html/206.htm, accessed January 22, 2010.
41. cbc.ca/news/features/water/atlanta.html, accessed August 8, 2009.
42. reason.org/news/show/122661.html, accessed August 8, 2009.
43. epa.gov/water/wel, accessed August 8, 2009.
44. atlantawatershed.org/answers/RateIncreaseJuly12009.htm, accessed August 8, 2009.
45. northgeorgiawater.com/html/217.htm, accessed August 8, 2009.
46. atlantawatershed.org/news/pressrel/2009/r090417a.htm, accessed August 8, 2009.
47. atlantaga.gov/media/citynewsbytes_012908.aspx#toilet, accessed August 8, 2009.
48. Green*Plumbers* is a trademark of Master Plumbers & Mechanical Services Association of Australia.
49. conservewatergeorgia.net/documents/waterSmart.html#tools, accessed August 8, 2009.

50. atlantawatershed.org/answers/DWMfrom2002-2008.htm, accessed August 8, 2009.
51. google.com/hostednews/ap/article/ALeqM5j7WAc28al0-r3Q6Rvy0Oi4 OwobJAD99J1P6O0, accessed August 8, 2009.
52. georgiawcip.org/Pages/WCIP_Welcome.aspx, accessed August 8, 2009.
53. georgiawcip.org/Pages/WCIP_Welcome.aspx, accessed August 8, 2009.
54. ajc.com/news/georgia-politics-elections/perdue-backs-water-conservation -290093.html, accessed February 4, 2010.
55. quickfacts.census.gov/qfd/states/06/06073.html, accessed November 23, 2009.
56. sdcwa.org/about/annual_2008.pdf, accessed August 8, 2009.
57. sdcwa.org/manage/pdf/Conservation/Conservation_factsheet.pdf, accessed August 8, 2009.
58. Ibid.
59. sandiegonewsroom.com/news/index.php?option=com_content&view=art icle&catid=41:water&id=21657:mwd-imposes-13-cut-mandatory-cutbacks -likely&Itemid=58, accessed August 8, 2009.
60. 20gallonchallenge.com/whatisit.html#supplies, accessed August 8, 2009.
61. sdcwa.org/news/2009_0423_sdcwa8percentcutback.phtml, accessed August 8, 2009.
62. sandiego.gov/water/conservation/drought/droughtlevels2.shtml, accessed August 8, 2009.
63. sandiego.gov/water/conservation/selling.shtml, accessed August 8, 2009.
64. sandiego.gov/water/conservation/clsp.shtml, accessed August 8, 2009.
65. sdcwa.org/manage/pdf/Conservation/Conservation_factsheet.pdf, accessed August 8, 2009.
66. sdcwa.org/about/annual_2008.pdf, accessed August 8, 2009.
67. sdcwa.org/manage/pdf/2005UWMP/Sections_1-9.pdf, accessed August 8, 2009.
68. sdcwa.org/about/pdf/overview.pdf, accessed August 8, 2009.
69. sdcwa.org/manage/pdf/2005UWMP/Sections_1-9.pdf, accessed December 15, 2009.
70. As I discussed earlier in this chapter, Australia, with 20 million people occupying the driest inhabited continent in the world, has taken unprecedented and long-lasting steps toward embedding conservation and water recycling permanently in public consciousness, while still adding water supplies by building new desalination plants.

Chapter 4

1. quotegarden.com/water.html, accessed December 15, 2009.
2. mdleasing.com/djia.htm, accessed November 24, 2009.
3. nature.org/initiatives/climatechange/features/art29432.html?src=news, accessed December 15, 2009.
4. climatewizard.org, from The Nature Conservancy, accessed November 24,

2009, a midrange scenario based on the IPCC Fourth Assessment report, 2007, with High A2 emission scenario. Half the models predict a decrease in precipitation for these regions. See also, nature.org/initiatives/climate change/features/art29432.html?src=news, accessed November 24, 2009.

5. Ibid.

6. epa.gov/climatechange/science/futuretc.html#projections, accessed November 24, 2009.

7. ccnr.org/amory.html, accessed November 24, 2009.

8. California Energy Commission, *California's Water-Energy Relationship, Final Staff Report*, 2005, available at energy.ca.gov/2005publications/...2005.../CEC-700-2005-011-SF.PDF, accessed November 24, 2005.

9. Assumes water at $2/CCF (= $0.0025/gallon), gasoline at $2.50 per gallon and bottled water at $2.66 per liter ($10/gallon).

10. Author's water bill, December 2009.

11. bakersfield.com/news/local/x29579878/Are-we-paying-enough-for-water, accessed November 20, 2009.

12. Darren Haver, *Irvine Ranch Water District: A Case Study in Urban Water Conservation*, 2005, accessed November 24, 2009 at: lib.berkeley.edu/WRCA/WRC/pdfs/WRCC07aHaver.pdf. An acre-foot is defined in the Glossary in Appendix I.

13. Peter H. Gleick and Nicholas L. Cain, *The World's Water, 2004–2005: The Biennial Report on Freshwater Resources,"* Island Press, p. 124.

14. Smart meters provide two-way communication between the utility company and the user and in many cases allow the utility to cut off electric power to certain services during periods of peak demand.

15. Jerry Yudelson, *The Portland Water Abundance Plan*, 1999, for Cascade Policy Institute, accessed November 24, 2009, at: cascadepolicy.org/pdf/bgc/water.pdf.

16. Interview with Sajjad Ahmad, October 2009.

17. Ibid.

18. Ibid.

19. Ibid.

20. rssweather.com/climate/Nevada/Las%20Vegas, accessed November 25, 2009.

21. vegas.com/attractions/outside_lasvegas/lakemead.html, accessed November 25, 2009.

22. snwa.com/assets/pdf/wr_plan_exec_summary.pdf, accessed November 25, 2009.

23. snwa.com/html/wr_index.html, accessed November 25, 2009.

24. snwa.com/assets/pdf/wr_plan_exec_summary.pdfm accessed November 25, 2009.

25. According to US Geological Survey (USGS), per capita water use is calculated by dividing the total amount of water withdrawn from all water suppliers by the population. At USGS, water used for domestic, commercial, industrial and thermoelectric power, including water used for fire fighting, street washing, parks and swimming pools, is included. Water used for

irrigation and agriculture (including sub-metered commercial and urban residential irrigation) is not included.

26. snwa.com/assets/pdf/wr_plan_exec_summary.pdf, accessed November 25, 2009.
27. snwa.com/assets/pdf/wr_plan_chapter2.pdf, accessed November 25, 2009.
28. lvrj.com/news/51734727.html, accessed November 25, 2009.
29. snwa.com/assets/pdf/wr_plan_chapter2.pdf, accessed November 25, 2009.
30. snwa.com/html/wr_index.html, accessed November 25, 2009.
31. snwa.com/html/cons_wshome.html, accessed November 25, 2009.
32. snwa.com/html/cons_wet.html, accessed November 25, 2009.
33. A consumptive use is one that diminishes the quality or quantity of water and thus impairs or prevents the next use of the water. Examples of consumptive use include evaporation or contamination.
34. A non-consumptive use is one that does not diminish the quality or quantity of water. An example of non-consumptive use is a piece of equipment that uses a water-cooling process where the water does not evaporate or diminish in quality.
35. snwa.com/assets/pdf/cons_plan_strategies.pdf, accessed November 25, 2009.
36. Ibid.
37. Ibid., accessed December 15, 2009.
38. snwa.com/assets/pdf/wr_plan_chapter2.pdf, accessed November 25, 2009.
39. Ibid.
40. lvrj.com/news/51734727.html, accessed August 1, 2009.
41. snwa.com/assets/pdf/wr_plan_chapter2.pdf, accessed August 1, 2009.
42. Interview with Doug Bennett, September 2009.
43. usbr.gov/lc/region/programs/drop2/faqs.html, accessed August 1, 2009.
44. Total direct wastewater reuse for 2007 and 2008 was 26,845 acre-feet and 24,009 acre-feet respectively. The City of Las Vegas' was the smallest number. In 2007, Clark County reused 12,693 acre-feet, and the city of Henderson reused 8,338 acre-feet. About five percent of all wastewater is treated for direct reuse, and the remaining 95 percent is reclaimed for indirect reuse.
45. Todd Woody, "Alternative Energy Plants Stumble on a Need for Water," *New York Times*, September 30, 2009, nytimes.com/2009/09/30/business/energy-environment/30water.html?_r=1&scp=1&sq=todd%20woody%20September%2030%202009&st=cse, accessed November 24, 2009.
46. Interview with Mike Hightower, September 2009.
47. saws.org/our_water/recycling, accessed November 25, 2009.
48. cpsenergy.com/About_CPS_Energy/Who_We_Are/index.asp, accessed November 25, 2009.
49. Mike Hightower, "Energy and Water: Energy-Water Science & Technology Research Roadmap," presentation to Arizona Investment Council meeting, Tucson, AZ, August 28, 2009.
50. Western Water, Stephanie Gillespie, presentation at OzWater '09, Melbourne, March 2009.

51. "The Water Energy Carbon Footprint," Gary Klein, Affiliated International Management, Water Efficiency Conference, Newport Beach, CA 2009, and "Accounting for the Water-Energy-Greenhouse Gas Connection," Water-Smart Innovations Conference, Las Vegas, NV 2009.

52. California Energy Commission, 2005, op. cit.

Chapter 5

1. quotegarden.com/water.html, accessed December 15, 2009.

2. sydneywater.com.au/Water4Life/InYourBusiness/images/Officegraph.gif, accessed December 10, 2009.

3. smh.com.au/environment/water-plan-rubs-salt-into-ratepayers-wounds -20091011-gsdo.html, accessed November 25, 2009.

4. "Water Efficiency Guide: Office and Public Buildings," Australian Government Department of the Environment and Heritage, October 2006, p. 2.

5. Personal communication, Thomas Auer, Transsolar Climate Engineering, Stuttgart.

6. "Best Practice Guidelines for Water Conservation in Commercial Office Buildings and Shopping Centres," Sydney Water, 2007, p. 130.

7. NABERS is the National Australian Built Environment Rating System.

8. AGES GmbH, "Energie und Wasserverbrauchskennwerte (2005) in der Bundesrepublik Deutschland, February 2007, pp. 29–30, available from ages-gmbh.de, copyright by ages-GmbH, Kosterstrasse 3, 48143 Münster, Germany, project leader Carl Zeine.

9. 15 to 30 liters/day/worker × 225 working days/year divided by 20 to 30 sq.m. per person average office space, per Thomas Auer.

10. Data from Jeffrey Martin, Caterpillar Financial, January 2010. Building is 323,000 sq.ft. A new ozone cleaning system for the cooling tower installed in 2008 reduced water use by nearly 30 percent in 2009 from 2006 levels.

11. Data from Byron Courts, Melvin Mark Companies, Portland, OR, December 2009. First building, 360,000 sq.ft., houses federal office workers. Second building is a 250,000 sq.ft. office building. Other office buildings in Portland operated by the same company show water use in this range.

12. Kim Fowler and Emily Rauch, "Assessing Green Building Performance: A Post-Occupancy Evaluation of 12 GSA Buildings," 2008, GSA/Pacific Northwest National Laboratory, Richland, WA, Report PNNL-17393, gsa.gov/Por tal/gsa/ep/contentView.do?programId=13852&channelId=-26364&ooid=2 8927&contentId=28929&pageTypeId=17109&contentType=GSA_BASIC& programPage=%2Fep%2Fprogram%2FgsaBasic.jsp&P=, accessed February 7, 2010. Buildings range from 68,000 to 327,700 gross sq. ft. Usage depends somewhat on cooling towers and outdoor irrigation.

13. McGraw-Hill Construction, 2009, *Water Use in Buildings: Achieving Business Performance Benefits through Efficiency*, construction.ecnext.com/ coms2/summary_0249-307522_ITM_analytics, accessed August 18, 2009.

14. Personal communication, Amin Delagah, Food Technology Research Center, December 2009.

15. Peter H. Gleick and Nicholas L. Cain, *The World's Water, 2004–2005: The Biennial Report on Freshwater Resources*, Washington, DC: Island Press, p. 39.

16. Ibid., Table 6.1, p. 133.

17. Ibid., p. 142.

18. Based on a presentation by Dr. Daniel Yeh, "Tools for Recovery of Embedded Renewable Energy, Water and Nutrients from Wastewater," Greenbuild Conference, Phoenix, 2009.

19. Source: the author.

20. US Department of Energy, Emissions of Greenhouse Gases in the United States 2002, October 2003, eia.doe.gov/oiaf/1605/archive/gg03rpt/index.html, accessed December 15, 2009.

21. Interview with John Koeller, May 2009. Koeller is technical advisor to both the Alliance for Water Efficiency and the California Urban Water Conservation Council.

22. This information is current as of the end of 2009, but keep checking, as the legislation in this field is constantly changing.

23. Interview with Ike Casey, PHCC, April 2009.

24. Andrea Stahl, 2008, "Germany: Water Supply and Wastewater Disposal," US Commercial Service, Report 14264596, p. 5.

25. adb.org/water/topics/non-revenue/default.asp, accessed January 17, 2010.

26. USGBC staff data, compiled monthly, supplied to the author.

27. sandia.gov/energy-water/nexus_overview.htm, accessed July 10, 2009.

28. pe.com/localnews/inland/stories/PE_News_Local_S_cuts15.45082a4.html, accessed July 10, 2009.

29. iccsafe.org/e/prodcat.html?catid=C-P-06i&pcats=ICCSafe,C,I-C-06&state Info=clkfdpAjbpElluan9523|3, accessed July 10, 2009.

30. *LEED-EBOM Reference Guide*, 2009, Washington, DC: US Green Building Council, p. 93.

31. lacitysan.org/fmd/submtrcom.htm, accessed August 19, 2009.

32. Ibid.

33. CALGREEN requires separate water meters for non-residential buildings' indoor and outdoor water use, with a requirement for moisture-sensing irrigation systems for larger landscape projects, gov.ca.gov/press-release/14186/, accessed January 21, 2010.

34. Personal communication, Andrew Forster-Knight, South East Water, July 2009, usus.com.au.

35. Ibid., p. 101.

36. sloanvalve.com/UPPERCUT.aspx, accessed December 15, 2009.

37. Interview with Mark Morello, May 2009, infinityh2o.com, accessed May 28, 2009.

38. Interview with Wade Lange, April 2009.

39. LEED-EBOM 2009 Reference Guide, p. 116.

40. epa.gov/watersense/water/why.htm, accessed May 28, 2009.

41. Interview with Bill Hoffman, June 2009.

42. "Makeup water is fed into a cooling tower system to replace water lost

through evaporation, wind drift, bleed-off or other causes," LEED Reference Guide, p. 500.

43. LEED-EBOM, 2009 edition, p. 118.

44. saws.org/Latest_News/Newsdrill.cfm?news_id=139, accessed August 18, 2009.

45. buildinggreen.com/auth/article.cfm/ID/3903/, accessed August 18, 2009.

46. Ibid.

47. azstarnet.com/metro/296460, accessed August 18, 2009.

48. Over the longer run, it seems possible that water utilities could find rate structures that would be "revenue neutral" at various levels of conservation and overall consumption. I believe that "revenue neutral" is a key political consideration, as is the social equity issue of reducing water costs for lower-income residents.

49. See, for example, the new Plumbing Efficiency Research Coalition announcement, phccweb.org/Newsroom/PRdetail.cfm?ItemNumber=6940& navItemNumber=534, accessed August 18, 2009.

50. "Newly Named 'Plumbing Efficiency Research Coalition' (PERC) Identifies Drainline Transport as First Joint Project," February 18, 2009, phccweb. org/Newsroom/PRdetail.cfm?ItemNumber=6940&navItemNumber=534, accessed January 27, 2010.

51. Interview with Russ Chaney, April 2009.

52. "Water Conservation Tests Germany's Sewer Infrastructure," deutsche-welle .com/dw/article/0,,4582438,00.html, accessed August 26, 2009.

53. Andrea Stahl, ibid., p. 2.

54. "Water Conservation Tests Germany's Sewer Infrastructure," deutsche-welle .com/dw/article/0,,4582438,00.html, accessed August 26, 2009.

55. Guenter Hauber-Davidson, Power Point presentation, "Towards a Greater Sustainable Water Supply for our Office Buildings Through Greywater Recycling," March 2007, p. 6. Personal communication, August 2009.

Chapter 6

1. cyber-nook.com/water/p-quotes.htm, accessed December 15, 2009.

2. Peter H. Gleick, Nicholas L. Cain, *The World's Water, 2004–2005: The Biennial Report on Freshwater Resources*, Washington, DC: Island Press, p. 106.

3. epa.gov/WaterSense/products/in_the_pipeline.html, accessed December 15, 2009.

4. epa.gov/WaterSense/calculator/index.htm, accessed November 29, 2009.

5. US Department of Energy, *Buildings Energy Data Book*, October 2009, section 8, p. 8.

6. ecohomemagazine.com/green-products/flush-with-options.aspx, accessed November 9, 2009.

7. reevesjournal.com/Articles/Feature_Article/BNP_GUID_9-5-2006_A_100 00000000000569247, accessed January 28, 2010.

8. cuwcc.org/MaPTesting.aspx, accessed January 27, 2010.

9. cuwcc.org/MaPTesting.aspx, accessed December 15, 2009.

10. Personal interview with John Koeller, May 13, 2009.

11. allianceforwaterefficiency.org, accessed November 29, 2009.

12. epa.gov/WaterSense/pp/find_het.htm, accessed November 29, 2009.

13. epa.gov/watersense/news/current/index.htm, accessed November 29, 2009.

14. Based on a presentation by Dr. Daniel Yeh, "Tools for Recovery of Embedded Renewable Energy, Water and Nutrients from Wastewater," Greenbuild Conference, Phoenix, 2009.

15. roca.com.es/w+w/w+w/en/index.html, accessed February 8, 2010.

16. jetsongreen.com/2010/02/roca-dual-wash-basin-water-closet.htmlaccessed, accessed February 8, 2010.

17. epa.gov/WaterSense/specs/homes_certification.htm, accessed November 29, 2009.

18. EPA WaterSense Homes, "Draft Guidelines," May 8, 2009, p. 1.

19. epa.gov/ogwdw/faq/faq.html, #ccr, accessed November 29, 2009.

20. W. Ahmed, et al., "Quantitative Detection of Pathogens in Roof Harvested Rainwater in Queensland Indicates Potential Health Risks," paper presented at OzWater '09 conference, Melbourne, Australia, March 2009.

21. National Sanitary Foundation, nsf.org/consumer/drinking_water/dw_con taminant_guide.asp?program=WaterTre, accessed November 29, 2009.

22. usgovinfo.about.com/gi/dynamic/offsite.htm?site=h2ouse.org/tour/details/ element_actions.cfm%3FelementID=75008840-13D7-4855-9013CC8A59 F03381, accessed December 2, 2009.

23. (a) epa.gov/WaterSense/pubs/toilets.htm, accessed December 2, 2009; (b) Non-conserving shower heads consume up to 40 gallons of water for a single five-minute shower, fypower.org/res/tools/products_results.html?id= 100160, accessed December 2, 2009; (c) A typical dishwasher uses between 8 and 15 gallons per load of dishes with an average of about 9.3 gallons per load. A high-efficiency dishwasher can wash a load of dishes using 5 to 7 gallons of water, usgovinfo.about.com/gi/dynamic/offsite.htm?site=h2ouse .org/tour/details/element_actions.cfm%3FelementID=75008840-13D7-4855 -9013CC8A59F03381, accessed December 2, 2009; (d) Traditional clothes washers use approximately 41 gallons per load (gpl) while high efficiency machine use only 23 gpl usgovinfo.about.com/gi/dynamic/offsite.htm?site= h2ouse.org/tour/details/element_actions.cfm%3FelementID=75008840- 13D7-4855-9013CC8A59F03381, accessed December 2, 2009; (e) socalwater smart.com/index.php?option=com_content&view=article&id=47&Itemid= 34, accessed December 2, 2009; (f) For a family of four that replaces both kitchen and bathroom faucet aerators, usgovinfo.about.com/gi/dynamic/off site.htm?site=h2ouse.org/tour/details/element_actions.cfm%3FelementID= 75008840-13D7-4855-9013CC8A59F03381, accessed December 2, 2009; (g) For a three-person household, ci.sierra-vista.az.us/calendar/download_ attachment.php?aid=2348, accessed December 2, 2009; (h) For a family of four, usgovinfo.about.com/gi/dynamic/offsite.htm?site=h2ouse.org/tour/ details/element_actions.cfm%3FelementID=75008840-13D7-4855-9013CC8

A59F03381, accessed December 2, 2009; (i) csa.com/discoveryguides/water/overview.php, accessed December 2, 2009; (j) bewaterwise.com/tips01.html, accessed December 2, 2009. && bewaterwise.com/tips01.html, accessed December 2, 2009; (k) Ibid; (l) Ibid; (m) usgovinfo.about.com/gi/dynamic/offsite.htm?site=h2ouse.org/tour/details/element_actions.cfm%3Felement ID=75008840-13D7-4855-9013CC8A59F03381, accessed December 2, 2009. Stopping leaks of 30 gallons per day is equivalent to about 11,000 gallons per year of savings.

24. One such device is Metlund's Hot Water D'MAND system, gothotwater.com, accessed November 29, 2009.
25. askthebuilder.com/413_Hot_Water_Recirculating_Pumps.shtml, accessed November 29, 2009.
26. gothotwater.com/D%27MAND/Benefits/rebates.asp, accessed November 29, 2009.
27. For a list of incentive programs in your area, see dsireusa.org, accessed January 21, 2010.
28. h2ouse.org/tour/details/element_action_contents.cfm?elementID=1D4BA BB7-8E4C-4524-98836EECCC5AEE08&actionID=B70C165D-B4B0-4A39 -82A618B56149640B, accessed December 2, 2009.
29. usgovinfo.about.com/gi/dynamic/offsite.htm?site=h2ouse.org/tour/details/element_actions.cfm%3FelementID=75008840-13D7-4855-9013CC8A59 F03381, accessed December 2, 2009.
30. fypower.org/res/tools/products_results.html?id=100160, accessed December 2, 2009.
31. tucsonaz.gov/water/rebate.htm, accessed December 2, 2009.
32. saws.org/conservation/h2ome/washright/, accessed December 2, 2009.
33. harvestingrainwater.com/rainwater-harvesting-inforesources/water-harvesting-tax-credits/, accessed December 2, 2009.
34. smgov.net/Departments/OSE/Categories/Urban_Runoff/Rainwater_Harvesting.aspx, accessed December 2, 2009.
35. harvestingrainwater.com/rainwater-harvesting-inforesources/water-harvesting-tax-credits/, accessed December 2, 2009.
36. valleywater.org/Programs/LandscapeReplacementRebates.aspx, accessed December 2, 2009.
37. valleywater.org/Programs/IrrigationEquipmentUpgradeRebates.aspx, accessed December 2, 2009.
38. citypopulation.de/Australia-UC.html, accessed November 29, 2009.
39. "Brisbane Writes a Case Study on Saving Water," *Los Angeles Times*, November 24, 2009, latimes.com/news/local/la-me-conserve-brisbane24-2009nov 24,0,5700605.story, accessed November 29, 2009.

Chapter 7

1. gardendigest.com/water.htm, accessed December 15, 2009.
2. Adam Bluestein, "Blue Is the New Green," *Inc. Magazine*, October 2008, inc.com/magazine/20081101/blue-is-the-new-green.html, accessed November 28, 2009.

3. pacinst.org/reports/business_water_climate/full_report.pdf, accessed November 27, 2009.
4. Ibid., pp. 1–2.
5. environmentalleader.com/2009/04/29/starbucks-cuts-monthly-water-use-to-24-gallons-per-sf/,accessed November 27, 2009.
6. theartemisproject.com/newsletter_vol1_0909.html, accessed November 27, 2009. See also walmartstores.com/download/3338.pdf, accessed November 27, 2009.
7. ipcg.com/.../Artemis_Project_Top_50_Water_Companies_Competition_Winners_Release.pdf, accessed November 27, 2009.
8. theartemisproject.com/competitionpage.html, accessed November 28, 2009.
9. "Water Matters: Venture Investment Opportunities in Innovative Water Technology," 2008, The Artemis Project, downloaded from theartemisproject.com/publications.html, accessed November 28, 2009.
10. Interview with Chris Spain, September 2009.
11. tucsonaz.gov/water/ordinances.htm, accessed December 15, 2009.
12. Hansgrohe AG, PowerPoint presentation "Pontos AquaCycle: Use Your Water Twice — It's the Smart Way," p. 4.
13. Interview with Guenter Hauber-Davidson, September 2009.
14. Jerry Yudelson, *Green Building through Integrated Design*, 2008, New York: McGraw-Hill, pp. 192, 205.
15. Jerry Yudelson (ed.), "Engineering a Sustainable World," 2005, Interface Engineering, Portland, OR, 26–28, download available at interfaceengineering.com/sustainable-engineering/energy-strategies, accessed November 26, 2009.
16. Personal communication, Andrew Frichtl and Jonathan Gray, Interface Engineering.
17. Personal communication, Thomas Auer and Helmut Meyer, Transsolar, October 2009.
18. Interview with Mathias Rudolph and Helmut Meyer, October 2009.
19. Meyer and Rudolph point out that there is another type of "hybrid" cooling tower in the US than their European dry-cooling approach, so they caution not to get confused with the terminology.
20. To learn more about Transsolar's choice of hybrid cooling tower, go to jaeggi.us, accessed December 15, 2009.
21. docksidegreen.com/sustainability/overview/overview.html, accessed January 31, 2009.
22. perkinswill.com/news/newsarticle.aspx?id=301, accessed December 15, 2009. See also docksidegreen.com, accessed December 15, 2009.
23. docksidegreen.com/sustainability/eco-friendly/onsite-reclaimed-water-treatment.html, accessed December 15, 2009.
24. Ibid.
25. docksidegreen.com/sustainability/eco-friendly/potable-water-reduction-in-buildings.html, accessed December 15, 2009.
26. Susan Berfield, "There Will Be Water," *Business Week*, June 12, 2008; business

week.com/magazine/content/08_25/b4089040017753.htm, accessed November 30, 2009.

Chapter 8

1. brainyquote.com/quotes/keywords/water.html, accessed December 15, 2009.
2. graywater.net, accessed November 27, 2009.
3. Ibid.
4. allianceforwaterefficiency.org/Package_Graywater_Recovery_and_Treatment_Systems.aspx, accessed August 20, 2009.
5. Personal communication, Gunnar Baldwin, Toto U.S.A., June 2009.
6. Interview with Andy Kruse, April 2009.
7. greywateraction.com, accessed December 15, 2009.
8. wahaso.com, accessed December 15, 2009.
9. wahaso.com/services/greywatersystems.asp, accessed December 15, 2009.
10. Pontos AquaCycle 4500 specification sheet.
11. hansgrohe.de/int_en/86087.htm, accessed August 18, 2009.
12. tuv.com/us/en/index.html, accessed November 27, 2009.
13. The 1976 Bathing Water Quality Directive, Directive 76/160/EEC. ec.europa.eu/environment/water/water-bathing/index_en.html, accessed November 27, 2009.
14. perpetualwater.com.au, accessed November 26, 2009.
15. Interview with Don Giarratano, April 2009.
16. Berlin Senate Department for Urban Development, "Innovative Water Concepts: Service Water Utilisation in Buildings," 2007, p. 17.
17. Stephen W. Bilson, "The Monetary Value of Greywater Irrigation Systems: San Diego County Analysis," rewater.com/consulting.htm, accessed August 20, 2009.
18. sloanvalve.com/Our_Products/AQUS_Greywater_Systems.aspx, accessed November 27, 2009, and watersavertech.com/AQUS-System.html, accessed November 27, 2009.
19. Assuming four flushes per day at the low-flow setting (0.8 gpf) and 350 days per year use, one would save about 1,100 gallons per year.
20. bracsystems.com/index.html, accessed November 27, 2009.
21. Presentation by John Koeller, "Graywater Treatment and Reuse Systems," WaterSmart Innovations Conference, Las Vegas, NV, October 2009, koeller@earthlink.net.
22. Art Ludwig, *Design an Oasis with Greywater*, 2006, 5th edition, available from oasisdesign.net.
23. Marc B. Haefele, "A Solution to California's Water Shortage Goes Down the Drain," opinion in the *Los Angeles Times*, April 19, 2009.
24. oasisdesign.net, accessed November 27, 2009. "Using Gray Water at Home," Arizona Department of Environmental Quality pamphlet, az.gov/webapp/portal/SiteSearch?sitehome=http%3A%2F%2Fazdeq.gov&sitename=ADEQ&returnlink=http%3A%2F%2Fazdeq.gov%2Fenviron%2Fwater%2Findex.html&template=http%3A%2F%2Fazdeq.gov%2Fsearch.html&q=cache:S9Ou

XLjcBfUJ:azdeq.gov/environ/water/permits/download/graybro.pdf+gray+
water&site=adeq&client=azportal&output=xml_no_dtd&proxystylesheet=
azportal&ie=UTF-8&access=p&oe=UTF-8, accessed January 22, 2010.

Chapter 9

1. gardendigest.com/water.htm, accessed December 15, 2009.
2. Texas Water Development Board, *Texas Guide to Rainwater Harvesting*, 3rd edition, 2005, p. 1, twdb.state.tx.us, accessed February 3, 2010.
3. Personal communication, Steven A. Straus, P.E., Glumac, Portland, OR, December 11, 2009.
4. Berlin Senate Department for Urban Development, "Innovative Water Concepts: Service Water Utilisation in Buildings," 2007, p. 16.
5. Interview with Mike Kotubey, June 2009.
6. See, for example, cibse.org/pdfs/SYPHONIC%20RAINWATER%20SYSTE MS.pdf, accessed November 28, 2009.
7. Personal communication, Heather Kincaide, ASLA, Forgotten Rain LLC, July 2009.
8. See for example, Jonathan Gray and Jerry Yudelson, "Taking the LEED in Water Conservation," March 2002, *Consulting-Specifying Engineer*, csemag .com/article/179227-Taking_the_LEED_in_Water_Conservation.php?q= jonathan+gray, accessed August 18, 2009.
9. Ibid.
10. jrsmith.com/green_building/rwh_harvesting_steps_catchment.htm, accessed August 18, 2009.
11. Heather Kinkade, a landscape architect, comments: "We have had a lot of complaints on the tannins in the water from a green roof. Especially when using the water for flushing toilets, it looks like the toilets have already have been used, causing additional flushing." Personal communication, January 2010.
12. Download from twdb.state.tx.us, *Texas Manual on Rainwater Harvesting*, 3rd edition, accessed August 18, 2009.
13. jrsmith.com/green_building/rwh_harvesting_steps_catchment.htm, accessed August 18, 2009.
14. pentair.com/twins/Assets/ReleaseTwinsPentairSponsorship.pdf, accessed February 12, 2010.
15. Interview with Heather Kinkade, September 2009. See also similar products manufactured by Australia's Atlantis, atlantiscorp.com.au, accessed January 7, 2010.
16. jaxairnews.com/stories/022609/mil_J5.shtml, accessed December 13, 2009.
17. jrsmith.com/green_building/rainwater_harvesting_advantages_benefits .htm, accessed February 3, 2010.
18. plumbingengineer.com/april_09/rainwater_feature.php, accessed February 3, 2010.
19. allianceforwaterefficiency.org/Alternative_Water_Sources_Intro.aspx, accessed February 3, 2010.

20. lwf.ncdc.noaa.gov/oa/climate/online/ccd/nrmlprcp.html, accessed December 16, 2009.
21. npr.org/templates/story/story.php?storyId=104643521, accessed February 3, 2010.
22. Stephanie Simon, "Currents: Out West: Catching Raindrops Can Make You an Outlaw," *Wall Street Journal* (Eastern edition), March 25, 2009, p. A.14, retrieved June 12, 2009, from ABI/INFORM Global database. (Document ID:1666498501).
23. arcsa.org/resources.html, accessed February 3, 2010.
24. cmhc-schl.gc.ca/publications/en/rh-pr/tech/03-100-e.htm, accessed August 18, 2009.
25. plumbingengineer.com/april_09/rainwater_feature.php, accessed August 18, 2009.
26. allianceforwaterefficiency.org/Alternative_Water_Sources_Intro.aspx, accessed August 18, 2009.
27. opa.yale.edu/news/article.aspx?id=6571, accessed February 3, 2010. Personal communication, Shanta Tucker, Atelier Ten, February 2010.
28. greensource.construction.com/green_building_projects/2009/0909_Kroon-Hall.asp, accessed February 3, 2010.
29. Personal communication, Nicole Holmes, Nitsch Engineering, February 4, 2010.
30. environment.yale.edu/news/5508, accessed February 3, 2010.
31. Personal communication, Paul Stoller, Atelier Ten, February 3, 2010.
32. LEED submittal documents, personal communication, Nicole Holmes, Nitsch Engineering, Boston, February 2010.
33. Ibid.
34. Kenneth L. Seibert, "An Energy Education," *High Performing Buildings*, Winter 2010, pp. 44–55.
35. Ibid., p. 52.
36. Interview with Winston Huff, April 2009.
37. Guenter Hauber-Davidson, "Towards a Greater Sustainable Water Supply for Our Office Buildings Through Grey Water Recycling," Power Point presentation, March 2007, p. 5.
38. lowimpactdevelopment.org/raingarden_design/whatisaraingarden.htm, accessed November 28, 2009.
39. Example taken from Jerry Yudelson, *Green Building Trends: Europe*, 2009, Washington, DC: Island Press, pp. 73–74.
40. Herbert Dreiseitl and Dieter Grau, *New Waterscapes: Planning, Building and Designing with Water*, 2005, Basel: Birkhäuser, p. 55.
41. fbr.de/englisho.html, accessed November 28, 2009.
42. Information provided by Klaus W. König.
43. Klaus W. König, *Rainharvesting in Building: Fundamentals, Practical Aspects, Outlook*, 2001, WILO-Brain: Dortmund, Germany.
44. Interview with Klaus W. König, September 2009.
45. Email from Klaus W. König, September 15, 2009.

46. Klaus W. König, "Rainwater for 176 Washing Machines," article furnished to the author.
47. Personal communication, Björn Rohle and Stefan Holst, Transsolar, December 2009. Analysis for a confidential client.
48. According to the engineering analysis, retail water supply and wastewater treatment cost in Frankfurt is 3.64 Euros per cubic meter (about 266 gallons), or about $20 per 1,000 gallons, much higher than in the US, which makes replacing potable water from the city with rainwater fairly attractive.
49. Personal communication, Guenter Hauber-Davidson, March 2009, water group.com.au.
50. Guenter Hauber-Davidson, "Large Scale Rainwater Harvesting Down Under," fbr.de/rainwaterharvesting.html, accessed November 28, 2009.
51. Personal communication, Guenter Hauber-Davidson, December 2009.
52. Rainfall data from weather.com/outlook/travel/businesstraveler/wxclimatol ogy/monthly/graph/USMO0787?from=36hr_bottomnav_business, accessed November 21, 2009.

Chapter 10

1. gmd4.org/quotes.html, accessed December 15, 2009.
2. greensource.construction.com/green_building_projects/2009/0911_Vision aire.asp, accessed December 5, 2009.
3. Ruth Slavid, "New York's First Platinum-rated Condo by Atelier Ten," *Building Sustainable Design*, September 2009, bsdlive.co.uk/story.asp?story code=3146735, accessed December 5, 2009.
4. Ibid.
5. aiatopten.org/hpb/overview.cfm?ProjectID=273, accessed December 5, 2009.
6. Interview with John An, Atelier Ten, September 2009.
7. From the General Electric project fact sheet, gewater.com/products/equip ment/mf_uf_mbr/mbr.jsp, accessed August 20, 2009.
8. reuters.com/article/mnGreenBuildings/idUS10241523020091130, accessed November 30, 2009.
9. gewater.com/products/equipment/mf_uf_mbr/mbr.jsp, accessed December 5, 2009.
10. dnr.state.wi.us/org/water/wm/ww/tech/asludge.htm, accessed December 7, 2009.
11. gewater.com/products/equipment/mf_uf_mbr/mbr.jsp, and gewater.com/pdf/Case%20Studies_Cust/Americas/English/CS-VANC-COMWW-1206 -NA.pdf, accessed December 7, 2009.
12. ecocycledesign.com, accessed December 5, 2009.
13. issuu.com/jocke/docs/cleantech_001-132_webb/73, accessed December 5, 2009.
14. clivusmultrum.com/proj_greenbuilding.shtml, accessed December 5, 2009.
15. Jerry Yudelson, *Green Building A to Z*, New Society Publishers, 2007, pp. 184–185.

16. Ibid.
17. natsys-inc.com/resources/about-constructed-wetlands, accessed December 5, 2009.
18. livingmachines.com/resources/, accessed August 20, 2009.
19. Interview with Eric Lohan and Will Kirksey, June 2009.
20. worrellwater.com/resources, accessed December 10, 2009.
21. ilbi.org/the-standard/version-2-0, accessed December 5, 2009. Standard effective July 2009.
22. eomega.org/omega/about/ocsl/eco-machine/?image=22&category=eco -machine, accessed December 5, 2009.
23. Interview with Steve McDowell and Laura Lesniewski, September 2009.
24. See biomimicry.net and biomimicryguild.com, accessed January 22, 2010.
25. Case study adapted from "Water That Works: Sustainable Water Management in the Commercial Sector," CEDA (Committee for the Economic Development of Australia), Melbourne, ceda.com.au, February 2007, p. 75. Case study authored by Romilly Madew, CEO of the Green Building Council of Australia, gbca.org.au.

Chapter 11

1. jperret.tripod.com/water.html, accessed December 15, 2009.
2. The term "purple pipe" refers to the color of the pipe carrying reclaimed wastewater. The 2009 International Plumbing Code requires that any water not of drinking water quality should be in a purple pipe, while many wastewater treatment authorities want it to refer specifically to their processed sewage "product." See, for example, cdm.com/knowledge_center/monthly_ viewpoint/purple_pipe_issue.htm, accessed December 9, 2009.
3. epa.gov/owow/nps/whatis.html, accessed December 10, 2009.
4. latimes.com/news/local/la-me-rain-barrels1-2010feb01,0,1154413.story, accessed February 7, 2010.
5. queensbotanical.org/103498/sustainable?tid=6976, accessed December 9, 2009.
6. Metropolis, February 2008, metropolismag.com/story/20080220/a-garden -blooms-in-queens, accessed December 7, 2009.
7. queensbotanical.org/103498/sustainable, accessed December 7, 2009.
8. Herbert Dreiseitl and Dieter Grau, New Waterscapes, 2005, Basel: Birkhäuser, p. 60.
9. aiatopten.org/hpb/site.cfm?ProjectID=1018, accessed December 7, 2009. For a description of bioswales, see buildgreen.ufl.edu/Fact_sheet_Bioswales_ Vegetated_Swales.pdf, accessed December 9, 2009.
10. Dreiseitl and Grau, op.cit.
11. Shanghai Wisepool Real Estate Co. Ltd. is the developer. Architects are Schaller/Theodor Architekten und Stadtplaner and Stefan Schmitz Architekten und Stadtplaner, both of Köln (Cologne). schallertheodor.de/pdfs/ Zhangjiawo_Staedtebau.pdf, accessed December 10, 2009.
12. Information and photos provided by Atelier Dreiseitl GmbH, landscape ar-

chitects for the project, dreiseitl.de/index.php?id=525&lang=en&choice=33, accessed December 10, 2009.

13. greenroofs.org/index.php/mediaresource/industry-survey-2008, accessed December 7, 2009.

14. greenroofs.org/index.php/about-green-roofs/green-roof-benefits, accessed December 7, 2009.

15. artic.edu/webspaces/greeninitiatives/greenroofs/main_map.htm, accessed July 7, 2009.

16. inhabitat.com/2006/08/01/chicago-green-roof-program/, accessed May 28, 2009.

17. thesolaire.com/documents/rooftop.html, accessed May 29, 2009.

18. Jerry Yudelson, *Green Building A to Z*, New Society Publishers, 2007, p. 82.

19. irrigation.org/swat/Industry/, accessed December 10, 2009.

20. Regency Centers press release, October 7, 2009, regencycenters.com/company_information/press_detail.php?id=134, accessed December 7, 2009.

21. Ibid.

Chapter 12

1. ushistory.org/franklin/quotable/quote25.htm, accessed November 30, 2009.

2. There is an exception for water that must be from potable sources due to local health regulations, including sinks, faucets and showers but excluding irrigation, toilet flushing, janitorial uses and equipment uses. However, due diligence to comply with this imperative must be demonstrated by filing an appeal(s) with the appropriate agency (or agencies). ilbi.org/the-standard/version-2-0.

3. An exception is made for an initial water purchase to get cisterns topped off. The basic concept is that a Living Building fills its water storage tank or cistern only once and only imports water for those uses that are required by health codes to use potable water.

4. Acceptable onsite storm water management practices are defined in the *Living Building Challenge User's Guide*. Municipal storm sewer solutions do not qualify. For building projects that have a floor-to-area ratio equal to or greater than 1.5, a conditional exception may apply, which allows some water to leave the site at a reduced rate and depends on site and soil conditions and the surrounding development context. Greater flexibility is given to projects with higher densities. Onsite stormwater should feed the project's internal water demands or be released onto adjacent sites for management through acceptable natural time-scale surface flow, groundwater recharge, agricultural use or adjacent building needs.

5. yesmagazine.org/planet/a-living-built-environment, accessed December 6, 2009.

6. record.wustl.edu/news/page/normal/14246.html, accessed December 6, 2009.

7. ecolifestl.com/Feature-Story/Living-Learning-Center-First-Living-Building-in-Country.aspx, accessed December 6, 2009.

8. Interview with Dan Hellmuth and Matt Ford, October 2009.
9. greenbuildingsnyc.com/2009/01/12/bnim-architects-omega-center-for-sus tainable-living, accessed November 30, 2009.
10. renewableenergyworld.com/rea/partner/alteris-4286/news/article/2009/08/ omega-institute-turns-on-americas-first-zero-impact-living-building, accessed November 30, 2009.
11. jetsongreen.com/2009/07/ocsl-leed-platinum-living-building.html, accessed November 30, 2009.
12. Interview with Laura Lesniewski and Steve McDowell, September 2009.
13. Of course, it would be better if all water use were metered, to ensure that the "net-zero" requirement was met by rainwater falling on the property.
14. BNIM Architects, "Flow" booklet about the Omega Center, personal communication, September 2009.

Chapter 13

1. From "The Continent's End," *The Collected Poetry of Robinson Jeffers*, 1988, Stanford University Press, accessed December 11, 2009 at poetryfoundation. org/archive/poem.html?id=182232.
2. online.wsj.com/article/SB120053698876396483.html?mod=googlenews_wsj, accessed December 6, 2009; The International Desalination Association, idadesal.org, accessed December 6, 2009.
3. Assuming 145 gallons per day per person, if all desalination plants provided output at full capacity, the water supply would satisfy the needs of about 11 million people, about 3.6 percent of the US population of 305.5 million in January 2009, usnews.com/articles/opinion/2008/12/31/us-population -2009-305-million-and-counting.html, accessed December 6, 2009.
4. Peter Gleick, *The World's Water 2006–07*, 2007, Washington, DC: Island Press, p. 58.
5. zawya.com/projects/project.cfm/pid110307063924/DEWA%20-%20Jebel% 20Ali%20M%20Station%20Desalination%20Plant?cc, accessed December 6, 2009.
6. www2.tbo.com/content/2007/dec/22/na-applause-at-last-for-desalination -plant/, accessed December 6, 2009.
7. Ibid.
8. Bradley J. Fikes, "Water: Poseidon Seeks Additional $50 Million for Desal Bonds," *North County Times*, November 2, 2009, nctimes.com/business/ article_d87233fe-688e-5dad-a882-eab1483d32a4.html, accessed December 7, 2009.
9. "MWD Approves Subsidy for Carlsbad Desalination Plant," *San Diego News Room*, November 10, 2009, sandiegonewsroom.com/news/index.php? option=com_content&view=article&id=37850:mwd-approves-subsidy-for -carlsbad-desalination-plant&catid=41:water&Itemid=58
10. circleofblue.org/waternews/2009/world/peter-gleick-doing-desalination -wrong-poseidon-on-the-public-dole/, accessed December 6, 2009.
11. "A World Without Water," *The Nation* interview, February 16, 2009.

12. texaswater.tamu.edu/readingstexaswater.tamu.edu/readings/desal/Introto Desal.pdf, accessed December 7, 2009.

13. Ibid. Mgd = million gallons per day.

14. "Review of the Desalination and Water Purification Technology Roadmap," 2004, p. 3, nap.edu/nap-cgi/skimit.cgi?isbn=0309091578&chap=1-7, National Research Council, accessed December 7, 2009.

15. Ibid., p. 4.

16. A good discussion can be found at: waterrecycling.blogspot.com/2007/07/desal-brine-disposal.html, accessed January 11, 2010. The following illustrates the issue: "The environmental impacts of ocean disposal are mainly marine disturbances in the vicinity of the outlet due to the higher salinity and often chemical constituents in the brine waste. The high specific weight of the brine creates a plume at the outlet and this prevents mixing and makes the brine plume sink to the bottom. What is created is a "salty desert" in the area near the outlet affecting the benthic environment negatively. The chemicals used are also a concern regarding the marine organisms and plants." From Marcus Svensson, "Desalination and the Environment: Options and Considerations for Brine Disposal in Inland and Coastal Locations," 2005, SLU Department of Biometry and Engineering, Uppsala, Sweden, ISSN 1652-3245, p. 28.

17. Ibid., pp. 27, 34.

18. Ibid., p. 15. Cost is typical for urban coastal communities in the United States.

19. Ibid., p. 5.

20. wrd.org/engineering/seawater-intrusion-los-angeles.php, accessed December 6, 2009.

21. Peter Gleick, *The World's Water 2000–02*, 2002, Washington, DC: Island Press, p. 142.

22. ufdp.dri.edu/projects/tresrios.htm, accessed December 6, 2009.

23. Future: Full Scale Wetlands, phoenix.gov/TRESRIOS/future.html, accessed November 30, 2009.

24. sydneywater.com.au/Water4Life/RecyclingandReuse/, accessed December 6, 2009.

25. sydneywater.com.au/Water4Life/RecyclingandReuse/RecyclingAndReuseIn Action/RouseHill.cfm, accessed December 6, 2009.

26. Craig Berry and Peter Anusas, "Western Corridor Recycled Water Project, Alliance Delivery Experience: The Race Against the Drought," paper delivered at OzWater'09 conference, Melbourne, March 2009.

27. tucsonaz.gov/water/reclaimed.htm, accessed December 6, 2009

28. Interview with Jeff Biggs, October 2009.

29. tucsonaz.gov/water/pubs-gi.htm, accessed December 6, 2009.

Chapter 14

1. gmd4.org/quotes.html, accessed December 14, 2009.

2. saws.org/who_we_are/service.shtml, accessed February 16, 2010.

3. statesman.com/news/content/news/stories/local/2009/08/06/0806conserva tion.htmlm accessed August 6, 2009.

4. saws.org/conservation/aquifermgmt/, accessed August 5, 2009.

5. saws.org/latest_news/NewsDrill.cfm?news_id=608, accessed August 5, 2009.

6. saws.org/conservation/commercial/audit.shtml, accessed August 5, 2009.

7. saws.org/conservation/commercial/carwash/, accessed August 5, 2009.

8. saws.org/conservation/commercial/restaurants/, accessed August 5, 2009.

9. Interview with Karen Guz, October 2009.

10. ladwp.com/ladwp/cms/ladwp000509.jsp, accessed August 6, 2009.

11. Ibid.

12. laalmanac.com/weather/we13.htm, accessed August 6, 2009.

13. Ibid.

14. ladwp.com/ladwp/cms/ladwp009868.pdf, accessed August 6, 2009.

15. ladwp.com/ladwp/cms/ladwp001149.pdf, accessed August 6, 2009.

16. Ibid.

17. ladwp.com/ladwp/cms/ladwp009949.jsp, accessed August 6, 2009.

18. latimesblogs.latimes.com/lanow/2009/07/watersaving-fixtures-now-requir ed-in-new-los-angeles-buildings.html, accessed August 6, 2009.

19. forms.iapmo.org/newsletter/green/2009/Aug09.htm, accessed August 6, 2009.

20. ladwp.com/ladwp/cms/ladwp001799.jsp, accessed August 6, 2009.

21. ladwp.com/ladwp/cms/ladwp001225.jsp, accessed August 6, 2009.

22. mwdsaveabuck.com/download-documents.php, accessed August 6, 2009.

23. ladwp.com/ladwp/cms/ladwp001820.jsp, accessed August 6, 2009.

24. ci.austin.tx.us/watercon/taskforce.htm, accessed August 1, 2009.

25. "Water Efficiency in Austin, Texas, 1983–2005: An Historical Perspective," ci.austin.tx.us/watercon/downloads/JAW200702_well03gregg.pdf, accessed August 1, 2009.

26. statesman.com/news/content/news/stories/local/2009/08/06/0806conserva tion.html, accessed August 1, 2009.

27. c40cities.org/bestpractices/water/austin_conservation.jsp, accessed August 1, 2009.

28. ci.austin.tx.us/watercon/systemaudits.htm, accessed August 1, 2009.

29. c40cities.org/bestpractices/water/austin_conservation.jsp, accessed August 1, 2009.

30. ci.austin.tx.us/watercon/systemaudits.htmm accessed August 1, 2009.

31. ci.austin.tx.us/watercon/ctoilet.htmm accessed August 1, 2009.

32. "Water Efficient Equipment and Design", ci.austin.tx.us/watercon/down loads/EquipmentGuide.pdf, accessed August 1, 2009.

33. Ibid.

34. austin.wateriqknowyourwater.org/ad-campaign.php

35. enviromedia.com/enviroblog/?tag=water-iq

36. enviromedia.com/study-water-iq.php

37. statesman.com/news/content/news/stories/local/2009/12/14/1214toilets .html, accessed December 14, 2009.

38. ebmud.com/about_ebmud/publications/all_about_ebmud/default.htm, accessed July 10, 2009.
39. ebmud.com/about_ebmud/publications/all_about_ebmud/default.htm, accessed July 10, 2009.
40. ebmud.com/conserving_&_recycling/non_residential/clotheswasher_rebate/default.htm, accessed July 10, 2009.
41. ebmud.com/conserving_&_recycling/non_residential/commercial_rebates/default.htm, accessed July 10, 2009.
42. ebmud.com/drought/restrictions.html, accessed July 10, 2009.
43. EBMUD, "Nearly five months since declaring a drought emergency EBMUD's aggressive effort to meet water savings goal shows positive results," October 2, 2008, ebmud.com/sites/default/files/pdfs/Drought Status Press Release.pdf, accessed February 16, 2010.
44. Ibid.
45. ebmud.com/about_ebmud/publications/annual_reports/EBMUD%2008%20Annual%20Report.pdf, accessed July 10, 2009.
46. ebmud.com/drought/drought_rates_and_allocations_faqs.html, accessed July 10, 2009.
47. https://portal.ebmud.com/drought/alloc_in.cfm, accessed December 10, 2009.
48. cuwcc.org/mou/terms-section-2-purposes.aspx
49. Interview with Chris Brown, September 2009.
50. cuwcc.org/mou-main-page.aspx, accessed July 23, 2009.
51. Interview with Chris Brown, op. cit.

Chapter 15

1. cyber-nook.com/water/p-quotes.htm, accessed February 3, 2010.
2. Every two years or so, the LEED minimum requirements ratchet up a notch, so what might be a "certified" project under 2010 standards might not make the grade under 2011 or 2012 standards.
3. A good source for starting the home water audit process is wateruseitwisely.com/100-ways-to-conserve/home-water-audit.php, accessed December 13, 2009.
4. In many places, this action will require changes in plumbing codes as well as installation of separate piping to carry non-potable water to points of use, along with storage tanks, filtration and treatment equipment, etc.
5. Water managers need to inform themselves of the best approaches for sending conservation messages that motivate long-term changes in behavior.
6. Amy Vickers, 2001, *Handbook of Water Use and Conservation: Homes, Landscapes, Business, Industries, Farms.*
7. Interview with Amy Vickers, September 2009.
8. plumberprotects.com/whats_new_champions_of_the_environment.htm, accessed February 16, 2010.
9. Interview with Troy Aichele, Stirrett-Johnsen, Inc., May 2009.
10. The classic study of "diffusion of innovations" is the work of Everett Rogers,

Diffusion of Innovation, 2003, 5th edition, New York: Free Press. For a brief discussion of this subject, see my book, *Marketing Green Building Services*, 2007, New York: Architectural Press, pp. 165–171.

11. Jerry Yudelson, "The Portland Water Abundance Plan: A Proposal to Use Managed Competition to Conserve and Extend the Portland Metropolitan Region's Water Supplies," 1998, Oregon Better Government Competition essay winner, available at: cascadepolicy.org/pdf/bgc/water.pdf, accessed December 11, 2009.

12. In economics, this is called "the price elasticity of demand." See Lars G. Hansen, "Water and Energy Price Impacts on Residential Water Demand in Copenhagen," *Land Economics*, February 1996, v. 72, n. 1, pp. 66ff.; Terry L. Anderson and Pamela Snyder, *Water Markets: Priming the Invisible Pump*, 1997, Washington, DC: Cato Institute.

13. City of Portland Bureau of Water Works, "Water System Demand Study," Portland, February 1992.

14. Personal communication, Beth Beeman, Director of Public Affairs, Irvine Ranch Water District, November 30, 2009.

15. According to IRWD, "An allocation-based conservation rate structure is a unique and effective conservation tool that allows a water provider to use property-specific water budgets and tiered pricing to provide customers with economic incentives for efficient water use." See citation below.

16. "Irvine Ranch Water District Allocation-Based Conservation Rate Structure," October 2009. Personal communication from IRWD, November 30, 2009.

17. aguanomics.com/2009/04/water-budgets.html, accessed December 1, 2009.

18. thearizonagreenplumbers.com, accessed February 12, 2010.

19. Sydney Water, "Best Practice Guidelines for Water Conservation in Commercial Buildings and Shopping Centres," December 2007, 138 pp., sydneywater.com.au/SavingWater/InYourBusiness/, accessed August 20, 2009.

20. Ibid., p. 46.

21. Climate can affect these percentages; for example, in a temperate climate, there is much less use of cooling towers, which are major water consumers.

22. ilbi.org/resources/research/CodeStudies/codestudy3/, accessed December 11, 2009.

23. Interview with Jonathan Gray, May 2009.

24. pmihome.org, accessed December 11, 2009.

25. Interview with Shawn Martin, June 2009.

26. iapmo.org, accessed December 9, 2009.

27. "Green Buildings + Water Performance," White Paper insert, *Building Design & Construction*, November 2009, p. 34, bdcnetwork.com, accessed December 9, 2009.

28. Interview with Russ Chaney, April 2009.

29. Interview with Winston Huff, Smith Seckman & Reid, May 2009.

30. Office of the Premier, State of Victoria, press release, April 8, 2009.

31. Personal communication, Tara Reynaud, Green*Plumbers* USA, December 2009.

32. greenplumbersusa.com, accessed December 8, 2009.

33. Interview with Tara Reynaud, September 2009.

34. greenplumbers.com.au/media/CalculatorIndoor.htm, accessed December 11, 2009.

35. greenplumbersusa.com, accessed December 11, 2009.

36. contractormag.com/green-contracting/urban_dams/, accessed December 11, 2009.

37. epa.gov/watersense/about_us/watersense_label.html, accessed December 11, 2009.

38. epa.gov/watersense/nhspecs/homes_final.html, accessed December 11, 2009.

39. "WaterSense Single Family New Home Specification, Version 1.0," cited above.

40. vanguardhomesnc.com/sustainability.asp, accessed December 13, 2009. These homes were part of the US EPA's WaterSense Homes pilot program.

41. energystar.gov/index.cfm?fuseaction=mil_homes.showSplash, accessed December 11, 2009.

42. Jerry Yudelson, *Choosing Green: The Homebuyer's Guide to Good Green Homes*, 2008, Gabriola Island, BC: New Society Publishers, 180–182.

43. For a full description of these options, see Sue Reed, *Energy-Wise Landscape Design: A New Approach for Your Home and Garden*, Gabriola Island, BC: New Society Publishers, 2010.

44. hometownstation.com/index.php?option=com_content&view=article&id= 18708:valencia-water-company-2009-12-14-12-47&catid=26:local-news& Itemid=97, accessed December 15, 2009.

45. Ibid.

46. valenciawater.com/conservation/watersmart.asp, accessed December 14, 2009.

47. sfgate.com/cgi-bin/blogs/gleick/detail??blogid+104&entry_id=55780, accessed January 24, 2010.

Chapter 16

1. Interview with John Devine, Senior Attorney, Water Program, Natural Resources Defense Council, September 2009.

2. european-waternews.com/news/id884-Call_for_Global_Water_Fund.html, accessed December 13, 2009.

3. european-waternews.com/news/id885-Global_Climate_Challenge_Is_ Global_Water_Challenge.html, accessed December 9, 2009.

4. Ram Nidumolu, C. K. Prahalad and M. R. Rangaswami, "Why Sustainability Is Now the Key Driver of Innovation," *Harvard Business Review*, September 2009, hbr.harvardbusiness.org/2009/09/why-sustainability-is-now-the-key -driver-of-innovation/ar/1, accessed December 11, 2009.

5. Anthony Pratt, "Green Fields Abound in Pots of Gold," opinion in *The Australian*, December 12, 2009, theaustralian.com.au/news/opinion/green -fields-abound-in-pots-of-gold/story-e6frg6zo-1225809433611, accessed December 12, 2009.

6. buyusa.gov/newhampshire/israel.html, accessed December 12, 2009.

7. bioisrael.com/Homeinc_coverstoryDetails.asp?Id=98, accessed December 12, 2009.

8. theclimategroup.org, accessed December 12, 2009.

9. Dr. Jim Gill, presentation at WaterSmart Innovations conference, Las Vegas, NV, October 7, 2009.

10. The best-known proponent of the public ownership and operation of water is Maude Barlow, now at the United Nations Organization. See for example, her 2007 book, *Blue Covenant: The Global Water Crisis and the Coming Battle for the Right to Water*, New York: The New Press.

11. serconline.org/waterPrivatization/fact.html, accessed December 11, 2009. Goldsmith is a strong advocate for "managed competition" for all city services, including water and wastewater. See his book, *21st Century City: Resurrecting Urban America*, 1999, Lanham, MD: Rowman & Littlefield.

12. Ibid.

13. See Andrew Schwarz and Sharon B. Megdal, "Conserve to Enhance," *Journal of the American Water Works Association*, January 2008, pp. 42–53, available at cals.arizona.edu/azwater/publications.php?rcd_id=77, accessed December 11, 2009.

14. Ibid., p. 45.

15. LEED registration information courtesy of USGBC staff, usgbc.org, accessed December 1, 2009.

16. Herbert Dreiseitl and Dieter Grau, *New Waterscapes*, 2005, Basel: Birkhäuser, p. 14.

17. Ibid., p. 42.

18. Ibid., pp. 44–45.

19. Theodor Schwenk, *Sensitive Chaos: The Creation of Flowing Forms in Water and Air*, London: Rudolf Steiner Press, 1965, p. 98.

20. Kenneth E. Boulding, *Feather River Anthology*, oaecwater.org/water-poetry, accessed December 12, 2009.

Appendix I.

1. allianceforwaterefficiency.org/Glossary.aspx?terms=glossary, accessed June 8, 2009.

2. Ibid.

3. Ibid.

4. Ibid.

5. Ibid.

Appendix II

1. Ohio Department of Public Health, "Plans for Developing a Rainwater Cistern or Hauled Water Supply," June 2004, atsdr.cdc.gov/sites/washington_marietta/docs/plans_for_developing.pdf, accessed January 9, 2010.

2. For other roof areas and rainfall amounts, the reader can interpolate using these numbers.

Index

About the Author

JERRY YUDELSON, PE, MS, MBA, LEED AP, is the founder of Yudelson Associates, a green building and sustainable planning consultancy based in Tucson, Arizona. He holds BS and MS degrees in civil and water resources engineering from the California Institute of Technology and Harvard University, respectively, and an MBA (with highest honors) from the University of Oregon. He is a licensed professional engineer.

Besides his business and professional background, Jerry Yudelson served eight years as one of the original LEED national faculty members for the US Green Building Council (USGBC). He served on the USGBC's national board of directors and, from 2004 through 2009, chaired the USGBC's annual conference, *Greenbuild*, the largest green building conference in the US.

Jerry Yudelson has written 11 previous books, including *Green Building A to Z: Understanding the Language of Green Building*; *Choosing Green: The Homebuyer's Guide to Good Green Homes*; *Greening Existing Buildings*; *Green Building through Integrated Design*; *Green Building Trends: Europe*; *Sustainable Retail Development: New Success Strategies*; *The Green Building Revolution*; and *Marketing Green Building Services: Strategies for Success*.

Jerry and his wife, Jessica, along with their Scottish terrier, Bodhi, live in the Sonoran Desert bioregion in Tucson, Arizona.

If you have enjoyed *Dry Run*,
you might also enjoy other

BOOKS TO BUILD A NEW SOCIETY

Our books provide positive solutions for people who
want to make a difference. We specialize in:

Sustainable Living ◆ Ecological Design and Planning

Natural Building & Appropriate Technology ◆ New Forestry

Environment and Justice ◆ Conscientious Commerce

Progressive Leadership ◆ Resistance and Community

Nonviolence ◆ Educational and Parenting Resources

New Society Publishers
ENVIRONMENTAL BENEFITS STATEMENT

New Society Publishers has chosen to produce this book on recycled
paper made with 100% post consumer waste, processed chlorine free,
and old growth free.

For every 5,000 books printed, New Society saves the following resources:[1]

32	Trees
2,910	Pounds of Solid Waste
3,202	Gallons of Water
4,177	Kilowatt Hours of Electricity
5,291	Pounds of Greenhouse Gases
23	Pounds of HAPs, VOCs, and AOX Combined
8	Cubic Yards of Landfill Space

[1]Environmental benefits are calculated based on research done by the Environmental
Defense Fund and other members of the Paper Task Force who study the environmental
impacts of the paper industry.

For a full list of NSP's titles, please call 1-800-567-6772 or check out our web site at:

www.newsociety.com

NEW SOCIETY PUBLISHERS